Delictual Damages

For Mollie and Gilbert White

RMW

For Kathryn, Christopher and Mark

MJF

Delictual Damages

Robin M White LLB, LLM, Cert Soc Anth, AIL, JP
Senior Lecturer in Law, University of Dundee

Michael J Fletcher LLB, Solicitor
Sheriff of Lothian and Borders at Edinburgh

Butterworths
Edinburgh
2000

United Kingdom	Butterworths, a Division of Reed Elsevier (UK) Ltd, 4 Hill Street, EDINBURGH EH2 3JZ and Halsbury House, 35 Chancery Lane, LONDON WC2A 1EL
Australia	Butterworths, a Division of Reed International Books Australia Pty Ltd, CHATSWOOD, New South Wales
Canada	Butterworths Canada Ltd, MARKHAM, Ontario
Hong Kong	Butterworths Asia (Hong Kong), HONG KONG
India	Butterworths India, NEW DELHI
Ireland	Butterworth (Ireland) Ltd, DUBLIN
Malaysia	Malayan Law Journal Sdn Bhd, KUALA LUMPUR
New Zealand	Butterworths of New Zealand Ltd, WELLINGTON
Singapore	Butterworths Asia, SINGAPORE
South Africa	Butterworths Publishers (Pty) Ltd, DURBAN
USA	Lexis Law Publishing, CHARLOTTESVILLE, Virginia

A CIP Catalogue record for this book is available from the British Library.

ISBN 0 406 014469

ISBN 0-406-01446-9

9 780406 014467

Typeset by Phoenix Photosetting, Chatham, Kent
Printed by Bookcraft (Bath), Midsomer Norton

Visit us at our website: http://www.butterworthsscotland.com

Preface

This book flows from two perceptions. The first named author, while teaching a course called Accidents, Compensation and the Law, found that there was no up-to-date, readily accessible book explaining what damages could be obtained, by whom, and for how much. The second named author over a number of years as a solicitor and then sheriff, found that the standard of pleading in a number of sheriff courts left something to be desired in relation to damages.

The authors therefore hope that the book will answer those basic questions, provide a firmer basis for discussion of damages generally and help raise the effectiveness of litigators.

They would like to thank Butterworths staff both past and present; Fiona Raitt who, as Head of Department, assented to sabbatical leave for one of the authors to write the book and did not object when part of it was spent writing about nationality law in Hong Kong (and Colin Reid, her successor, for continuing support); David Cabrelli, a former student who did sterling service as research assistant; and Gordon Cameron, Bill McBryde, Sue Moody, Ian Willock of (or recently of) the Dundee Law Department, and David Collison and David Power of the Dundee Accountancy Department, all of whom read parts of the manuscript and offered suggestions (but who are not liable for the product). They would also like to thank their families for their forbearance.

The first named author is primarily responsible for chapters 1–6, the second named for chapter 7 and the Appendix. They have tried to state the law up to 31 October 1999. However, the House of Lords gave its decision in *McFarlane v Tayside Health Board* while this book was in proof, and the report on the Scottish Courts website allowed its last minute inclusion.

Robin M White
Michael J Fletcher
December 1999

Contents

Table of Statutes

Table of Orders, Rules and Regulations

Table of Cases

Abbreviations

AC	Law Reports, Appeal Cases (House of Lords and Privy Council) 1890–
All ER	All England Law Reports 1936–
App Cas	Law Reports, Appeal Cases (House of Lords) 1875–90
D	Dunlop's Session Cases 1838–62
F	Fraser's Session Cases 1898–1906
ICR	Industrial Case Reports 1972–
IH	Inner House (Court of Session)
KB	Law Reports, King's Bench Division 1900–52
KIR	Knight's Industrial Reports 1966–75
LR Eq	Law Reports, Equity (England) 1865–1875
Macph	Macpherson's Session Cases 1862–73
MLR	Modern Law Review 1937–
NLJ	New Law Journal (England) 1965–
OH	Outer House (Court of Session)
QB	Law Reports, Queen's Bench Division (England) 1952–
R	Rettie's Session Cases 1873–98
R (HL)	House of Lords cases in Rettie's Session Cases 1873–98
RPC	Reports of Patents, Designs and Trademark Cases 1884–
SC	Session Cases 1907–
SC (HL)	House of Lords cases in Session Cases 1907–
SCLR	Scottish Civil Law Reports 1987–
SLR	Scottish Law Reporter 1865–1925
SLT	Scots Law Times 1893–1908 (preceded by year and volume number) 1909– (preceded by year)
SLT (Notes)	Notes of Recent Decisions in Scots Law Times 1946–81
WLR	Weekly Law Reports 1953–
WN (NSW)	Weekly Notes (New South Wales) 1884–

Textbooks

Atiyah	*Atiyah's Accidents, Compensation and the Law* (6th edn, 1999, ed Cane)
Bankton	*An Institute of the Laws of Scotland* (3 vols) (1751–53)
Bell	*Commentaries on the Law of Scotland and on the Principles of Mercantile Jurisprudence* (2 vols) (7th edn, 1870) (T & T Clark)
Bennett (SA)	*Personal Injury Damages in Scotland* (1999) (Barnstone)
Erskine	*An Institute of the Law of Scotland* (2 vols) (8th edn, 1871)
Kemp & Kemp	*The Quantum of Damages in Personal Injury and Fatal Accident Claims* (1982) (4th edn, rev)
McEwan & Paton	*McEwan & Paton on Damages for Personal Injuries in Scotland* (2nd edn, 1989, looseleaf updated) (Greens)

Stair   *The Institutions of the Laws of Scotland* (5th edn, 1832
                      (reprinted 1981: Edinburgh University Press and Glasgow
                      University Press)
Stair Memorial   *The Laws of Scotland: Stair Memorial Encyclopaedia* (vol 15,
   Encyclopaedia   1996), (vol 18, 1993) (Butterworths)
Thomson (JM)   *Delictual Liability* (2nd edn, 1999) (Butterworths)

1. Compensation and the nature of delictual damages

WHAT DAMAGES ARE

THE GENERAL NATURE OF DAMAGES

Damages are the standard form of compensation through law. They are the usual remedy in delict, displaying its reparational aspect. Delictual damages are thus the compensation provided by law for the harm (or *damnum*) caused (or *datum*) by the wrong (or *injuria*)[1].

This traditional terminology is useful in avoiding confusion over whether compensation is made for the wrong, or for the harm. *Injuria absque damno* ('wrong without harm') is not compensated, any more than *damnum absque injuria* ('harm without wrong')[2].

Damages are paid, normally as a lump sum of money, to restore the pursuer, so far as possible, to his or her original position, an aim expressed in the maxim *restitutio in integrum*.

DELICTUAL DAMAGES AND THE INSTITUTIONAL WRITERS

The institutional writers refer to delictual damages, though say little.

Stair

Stair, in the title 'Reparation, where of Delinquencies and Damages thence Arising'[3], includes discussion of punishment as well as of reparation. He also uses the terms 'damage' or 'damages', chiefly to refer to harm suffered[4] (ie *damnum*). Nevertheless, discussing what is recognisably delict in present-day terms, he distinguishes delinquencies against God, which should receive penalties, and those against a person, in which 'the obligation [is] of repairing

---

1 Cf Thomson *Delictual Liability* (2nd edn, 1999) p 1: 'The essence of the modern Scots law of delict is the obligation of a person to compensate another who has suffered loss as a result of the wrongful actions of that person. This obligation to pay compensation is called reparation.'
2 Direct authority is meagre, presumably because the point is axiomatic. However, see eg *McFarlane v Tayside Health Board* 1998 SC 389, 1998 SCLR 126, 1998 SLT 307, at 310, per Lord Justice-Clerk Cullen: 'The right to raise an action of damages in quasi-delict [ie in negligence] depends on the concurrence of *injuria* with *damnum*.'
3 *Institutions* I, 9.
4 As in the title itself; in I,9,1; and most explicitly in I,9,3: 'Damage is called *damnum, a demendo* [*scil "ademendo"*: ie "harm, by deprivation"], because it diminisheth or taketh away something from another, which of right he had.'

[the pursuer's] damage by putting him in as good a condition as he was in before the injury'[1].

Later, he observes that:

'[r]eparation is either by restitution of the same thing in the same case, that it would have been, if it had remained with the owner, and this is most exact; or, where that cannot be, by giving the like value, or that which may come nearest to make up the damage, according to the desire of the damnified. And if none be found fitter, reparation must be made in money, which is the common token of exchange, and that it hath in it the value of everything estimable'[2].

In relation to each of the interests protected by this branch of the law[3], he remarks on the nature of the reparation[4]. His discussion of the various means of vindicating delicts[5] also contains such observations[6]. Further, at least in relation to reparation for damage to the interest of 'content, delight and satisfaction' in property, he declares that the quantum might be the *pretium affectionis*[7] rather than the market value, and that it could be arrived at by the pursuer's 'oath to declare how much he accounted himself damnified: the exorbitancy whereof might have been taxed by the judge'[8].

Bankton

Bankton, in his title 'Reparation arising from Crimes or Delinquencies'[9], follows Stair, but is fuller. While distinguishing between a fine and damages, he maintains the relative lack of differentiation between crime and delict and also uses 'damage' to refer to particular forms of *damnum*[10]. While considering the 'nominate delicts', he discusses some issues as to the nature of damages as the term is now understood.

Thus in relation to 'Injury' (ie *damnum* including assault and defamation), he writes that 'commonly with us, the estimation is at the arbitrement of the judges, without taking the party's oath *in litem*'[11]. In relation to 'Damage' (*damnum* including damage to property generally), he writes that '[t]he real value of the thing, with the interest and expences [*sic*] of suit, is always given to the party damnified', also that '[t]he rule in ordinary cases, for reparation of damage, on this title, *viz* where it occurs through fault, but without fraud

---

1 I,9,2.
2 I,9,4.
3 Ie infringement of life, members and health; infringement of liberty; infringement of fame, reputation and honour; infringement of our content, delight or satisfaction which attaches 'affectionately' to something we own; and damages to goods and possession (I,9,4).
4 Thus, in relation to injury to fame, reputation and honour, 'firstly by making up the damage that is inferred in men's goods by the hurt of their fame, whereby their gain ceaseth.'
5 Ie the 'nominate delicts' of assythment, extortion etc.
6 Eg I,9,7; I,9,8; I,9,12.
7 Ie 'sentimental value'.
8 I,9,4.
9 *Institute*, I,10.
10 As in I,10,4, where it is described as 'a general term, but here it is partially understood of that damage which arises for Diminishing, Spoiling or Destroying one's goods, without any advantage to the offender; and is not only distinct from Injury, properly so termed, but likewise from Theft and Robbery, which are for Lucre'.
11 Ie 'in the proceedings': I,10,3.

of the party, is, that other things damnified should not be valued according to the affection of the owner, or their usefulness to him, or any other party, but at the common estimation or current price'[1].

Erskine

Erskine, distinguishing damages from punishment more clearly, under the general rubric 'Of Obligations and Contracts in General [Etc]' declares that *'Alterum non laedere*[2] is one of the three general precepts laid down by Justinian ... In consequence of this rule, every one ... is naturally obliged to make up the damage befalling his neighbour from a wrong committed by himself'[3].

In the same section, he also uses 'damage' to refer to *damnum* and notes that the reparation received 'never ought to rise higher than the loss truly sustained' and that '[w]here the person injured can be restored precisely to his former state, that method ought to be followed ... [b]ut where through the extinction or deterioration of the subject, that method of reparation cannot be affected [*sic*], the value of the damage in money must be ascertained by the judge ... All are agreed that the extent of the damage, where the delinquency is not attended by fraud, ought to be estimated by its real worth, and not by the *pretium affectionis*... In special cases, however, the judge ought to estimate the loss of the party higher than the subject destroyed or damaged would have been worth to any other; *ex gr* [ie 'eg'] when the trees near a gentleman's seat are cut down or hurt, which served for policy or shelter[4]'.

Bell

Bell, within the chapter entitled 'Of Interest of Money, of Damages, and of Penalties', in a section called 'Of Claims for Damages', distinguishes damages from penalties. He observes that:

'[c]laims of damage may arise either from injuries inflicted as by personal assault, libel, seduction, adultery, etc; or from breach of contract; or from the neglect of due diligence which the law requires in particular situations and contracts'[5].

Thereafter, he goes on to refer to remoteness of damage, to draw attention to the creation of the Jury Court to decide such matters, and to discuss the relationship of damages and bankruptcy.

The relevance of the institutional writers

These conclusions of the institutional writers provide some food for thought but are of little consequence. It is generally accepted that the current law of delict emerged largely in the nineteenth and twentieth centuries.

---

1 I,10,4.
2 Ie 'Not to harm others'.
3 III,1,13.
4 His footnote 13 refers to *solatium*, but only in relation to breach of promise and the death of a close relative.
5 *Commentaries* III, 699.

Principles must therefore be sought in sources of that period, and institutional dicta treated with respect, but without expectation of assistance.

DELICTUAL DAMAGES AND PRECEDENT

Damages are, in fact, essentially a creation of precedent. Surprisingly, how-ever, there is a dearth of authoritative judicial definition of delictual damages[1], and resort to academic writing is necessary.

Nevertheless, it is from the cases that most of the principles emerge as to the types of damages available, the principles upon which they are quantified, and how those principles are worked out in practice, as shown in the remainder of this book.

DELICTUAL DAMAGES AND STATUTE

There is legislation on delictual damages, not least the Damages (Scotland) Act 1976 (as amended). In some cases, statute makes considerable direct change to the common law, for instance the creation of damages for provision of necessary services to an injured person by s 8 of the Administration of Justice Act 1982. In others, considerable indirect effect flows from related statutory innovation, for instance the protection for motor vehicle accident pursuers through compulsory third party insurance legislation. Further, damages for infringement of intellectual property rights depend almost entirely upon liability created by statute such as the Copyright, Designs and Patents Act 1988, although the legislation says little about such damages. Damages for breach of a Convention right under the Human Rights Act 1998 (which can be regarded as effectively delictual) are entirely the product of that legislation, although it, too, says little, and refers to the principles laid down by the European Court of Human Rights.

In any event, statute gives no definitions of delictual damages and few statements of explicit general principle, so the area remains essentially common law.

DELICTUAL DAMAGES AND ACADEMIC AND OTHER CONTEMPORARY WRITERS

Academic writers have tended to concentrate on the delictual, rather than the reparational, aspect of the subject. They, and other contemporary writers, have generated definitions, although these have tended to be definitions of damages as such, rather than of delictual damages, and writers concerned with delictual damages have tended to eschew definitions and ignore all but personal injury cases[2].

---

1 See however *Hamilton v British Transport Commission* 1957 SC 300, noted below.
2 Eg McEwan & Paton *McEwan & Paton on Damages for Personal Injury in Scotland* (2nd edn, 1989) (looseleaf updated), Bennett *Personal Injury Damages in Scotland* (1999).

Walker, much the most prolific writer on the topic, offers:

'Damages may be defined as the sum of money payable under the order of a competent judicial tribunal by one juristic person to another in compensation for the prejudice suffered by the latter in consequence of the breach by the former of a duty to or right of obligation vested in the latter person[1]'.

He also lists half a dozen other definitions, taken variously from other academic sources, English and American, and presumably considered inadequate. However, he does not derive his definition from Scottish cases, but from *Hall Bros v Young*[2] in which Lord Greene MR asserted:

'"Damages" to an English lawyer, imports this idea, that the sums payable by way of damages are sums which fall to be paid by reason of some breach of duty or obligation, whether that duty is imposed by contract, the general law, or by legislation'.

Walker notes[3] that this was quoted approvingly in *Hamilton v British Transport Commission* by the Lord Ordinary (Cameron)[4], and in his various works discusses divers principles of delictual damages.

More succinctly, T B Smith observes that:

'Damages are awarded in reparation with a view to restoring the pursuer to the same position as he would have been had he not sustained the injury of which he complains'[5].

This relates to delictual damages only, but is clearly not a definition. It does, however, usefully refer to an underlying principle, and the passage goes on to consider its application in relation to various sorts of loss, and questions of remoteness and causation.

The learned author of 'Judicial and Other Remedies' in the *Stair Memorial Encyclopaedia* refers to other definitions, but prefers Walker's[6]. In more recent works on delict, Thomson[7] devotes one chapter to damages, considering various issues briefly, but does not include a definition, or discussion of general principle, and Stewart[8] has a few sections only, discussing practical matters.

---

1 This formulation originally appeared in his *Law of Damages in Scotland* (1955) p 1, and was repeated in *Law of Civil Remedies in Scotland* (1974) p 389. It also appears in *Law of Delict in Scotland* (1st edn, 1966) p 465; (2nd edn 1981) p 460. Interestingly, a somewhat different version appears in *Principles of the Law of Scotland* (4th edn, 1989) vol IV p 296.
2 [1939] 1 KB 756.
3 *Law of Civil Remedies in Scotland* p 389, n8.
4 1957 SC 300, at 304 where Lord Cameron observed, before quoting *Hall*, that '[t]he word "damages" is in law one which has a recognised technical meaning and is one which in addition can comprise and include a varying but identifiable number of elements or items'. However, he gave no technical meaning beyond adopting Lord Greene's words, and did not identify the elements or items. Walker modestly forebears to note that Lord Cameron mentions that the dictum was drawn to his attention by counsel quoting Walker's *Law of Delict in Scotland*.
5 *Short Commentary on the Law of Scotland* (1962) p 709.
6 Vol 13 (1992) para 72, *sub voc* 'Compensatory Remedies': cf vol 15 (1996) 'Obligations', *sub voc* 'Substitutionary Remedies (Damages)' which avoids definition.
7 *Delictual Liability* ch 16.
8 *Delict and Related Obligations* (3rd edn, 1998).

DAMNUM, COMPENSATION AND TYPES OF DAMAGES

DAMNUM

As traditional treatment of delict deals chiefly with *injuria*, *damnum* is not examined as closely. It is treated as implicit in the *injuria*, so defined by reference to it, or is examined only indirectly through discussion of causation, remoteness etc, and loosely described simply as either 'patrimonial' (or 'pecuniary') or otherwise. Also, statements of principle referring to losses (or harms, or injuries, or damage, or prejudice) 'arising naturally and directly out of the wrong done'[1], emphasise liability for the adverse consequences generally of any *injuria*. Further, various devices such as remoteness, are employed to restrict the effect of such broad principle, but closer definition of *damnum* has not been among them. Finally, the *damnum* in respect of any particular delict is commonly clear.

All this might suggest that close examination of the concept is unnecessary. However, what can be *damnum* in principle remains less than wholly clear, and loose classifications of types of *damnum*, such as 'patrimonial', are too vague and over-inclusive. This makes it difficult to answer with any precision apparently straightforward questions such as what delictual damages are paid for.

Some of the consequential difficulties of the vagueness of the position (and the dangers of unthinkingly translating *damnum* as 'loss', 'harm' etc) are neatly demonstrated by the Inner House decision in *McFarlane v Tayside Health Board*[2], a 'wrongful conception' negligence case arising out of a failed vasectomy. The mother claimed £10,000 *solatium* for having to undergo pregnancy and confinement, and the pain and distress of delivery, and she and the father together claimed £100,000 for extra expenditure on feeding and clothing the child etc, and in moving to a larger house. It also appears that they claimed for the mother's lost earnings, but not for the time and trouble of bringing up a child. The Lord Ordinary (Gill) held the claim irrelevant.

On appeal to the Inner House, the defender's principal argument was that this was *injuria absque damno*. Pregnancy and birth did not constitute a 'harm', nor a 'personal injury', but constituted a 'natural process'. Extra expenditure on a child could not be considered 'wasted'. The Second Division sidestepped all of these contentions as misinterpreting the pursuers' claim. 'Personal injury' is not the only form of *damnum*, and the birth was not the *damnum* claimed for, but the occasion of it. The *damnum* was actually the pain and suffering and the economic costs which resulted[3]. The claim, moreover, was not that pregnancy was not a 'natural process' but that the couple had been prevented from avoiding that 'natural process'. Similarly, expenditure on children might or might not be wasted, but the

---

1 *Allan v Barclay* (1864) 2 M 873, at 874.
2 1997 SLT 211 (OH). 1998 SC 389, 1998 SLT 307, 1998 SCLR 126 (2nd Div); (1999) Times, 26 November, HL.
3 In 1998 SLT 307, at 310I, Lord Justice-Clerk Cullen put the point in terms of 'interests', ie the mother's 'interest in her bodily integrity', which concerned the physical consequences of pregnancy, and both parents' 'pecuniary interest', etc.

claim was not that it was wasted, but that negligence had prevented the parents from avoiding it altogether[1].

However, there was no sustained attempt to define *damnum*. Lord Cullen described it as 'the prejudice suffered by the pursuer in respect of some interest which is recognised by law'[2]. Lord McCluskey gave similar descriptions[3], explicitly rejecting terms such as 'injury' and 'harm' and indeed suggesting that the Lord Ordinary had fallen into error by using the term 'injury'[4].

Classification of delict by interests is popular[5]. However, while it is relatively helpful in relation to damages for nominate delicts such as assault or defamation where the 'interest' protected is fairly clear, it tends to be repetitive (since most interests attract the same sorts of damages) and is less useful in relation to negligence (for the interest protected is less clear). In any case, it suffers from the lack of an authoritative list of protected interests. Thus, in *McFarlane*, both Lord Cullen and Lord McCluskey, despite agreeing that the case involved analysis of the concept of *damnum*, found themselves in the conventional position of tacitly defining it by reference to the *injuria*, and simply listing the things the pursuer complained of[6].

A way of attempting better understanding is to look at the concept of compensation, and examine the cases and discover what *damnum* has in fact been compensated.

COMPENSATION

The term 'compensation' is not itself free from ambiguity. It is often used to describe what is paid when there is no legal wrong done, for example in compulsory purchase. Equally, it is used in a wide range of situations, from repaying outgoings to recognising bereavement. On the other hand, simple return of something taken is restitution or restoration rather than compensation.

Dictionary definitions (with implicit reference to that central metaphor of the legal system, the 'scales of justice') emphasise the notion of 'counterbalancing'[7]. This notion contains the idea of comparison as well as that of redress.

---

1 The defenders also argued that, in any case, the benefits of a child outweighed any detriments, and that the cause of the expenditure was the parents' love of the child, thus breaking the chain of causation. The Second Division rejected these arguments at some length.

2 1998 SLT 307 at 310 F.

3 Above at 313 K, 314 K, 316 A.

4 Above at 315 G–I.

5 Walker catalogues delict this way in the 'Special Part' of his *Law of Delict in Scotland* and in the Introduction describes different classification schemes, regarding his as an adaption of Stair's (though terminology and substance seem to owe as much to Pound, as footnotes reveal). The learned author of the relevant section of vol 15 ('Obligations') of the *Stair Memorial Encyclopaedia* takes the same approach. Walker also uses it in *The Law of Civil Remedies in Scotland*. Convention rights under the Human Rights Act 1998 (not fully in force at the time of writing), breach of which by a 'pubic authority' is effectively delictual, are listed in this way.

6 1998 SLT 307 at 314C–G, Lord McCluskey referred to the defender's duty 'to take reasonable care to give ... accurate advice about his fertility', and the father's corresponding right to receive such advice and the mother's corresponding 'right not to be made pregnant without her knowing consent' etc. It would be difficult to contain these in a list of interests without being impossibly detailed or unhelpfully general. The House of Lords overturned the decision of the Inner House in relation to extra expenditure, but did not reject this analysis. Indeed, Lord Hope described it as 'the traditional view of delictual liability'. However, their Lordships were unanimous in finding another principle or principles to override the consequences of such analysis in that case: see (1999) Times, 26 November, HL. See also ch 3.

7 See eg *Shorter Oxford English Dictionary* (3rd edn, rev).

Whether redress is necessary, and whether it has been achieved, are determined by comparison. The pans of the scales are compared to see if one is lower than the other; the success of the redress is shown by comparing them to see if they have returned to equilibrium. This return to equilibrium is commonly expressed as *'restitutio in integrum'* (or in Stair's phrase, quoted above, 'putting [the pursuer] in as good a condition as he was in before the injury')[1].

ATIYAH'S ANALYSIS OF COMPENSATION

Atiyah analyses compensation in a delictual context[2]. He distinguishes 'corrective compensation' and 'redistributive compensation'. Simply put[3], redistributive compensation counterbalances by comparing different people, redress being shown by equality between them. Corrective compensation counterbalances by comparing one person at different times, typically before and after an event, redress being shown by restoration of the status quo.

Within 'corrective compensation', Atiyah draws another distinction of some significance between 'equivalent compensation' and 'substitute or solace compensation', and indeed, within them[4].

Equivalent compensation and substitute or solace compensation

Equivalent compensation occurs where something is given as an 'equivalent for what has been lost'[5]. Atiyah divides it into three sub-types in terms of the sort of loss. These are:

(i)   'money or some other asset which can be replaced by money': eg losses such as a destroyed or damaged car or house, but also past lost income;

(ii)   'costs incurred by a victim of injury or damage': eg losses, such as medical costs[6], incidental to the basic loss; and

1 Cf 'just satisfaction' in the Human Rights Act 1998, s 8(2) and art 41 (previously 50) of the European Convention on Human Rights.
2 Cane (ed) *Atiyah's Accidents, Compensation and the Law* (6th edn, 1999) pp 349–352, especially 351–352. He considers the matter principally in terms of personal injury actions, but his conclusions apply more widely.
3 In fact, the comparisons are more complicated. Redistributive compensation compares two positions: those of the claimant and of the comparator. Corrective compensation seemingly indicates three: those of the claimant's actual former position, actual present position, and hypothetical present position had the event to be corrected not occurred. The real comparison is not between the claimant's former position and his or her present position, but between the claimant's actual present position, and his or her hypothetical present position (as inferred from the former actual position). The difficulties increase if compensation is for 'future losses', since comparison involves a predicted future position inferred from the actual present position and another hypothetical future position inferred from the hypothetical present position.
4 In previous editions, compensation was divided into 'equivalence' (*sic*), 'substitute or solace' and 'equalisation' (5th edn, pp 350–351). In the latest, the last-mentioned has been given greater prominence and a useful change of title to 'redistributive'. The passage on p 350 of the 6th edition, introducing the newer classification, does not make it immediately clear that 'equivalent' and 'substitute and solace' can be sub-types of 'corrective', but reading the text confirms that this is so. There are some other differences in the new text. Regardless of the benefit of the new form of classification, the text in the 5th edition may be easier to follow.
5 This phrase (5th edn, p 350) has been dropped from the 6th edition, but seems still apposite.
6 In the 5th edition (p 325) Atiyah noted that in the United Kingdom much of this is borne by the National Health Service. It thus operates as a separate, no-fault, compensation system.

(iii) 'lost expectations' consequential upon the original loss: eg typically, lost future income[1].

Substitute or solace compensation is attempted where there is no equivalent for what is lost. In such cases, the aim is to provide 'a substitute source of satisfaction or pleasure . . ., or . . . to comfort the victim or provide him or her with solace for what has happened'[2]. Atiyah loosely distinguishes between 'substitute' and 'solace' by seeing the former as having an element of equivalence in that a genuine substitute is possible, and the latter applying where no possible substitute exists.

INSIGHTS FROM ATIYAH'S ANALYSIS

Atiyah's analysis sheds light on the nature of damages, the concept of *damnum*, conventional classifications of damages and methods of quantification, and underpins a typology of damages suggested below.

Compensation and the aims of delict

'Corrective compensation' is the province of delict. Comparison is made between the positions of the claimant before and after the *injuria*, the difference being the *damnum*. Redress is putting the claimant back in the position in which he or she was, so far as can be done (which may be called '*restitutio in integrum*').

'Redistributive compensation' has no interest in *damnum* and *injuria*, and the comparison made is between the claimant and another person[3]. This may include a notional person, and is the province of social security.

'Pecuniary' and 'non-pecuniary' damages and *restitutio in integrum*

Damages are conventionally, if loosely, classified into two categories, sometimes referred to as 'patrimonial' and 'non-patrimonial', sometimes as 'pecuniary' and 'non-pecuniary'. These clearly correspond to Atiyah's 'equivalent' and 'substitute or solace' types of compensation, respectively. Both aim to restore the claimant to his or her former position. The difference between them lies in the means by which this *restitutio in integrum* is attempted.

In the former, compensation is in principle possible by means of provision of an equivalent, expressed in money, so that there is a genuine possibility of substantial restoration of the status quo. In the latter, no equivalent is possible, and *restitutio in integrum* is attempted by the next best means, that is, a substitute, or, failing that, comfort in so far as this can be expressed in money.

Atiyah suggests that 'non-pecuniary' damages are harder to justify than 'pecuniary'. This is partly because it is not clear how quantification is possible, and partly on the *ad hoc* ground that such damages are in practice usually paid

---

1 As Atiyah notes, strictly speaking, the claim is for lost ability to earn, loss of future income being simply shorthand for a measure of that loss.

2 p 351.

3 However, see the opinions of Lord Clyde and Lord Steyn in *McFarlane v Tayside Health Board* (1999) Times, 26 November, HL.

by insurance companies out of premiums, and have a high opportunity cost. In other words, the money might be better spent elsewhere.

Damages themselves are, of course, always 'pecuniary', in that they are always expressed in terms of money, 'the universal solvent'[1].

Subdivisions of 'pecuniary' damages

'Patrimonial' or 'pecuniary' damages include the wide range of examples falling within Atiyah's equivalent compensation (though such equivalent may also be provided by other compensation systems, such as first party commercial insurance.)

They are sometimes further loosely divided into 'out-of-pocket expenses' and 'loss of income', to reflect the fact that the category is very wide, and contains disparate elements. These subdivisions loosely equate to Atiyah's three sub-types which are a little subtler. For example his 'lost expectations' emphasises the existence of future losses and their rather different nature from past losses. However, Atiyah's own sub-types may not be quite subtle enough, and may be influenced by the division in English law between 'general damages' (which do not require to be specially proved), and 'special damages' (which do)[2].

Nevertheless, they draw attention to the conceptual differences between losses of assets as such and consequential expenditure (that is, assets which you had and have lost by reason of the *injuria*) on the one hand, and lost income (that is, assets which you never even received, by reason of the *injuria*) on the other. Likewise it clearly reveals the differences between all past losses (in principle determinable) and all future losses (inevitably speculative). All these categories are conceptually distinguishable, and present different problems of quantification.

Subdivisions of 'non-pecuniary' damages and *restitutio in integrum*

Loose division of non-pecuniary damages, or *solatium*, is conventionally made into 'pain and suffering', 'loss of faculty' etc. Atiyah provides some explanation of this with his concept of 'substitute or solace', in so far as 'loss of faculty' might roughly correspond to cases where a substitute is available, and other types, including 'pain and suffering' to those for which only comfort can be provided.

TYPES OF DAMAGES

From Atiyah's categories can therefore be derived a useful, if slightly unconventional, classification of damages into compensation for:

(i)   Patrimonial losses—I: Losses of assets:
        including losses to corporeal or incorporeal, heritable or moveable property (as opposed to loss of income);

---

1 See *Auld v Shairp* (1874) 2 R 191, at 19, per Lord Neaves.
2 Thus, loss of assets and loss of past income may be classified together and loss of future income separately, because the former two are 'general damages' and the latter is 'special'.

(ii)   Patrimonial losses—II: Consequential expenditure:
         including past and future medical and nursing expenses, child-care
         and domestic expenses, extra living, housing alteration and moving
         expenses, but also claims under the Administration of Justice Act 1982
         for 'necessary' and 'personal' services;
(iii) Patrimonial losses—III: Loss of profit, loss of income and loss of
         support:
         including past and future loss of profit and income, and loss of
         support claims;
(iv)   Personal losses: *Solatium* and 'loss of society':
         including past and future claims for 'pain and suffering', 'loss of
         faculty' etc, and loss of society etc.

This typology is expanded upon in ch 2, and forms the basis of the examination of quantification in practice in ch 5.

2. Types of damages and who may claim them

On the basis of a re-interpretation of Atiyah's analysis of the concept of compensation, and consideration of the cases, a broad four-fold typology of damages emerges, as outlined in the previous chapter. This chapter examines the typology, and who may claim such damages. Quantification in principle, and of each type, is examined in chs 3, 4 and 5, and their relationship with other compensation systems in ch 6.

1. PATRIMONIAL LOSSES—I: LOSSES OF ASSETS

GENERAL

Losses of assets could be classified according to the *injuria* causing that *damnum*. Some traditional nominate and intentional delicts are specifically aimed at the protection of ownership, including intrusion and ejection, nuisance and spuilzie. So also are the various statutory remedies in relation to intellectual property[1]. Fraud and other breaches of statutory duty may cause losses of assets, as may negligence. Losses of assets might also flow from breach of a Convention right under the Human Rights Act 1998, for example breach of that for the protection of property[2]. However, different delicts do not involve different types of damages, and more than one delict may be involved (as in *Boots the Chemist Ltd v GA Estates plc*[3], where a pursuer who suffered flooding founded on both nuisance and negligence), so despite certain advantages to such a classification[4], it is somewhat repetitive.

The losses could be classified according to the nature of the loss itself, for example physical (as where corporeal property is destroyed or damaged by any means), or otherwise (as where rights in the property are prejudiced, for instance, by trespass or infringement of intellectual property rights). Thus, in *Hutchison v Davidson*[5], a cottage was destroyed; in *Pomphrey v James A Cuthbertson*[6], a car damaged; in *Bell v McGlennan*[7], radio apparatus detained; in *Oliver Homes (Manufacturing) v Hamilton*[8], copyright in building plans

---

1 For example, Patents Act 1977, s 61(1)(c); Copyright, Designs and Patents Act 1988, ss 96, 103(1) and 194 (copyright), 194 (performance rights) and 229 (unregistered designs); Trade Marks Act 1994, s 10(2); and Plant Varieties Act 1997, s 13.
2 Human Rights Act 1998, s 1(3), Sch 1, Pt II, First Protocol, art 1 (not in force at the time of writing).
3 1993 SLT 136, 1992 SCLR 859.
4 It was favoured by Walker in *Law of Civil Remedies in Scotland* (1974).
5 1945 SC 395.
6 1951 SC 147, 1951 SLT 191.
7 1992 SC 41, 1992 SLT 237.
8 1992 SLT 892.

breached; and in *Bristol & West of England Building Society v Rollo Steven & Bond*[1], a worse security over heritable property than expected obtained[2]. This classification clearly depends on the traditional classification of property law into heritable and moveable, corporeal and incorporeal. However, whether loss is by physical means or otherwise, all examples are in fact ones of prejudice to property rights, and that is the *damnum*[3]. For example, if you are denied use of moveable property by unlawful means you may vindicate your right, and it matters little whether the unlawful act destroyed the property or left it intact but in another's exclusive control. However, by definition, while rights in corporeal property can be prejudiced by physical means and non-physical means, those in incorporeal property can only be prejudiced by non-physical means.

Thus, although no classification is wholly satisfactory, it seems most sensible to rely on the traditional property law one, while bearing in mind that variations that may flow from different delicts, and distinctions such as the difference between total loss and lesser losses, might be useful. It should also be noted that infringement of intellectual property rights can be seen as reducing their capital value, thus producing a loss of asset, but has generally been treated as a loss of income.

Nevertheless, in all cases, Atiyah's 'equivalent' compensation is likely to be appropriate.

BOUNDARY AND OVERLAPPING CASES

Claims involving losses of assets may be difficult to disentangle from claims for extra expenditure[4].

PAST AND FUTURE LOSSES OF ASSETS

Losses of assets are past losses, though if infringement is treated as loss of income, this may extend into the future.

---

1 1998 SLT 9.
2 The loss of a legal right is loss of an incorporeal moveable asset: in *Kyle v P & J Stormonth Darling, WS* 1994 SLT 191, 1993 SCLR 18, the Inner House decided that what the pursuer had to prove was that the right had an ascertainable value.
3 It may be useful to recall the analysis of ownership, the greatest possible legal interest in a thing, in Honoré's 'Ownership' in *Oxford Essays in Jurisprudence* (ed Guest) (1961). He found eleven 'standard incidents', ie the right to possess, the right to use, the right to manage, the right to the income, the right to the capital, the right to security, the incident of trans-missibility, the incidence of absence of term, the prohibition of harmful use, liability to execu-tion, and the residuary character. The rights can be held by different persons, such as landlord and tenant, mortgagor and mortgagee, and anyone holding one suffers *damnum* if exercise is prejudiced.
4 Thus, in *Boots the Chemist Ltd v GA Estates* 1993 SLT 136, 1992 SCLR 859, where premises were flooded causing damage, the pursuer claimed for 'loss of stock', ie damage to moveable property, but also 'loss of sales' (presumably loss of profit, though the relationship of these two items was not explored) and for consequential expenditure, such as 'additional staff costs'. Repair costs might better be treated as losses of assets, as the repair merely evidences the existing *damnum*.

2. PATRIMONIAL LOSSES—II: CONSEQUENTIAL EXPENDITURE

THE NATURE OF CONSEQUENTIAL EXPENDITURE

Any delictual claim may involve the claimant in consequential expenditure, that is, costs which are not part of the *damnum* immediately or necessarily suffered, but consequential upon it, such as travel or nursing costs. This is clearly again Atiyah's 'equivalent compensation'.

In addition to actual consequential expenditure, there is notional consequential expenditure under s 8 or s 9 of the Administration of Justice Act 1982 for the cost of 'necessary' or 'personal' services, treated as *damnum* which is analogous to consequential expenditure even though supplied gratuitously.

ACTUAL CONSEQUENTIAL EXPENDITURE

Types of actual consequential expenditure

There is rather little by way of guidance from the Inner House as to what is permissible as consequential expenditure. Numerous cases exemplify what has been allowed.

Repair and associated costs have been included in property damage cases. In *Boots the Chemist v GA Estates Ltd*, for example, sums for 'supply and fitting of skirting', 'repair to electrical services', 'additional shopfitting costs' and 'additional staff costs' were agreed, although repair costs might better be regarded as losses of assets, for the repair is evidence of the existing *damnum* to the property. Building insurance premiums, legal and estate agency expenses and related costs were accepted in *Bristol & West of England Building Society*.

A wide variety has been allowed in personal injury cases, including the costs of goods (such as prostheses), services (such as nursing), and heritables (such as new or altered premises).

Thus, in *Tuttle v Edinburgh University*[1], a student had broken his back and suffered related medical conditions. Lord McDonald usefully reproduced a list of heads of damages from a report produced by the Spinal Injuries Association given in evidence[2]. These were:

(1) medical supplies (in fact disallowed as paid for by the National Health Service);
(2) appliances, aids and equipment (including an electric blanket, sheepskins, waterproof mattress cover, stand-up wheelchair, shower chair/commode, washing machine and dryer, and lifting pole);

---

1 1984 SLT 172.
2 Above, at 174–175. The report (apparently the first produced) was spoken to by the Association's 'claims consultant', and Lord Macdonald, at 173–174, 'found his report a helpful aid to identifying the requirements of a person so severely disabled as the pursuer' (but less so as to quantification). However, this consultant received scathing criticism from Temporary Judge Coutts in *McMillan v McDowall* 1993 SLT 311 at 314H–315A (as noted in ch 5).

(3)   future care and attendance provision (including regular assistance in keeping house and maintaining the garden);
(4)   additional motoring expenses (including vehicle replacement costs and running expenses, but not a 'terrain cycle' or a sporting wheelchair, the cost already being included in the *solatium*);
(5)   accommodation requirements (including house acquisition and conversion);
(6)   additional running costs of the home (including extra heating and fuel bills);
(7)   recreation and holidays (in fact included in *solatium*);
(8)   special clothing and dressing; and
(9)   employment (in fact included in *solatium* and future loss of earnings)[1].

Actions concerning children born handicapped after medical negligence or otherwise[2] have successfully claimed the costs of raising children as such (including goods, services and heritables), as in *Geddes v Lothian Health Board*[3], where the defenders were not liable, but the pursuer had claimed costs of moveables including a vehicle, heritables including adaptations to a house and future acquisition of another, maintenance costs on some of the property, and outlays on services including travel to medical centres. Most of these were accepted by the defenders, or objections to them repelled[4].

Other personal injury or like cases have included a curator's bond of caution, curator's fee and accountant's fee in *Forsyth's CB v Govan Shipbuilders*[5]; an 'excess' on insurance on a cancelled holiday in *Whyte v University of Dundee*[6]; kennelling costs and certain prescription charges in *Blackhall v McInnes*[7]; and in an assault case, *Downie v Chief Constable, Strathclyde Police*[8], pre-legal aid legal expenses.

In fatal accident cases the Damages (Scotland) Act 1976, s 1(3) permits expenses in connection with the deceased's funeral, incurred by a 'relative' as defined. The definition, in Schedule 1 to the Act, is the same as for 'loss of support' claims, discussed below.

Consequential expenditure claims, and particularly future care and accommodation cost claims, though significant only in comparatively recent years[9], is an area of expansion.

---

1   It is not clear what outlays in respect of employment were listed, though a sum for loss of opportunity was included in future loss of earnings. In principle they might have included training costs or equipment.
2   Although not necessarily unhandicapped children: see the House of Lords decision in *McFarlane v Tayside Health Board* (1999) Times, 26 November, HL, overturning in part 1998 SC 389, 1998 SLT 307, 1998 SCLR 126 (and impliedly *Allan v Greater Glasgow Health Board* 1998 SLT 580). Immediate extra expenditure, such as a 'layette', was accepted, but not the general costs of childcare.
3   1992 SLT 986, 1992 SCLR 214: see also *Anderson v Forth Valley Health Board* 1998 SLT 588, 1998 SCLR 97 and *McLelland v Greater Glasgow Health Board* 1999 SLT 543.
4   See also *McLelland v Greater Glasgow Health Board*, above, at 549L–550A (goods), 550B–553B and 553B–554J (costs of maintaining a child to 18), and 554J–557C (additional care costs on account of the child's handicap).
5   1987 SLT 321, 1987 SCLR 604.
6   1990 SLT 454.
7   1997 SLT 649.
8   1998 SLT 8, 1997 SCLR 603.
9   The first reported future care case seems to be *Sellar's CB v Glasgow Victoria and Leverndale Hospitals* 1973 SLT (Notes) 3: see Lord President Hope in *O'Brien's CB v British Steel plc* 1991 SLT 477 at 481L–482K and 482J, 1991 SCLR 831.

Boundary and overlapping cases

Questions arise as to whether items should be regarded as consequential expenditure or as something to be taken out of compensation for lost income (as with holiday costs in *Gardner v Howard Doris*[1] per Lord Grieve) or *solatium* (as with costs of a 'terrain cycle', sporting wheelchair and holiday costs in *Tuttle v Edinburgh University*[2], per Lord McDonald). This issue raises important questions as to the nature of 'equivalent compensation' and double compensation.

The matter was more fully discussed in *O'Brien's CB v British Steel plc*[3]. It was common ground that a proportion of the costs of a residential home was a 'domestic element'. This represented the cost of living had there been no accident, so was not consequential expenditure. It should thus be met out of compensation for lost income, since it would have been paid out of actual income. Lord President Hope concluded that, on the facts, food was the only 'domestic element', for it was justifiable for the incapax's wife and children to maintain a separate household to which the compensation for lost income would largely be applied[4].

McMillan v McDowall[5] raised similar questions (though without reference to *O'Brien's CB*) in relation to board and lodging received as part of a 'package of remuneration'[6]. Future board and lodging provided by the pursuer's parents were thus 'benefits of a benevolent character' and, by virtue of the Administration of Justice Act 1982, s 10[7], to be disregarded in assessing damages. Also, certain items treated in the pleadings as consequential expenditure turned out to have been purchased by the pursuer's parents, so were treated as 'necessary services' by 'relatives', by virtue of s 8 of the same Act (which is discussed below).

Past and future actual consequential expenditure

Actual consequential expenditure can be a single or occasional expense or a continuing one. If occasional or continuing it may extend into the future, and fall to be regarded as occasional or continuing future loss for the purposes of quantification and interest.

NOTIONAL CONSEQUENTIAL EXPENDITURE

Types of notional consequential expenditure

Claims are also possible in a personal injury action for certain notional consequential expenditure, that is, for services similar to those which might

---

1 1983 SLT 672 at 674.
2 1984 SLT 172 at 174.
3 1991 SLT 477, 1991 SCLR 831.
4 1991 SLT 477 at 480A–D.
5 1993 SLT 311.
6 Distinguishing *Edgar v Lord Advocate* 1965 SC 67, 1965 SLT 158, where a majority of the Inner House held that a wife's foregone wages were no loss to her husband.
7 Discussed in ch 6.

be paid for, but which are in fact provided free by or for a relative. These are defined as 'necessary services' and 'personal services' under the Administration of Justice Act 1982, ss 8 and 9, respectively, read with s 7. They may still be seen as Atiyah's 'equivalent compensation'.

Section 8: 'necessary services'

Section 8 services are ones which, as a result of injury, a relative renders to the injured person[1]. They are typified by the services of a 'carer', and include those the injured person can no longer carry out (such as washing), and those necessitated by the injury (such as nursing). The Administration of Justice Act 1982, s 8(1) declares that:

'Where necessary services have been rendered to the injured person by a relative in consequence of the injuries in question, then . . . [the defender] shall be liable to pay to the injured person by way of damages such sum as represents reasonable remuneration for those services and payment of reasonable expenses incurred in connection therewith.'

Section 8(3)[2] extends this to '[w]here, at the date of an award of damages in favour of the injured person, it is likely that necessary services will, after that date, be rendered to him'.

Background and origins of s 8

The s 8 claim arose chiefly from recommendations of the Scottish Law Commission report on damages for personal injuries, but also in part from the views of the Pearson Commission, and the (English) Law Commission[3].

Common law was generally unsympathetic to claims by relatives. Two cases, *Thompson v Angus County Council* (unreported, but quoted, and followed, in *Murphy v Baxter's Bus Services*[4]), and *Murphy* itself, warily admitted claims for services by family members. Both were cases of injured wives suing for the costs of services where their husbands had given up jobs to provide them. However, in *Edgar v Lord Advocate*[5] (where an injured husband sued for loss of wages of his wife who had given up work to provide the services) the Inner House, by a majority, overruled them, and doubted the relevancy of such claims, at least in the absence of special factors.

In *Jacks v McDougall & Co (Engineers) Ltd*[6] both wife and injured husband sued for the wife's lost wages in caring for the husband, and her travelling expenses for medical care. The husband argued that both earnings defrayed

---

1 In *McLelland v Greater Glasgow Health Board* 1999 SLT 543 necessary services could not be claimed for, as they were rendered to a handicapped child whose birth, but not handicap, were the result of negligence, and so was not 'an injured person'.
2 Added by the Law Reform (Miscellaneous Provisions) (Scotland) Act 1990, s 69.
3 See *Damages for Personal Injuries: Report on (1) Admissibility of Claims for Services, (2) Admissible Deductions* (Scot Law Com no 51) (HC Paper 557 (1977–78)), paras 8–33; *Report of the Royal Commission on Civil Liability and Compensation for Personal Injury* (Cmnd 7054 (1978)), paras 343–351; and *Report on Personal Injury Litigation—assessment of damages* (Law Com no 56) (HC Paper no 373 (1972–73)), para 155.
4 1962 SC 589, 1961 SLT 435.
5 1965 SC 67, 1965 SLT 158.
6 1973 SC 13.

household expenses which was a special factor, and sought to distinguish *Edgar*. Lord Keith thought his claim in respect to the wife's wages a matter of remoteness, and allowed proof before answer, but in respect of her travelling expenses, that they were not the husband's loss. He also held the wife's claim irrelevant as no duty was owed to her in respect of her husband[1].

English courts, however, were much better disposed to such claims[2], and the Scottish Law Commission favoured this approach. It argued that if an injured person required services, he or she had suffered a loss. Whether that loss was made up contractually or gratuitously was an artificial distinction, and in any case provision of the services bore most heavily upon responsible close family members, including wives who gave up jobs to nurse husbands.

Types of s 8 'necessary services'

The Scottish Law Commission envisaged services 'such as nursing services to and attendance upon the injured person and such supply to him of medical and surgical requisites, apparel and household goods, as might seem to the court to be reasonably necessary', and rejected the suggestion that only services of an extraordinary nature should be included[3]. It decided against a statutory definition of such 'services' and considered 'necessary' self-explanatory[4].

Thus the courts have had to decide these matters. No Inner House cases are reported but in the Outer House the ordinary household tasks of washing, ironing, cooking and shopping were accepted in *Denheen v British Railways Board*[5]; general nursing services such as adjusting clothing, washing, bathing, shaving, cutting up food, helping up after a fall and accompanying out of doors, in *Forsyth's CB v Govan Shipbuilders*[6]; and more intimate and skilled nursing services, such as sucking out a tracheotomy tube, cleaning the hole, administering drugs, feeding by naso-gastric tube, physiotherapy, and constant watch, in *Fowler v Greater Glasgow Health Board*[7].

A considerable broadening was allowed in *McMillan v McDowall*[8], which allowed for general emotional support, practical assistance including running errands, visits, provision of a vehicle, and alterations to a house[9]. However, in

---

1 1973 SC 13 at 16–21. In holding the wife's claim irrelevant Lord Keith followed Lord President Inglis in *Eisten v North British Railway Co* (1870) 8 M 980 at 984, 7 SLR 638, and Lord Watson in *Clark v Carfin Coal Co* (1891) 18 R (HL) 63 at 65, distinguishing *Soutar v Mulhern* 1907 SC 723, and holding that *McBay v Hamlett* 1963 SC 282, 1963 SLT 18 was wrongly decided.

2 See particularly *Donnelly v Joyce* [1974] QB 454, [1973] 3 WLR 514, [1973] 3 All ER 475. In *Thompson v Angus County Council*, Lord Guthrie relied on *Roach v Yates* [1938] 1 KB 256 and *Hawkes v Torquay Corporation* [1938] 4 All ER 16.

3 *Damages for Personal Injuries* (Scot Law Com no 51) para 25.

4 *Damages for Personal Injuries* (Scot Law Com no 51) para 27.

5 1986 SLT 249.

6 1988 SLT 321, 1987 SCLR 604 (OH); nb see 1988 SC 421, 1989 SLT 91, 1989 SCLR 87 (IH).

7 1990 SLT 303.

8 1993 SLT 311.

9 Visits were assumed to be 'necessary services', but had been admitted in the equivalent claim in England, at common law, in *Hunt v Severs* [1994] 2 AC 350 (see Lord Bridge's remarks at 356H–357A), [1994] 2 WLR 602, [1994] 2 All ER 385. In *McMillan*, at 314G, provision of the vehicle was considered by Temporary Judge Coutts to be 'not only necessary . . . but vital', and at 314F, alterations to the house were admitted by amendment to the pleadings as 'it was clear and plain . . . that it was both necessary and reasonable'.

Duffy v Lanarkshire Health Board[1], the Lord Ordinary (Johnston), as a matter of policy, rejected the 'ingenious' claim of provision of an organ for transplant, noting the effect on the law regarding payments to providers of transplants.

It therefore seems unlikely that any normal service likely to be performed by a relative will be excluded, and that 'necessary' has been interpreted as 'reasonable'.

'Relative'

'Relative' for the purposes of s 8 is defined in s 13(1) of the Administration of Justice Act 1982. It is restricted to spouses; 'ascendants'; 'descendants'; siblings; and uncles and aunts. However, the accepted family web is wider than this suggests. Divorced spouses and 'common law spouses'[2] are included, as are those treated as children of the family[3] (which could require difficult decisions) and illegitimate children[4]. So indeed are stepchildren, and since 'any relationship of the half blood shall be treated as a relationship of the whole blood', and 'any relationship by affinity shall be treated as a relationship by consanguinity'[5], presumably a variety of relationships is included, such as half-siblings, uncles and aunts by marriage, and even 'grandparents-in-law', and combinations of these categories. Presumably mothers-in-law and daughters-in-law are included by parallel reasoning with *McAllister v Imperial Chemical Industries plc*[6] and *Monteith v Cape Insulation Ltd*[7], decided under Sch 1 of the Administration of Justice Act 1982.

'Reasonable remuneration and ... reasonable expenses'

A 'necessary services' claim is for 'reasonable remuneration for those services' and 'reasonable expenses incurred in connection therewith'.

This raises difficulties of interpretation, involving questions of principle, which the decided cases do not clearly set out. This is dealt with in ch 5 as a matter of quantification.

Accounting to the service provider and limits on a claim

Section 8 does not allow the relative providing the service to sue, nor compel the injured person to do so, but if the injured person does recover the remuneration or expenses, s 8(2) requires him or her to account to the relative for them. In *Blackhall v MacInnes*[8] and *Kennedy v Lees of Scotland*[9] it was considered that where more than one relative had rendered services this

---

1 1999 SLT 906, at 907L–908B.
2 Administration of Justice Act 1982, 13(1)(b): 'any person, not being the spouse of the injured person, who was, at the time of the act or omission giving rise to liability in the responsible person, living with the injured person as husband or wife'. *Quaere* as to 'same-sex spouses'.
3 AJA 1982, s 13(1)(e): 'any person accepted by the injured person as a child of his family'.
4 AJA 1982, s 13 tailwords (b).
5 AJA 1982, s 13 tailwords (a).
6 1997 SLT 351.
7 1999 SLT 116.
8 1997 SLT 649.
9 1997 SLT 510.

normally required the court to apportion damages between them (although this does not seem generally to have been done, and in the latter case was not done, by agreement).

The same requirement operates in English common law, where a further limit was created in *Hunt v Severs*[1]. Plaintiff and defendant married after the accident. Expenses which would be s 8 costs in Scotland were refused in the House of Lords. Lord Bridge of Harwich[2] pointed out that the aim of the rule was to compensate the carer, not the plaintiff. Where the carer was the defendant it was pointless to order him to pay his wife money in order that she pay him back.

Lord Bridge compared English and Scots law[3], concluding there was little difference[4], and in *Kozikowska v Kozikowski*[5], Lord Coulsfield reached the same conclusion on similar facts. It is not clear from the Note of the decision whether this was because such payment would not be 'reasonable remuneration' or 'reasonable expenses' (terms more readily going to size than justifiability) or whether as a matter of statutory interpretation, he was reading in an implicit exception to avoid an absurdity. There was a second defender, and the question of how far s 8 remuneration and expenses could be apportioned to him was admitted to probation.

Such decisions ignore the background fact that such a claim would only be made if the defender were insured, and thus the damages come from the insurance company, not the defender. Their effect is therefore to deprive the pursuer of such funds. Perhaps, then, the decisions reflect a fear that the defender would benefit from his or her own *injuria*.

A s 8 claim is also explicitly excluded if 'the relative expressly agreed in the knowledge that an action for damages has been raised or is in contemplation that no payment should be made in respect of those services'. What constitutes 'express agreement' has not been discussed, but lack of it clearly vetoes a s 8 claim, as in *Campbell v Dumfries and Galloway Health Board*[6] where in evidence a sister insisted that she would take no money for services rendered to her brother. Indeed, as this shows, 'agreement', implying consensus, is hardly the appropriate term.

Past and future s 8 services

Like actual consequential expenditure, s 8 notional consequential expenditure can be incurred into the future and fall to be regarded as occasional or continuing future loss for the purpose of quantification and interest. The original s 8 was limited to past services, but was extended by amendment[7].

---

1 [1994] 2 AC 350, [1994] 2 WLR 602, [1994] 2 All ER 385.
2 [1994] 2 AC 350, at 363D–E.
3 Above, at 361F–363B.
4 Above, at 363E he asserted that if the case had been brought in Scotland 'it would have been immediately obvious that such a claim was not sustainable', presumably because of the word 'reasonable' in the statute.
5 1996 SLT 386.
6 1991 SLT 616.
7 Law Reform (Miscellaneous Provisions) (Scotland) Act 1990, s 69.

Section 9 'personal services'

Section 9 claims relate to those services which the injured person used to render to a relative before the injury[1]. They might be characterised as 'housekeeping and child-minding services claims', but the term 'DIY claims' (an informal name sometimes attached to the common law English equivalent), better describes some cases.

The Administration of Justice Act 1982, s 9(1) declares that:

'The [defender] shall be liable to pay to the injured person a reasonable sum by way of damages in respect of the inability of the injured person to render [certain] personal services'.

Background and origins of s 9

Like s 8 of the Administration of Justice Act 1982, s 9 arose substantially from the Scottish Law Commission Report on damages for personal injuries, though initially raised by the Pearson Commission, and observations of the (English) Law Commission[2].

Traditionally, Scots law has frowned upon claims for damages for loss of any form of services. Direct authority is surprisingly thin, but the *locus classicus* is *Allan v Barclay*[3], with further support in, for example, *Reavis v Clan Line Steamers*[4].

The Scottish Law Commission admitted that the proposal 'at first sight seems startling'[5], but was persuaded on the ground that '[w]ithin the family group, for practical reasons, a system of division of labour and pooling of income obtains in which, though in law the services are rendered gratuitously, they are in practice a species of counterpart for the benefits which that member receives as a member of the family group. If by reason of an accident a member of the family group loses the ability to offer the appropriate counterpart for the benefits he receives, he should be compensated for this loss'[6]. Moreover, this was reasonably foreseeable.

Types of 'personal service' under s 9

While the term 'necessary services' for s 8 purposes is undefined, s 9(3) defines 'personal services' as those:

'(a) which were or might have been expected to have been rendered by the injured person before the occurrence of the act or omission giving rise to liability;
(b) of a kind which, when rendered by a person other than a relative would ordinarily be obtainable on payment; and
(c) which the injured person, but for the injuries in question, might have been expected to render gratuitously to a relative'.

---

1   The reasoning of *McLelland v Greater Glasgow Health Board* 1999 SLT 543 in relation to s 8 would apply equally here, *mutatis mutandis*. Thus a pursuer who is not the 'injured person' cannot sue even if receiving 'personal' services.
2   Respectively: *Damages for Personal Injuries* (Scot Law Com no 51) paras 34–43; Report (Cmnd 7054) paras 352–358; and *Report on Personal Injury Litigation* (Law Com no 56) paras 156–157.
3   (1864) 2M 873.
4   1925 SC 725.
5   *Damages for Personal Injuries* (Scot Law Com no 51) para 34.
6   *Damages for Personal Injuries* (Scot Law Com no 51) para 38.

This still leaves much discretion with the courts, but there are rather few reported cases.

An early case was *Worf v Western SMT*[1]. The Lord Ordinary (Mayfield) did not discuss the nature of s 9 services, but clearly accepted as such services by the deceased husband and father carrying out home improvements, gardening, mathematical tuition to his children, transport, and preparation of his own tax report, and the deceased was also regarded as a source of security against crime. (The family was normally resident in the USA.)

Another early case was *Fox v NCR (Nederland) BV*[2], in which board and lodging, clothes-buying, laundry and similar requirements and use of a car, for a son in the Merchant Navy were accepted by Lord Prosser as personal services provided by his deceased parents. It was argued by the defender that some of these were not 'personal' but commercial, and some were loss of support claims under the Damages (Scotland) Act 1976, s 1(3)[3]. The pursuer, however, persuaded Lord Prosser that s 9 of the 1982 Act extended s 1(3) of the 1976 Act. In the same case, provision of a grandchild's lunch on school days by the deceased grandparents, and regular overnight stays with them while the father was at sea, were also accepted on the facts although Lord Prosser expressed some doubt as to alimentary claims[4].

More complicated was *Brown v Ferguson*[5]. The deceased was a wife and mother. The first pursuer, who was husband and father, could not afford a housekeeper, so undertook some such tasks himself, with assistance from the second pursuer (the deceased's mother), with whom the child normally lived during the week, and who had given up her job to do this. The first pursuer paid the second and had bought her a car for which he paid the running costs. The sums paid to the second pursuer were accepted as a consequence of 'the inability of the injured person to render the personal services' by virtue of s 9, though not, apparently, the cost and running expenses of the car[6], nor the loss of earnings of the second pursuer[7].

The only Inner House case on s 9 services is *Ingham v John G Russell (Transport) Ltd*[8]. Here, the deceased was a husband and father. The pursuers were the wife and child. Inter alia, they claimed under s 9 in respect of servicing the central heating system, sweeping the chimney, maintaining electrical appliances, plumbing work, conversions to the house and making furniture (which skills the deceased was teaching his children). It also included seven to ten hours' work a week in winter in the garden and twice that in summer, and maintenance of the children's bicycles. Further, he babysat when his wife, a radiographer, was on call.

Claims in relation to gardening, bicycle maintenance and babysitting were accepted by the defender, but not the others, because they were not 'personal'.

---

1 1987 SLT 317.
2 1987 SLT 401.
3 The English courts do not allow such claims on (*mutatis mutandis*) precisely this ground.
4 1987 SLT 401 at 404G.
5 1990 SLT 274, 1988 SCLR 577.
6 Although noted by Lord Sutherland in his narrative of the s 9 claim, at 1990 SLT 274 at 276G, he did not mention it when quantifying the claim. It is not clear why those costs were excluded.
7 Lord Sutherland, at 276F–G, observed that this was not part of the pursuer's loss, and it is to be presumed that the sum paid to her by the first pursuer in fact compensated her for lost income.
8 1991 SLT 739, 1991 SCLR 596.

Lord Justice-Clerk Ross treated this as a matter of statutory interpretation (and was prepared to look at the Scottish Law Commission report, though he did not find it helpful[1]). He eschewed any attempt to classify s 9 services and concluded that the nature of the services was irrelevant[2]; that '[i]n the context in which these words appear ... "personal" means "in person"'; and that s 9(3) did not so much define personal services as restrict the range which could be claimed to those within a family. Thus, in the instant case, if the deceased had done DIY himself, there would be a claim, but if he had sent one of his employees to do it, there would not[3].

This confirms the wide interpretation in *Worf* and *Fox v NCR*, and that 'DIY claims' are as acceptable as housekeeping ones.

'Relatives'

The definition of 'relatives' for the purposes of s 9 is given in s 13(1), and is the same as for s 8.

'Reasonable sum' for s 9 services:

Section 9 entitles the injured person to claim a 'reasonable sum' in respect of the 'personal services'. There are some comparisons to be made with s 8 claims and standard consequential expenditure claims, but there are significant differences. There has been a paucity of Inner House cases, and again, the matter is dealt with in ch 5 as a matter of quantification.

Accounting to the service receiver

Section 9(4) specifies that the relative who received the service has no claim but, curiously, there is no specific provision requiring the pursuer who obtains s 9 damages to account to him or her, save where s 9(2) applies.

Section 9(2) provides that where the injured person has died, a relative who can claim loss of support by virtue of the Damages (Scotland) Act 1976, s 1(3), which is effectively the same definition as in s 13(1) of the 1982 Act, can claim an equivalent sum under that provision.

Past and future s 9 services

A s 9 claim can be for past or future notional consequential expenditure, and so fall to be regarded as occasional or continuing future loss for the purposes of quantification and interest.

THE RELATIONSHIP OF S 8 'NECESSARY SERVICES' AND S 9 'PERSONAL SERVICES'

An issue the legislation does not mention is that some services may straddle 'necessary services' under s 8, and 'personal services' under s 9. The most

1 1991 SLT 739 at 743I–L.
2 Above, at 743F–G.
3 A principle applied, for instance, (though without citation of *Ingham*) in *Campbell v Gillespie* 1996 SLT 503.

obvious examples are housekeeping and shopping. The service is done for the benefit of both members of a couple. Before the accident it was done by the now injured party. After the accident it must be done by the other.

This complication has appeared in several cases, and has practical effects, as shown in *Low v Ralston*[1]. The s 8 services claimed by the pursuer were assistance in housework by her husband and her mother, and the s 9 services claimed were home decorating. Lord Osborne's opinion clearly and unsurprisingly regarded housework as straddling both. Since s 8 damages had to be accounted for to the service provider, total damages had to be apportioned to each section. This in turn required a detailed account of how the remuneration was to be calculated. Lord Osborne in fact allotted past and future damages, one-quarter to s 8 and three-quarters to s 9, on a complicated basis[2].

The matter was further discussed in *Kennedy v Lees of Scotland*[3]. Lord Gill trenchantly observed that awards for s 8 and s 9 were distinct and could not overlap. The pursuer claimed under both sections for reliance on her husband, daughter and sister for help in dressing, bathing and housework. Lord Gill characterised her claim as asserting that 'if the pursuer is unable to do certain housework she will have a claim under s 9. If her husband then does that housework himself, the pursuer will be able to claim for his services under s 8'[4]. Again, unsurprisingly he concluded '[t]his argument is fallacious', though he went on to say that '[t]he claims may in practice become almost inextricable where the services consist of normal domestic tasks from which the pursuer and the relative benefit; for example where a relative prepares a family meal or does the family laundry'. In such cases 'the court must take a broad approach'[5].

Thus, all this appears to show is that a pursuer cannot claim twice for the same service, so certain services have to be apportioned, as in *Low v Ralston* (which was not referred to in *Kennedy*). That such allotments are inescapably arbitrary is clear. Lord Gill, without any explicit reasoning, allotted one-third of the damages he awarded to s 8 and two-thirds to s 9[6]. He also noted that although this was not an issue in the instant case because the parties had agreed otherwise, a court should normally apportion the s 8 award as between the relatives providing the care[7].

3. PATRIMONIAL LOSSES—III: LOSS OF PROFIT, LOSS OF INCOME AND LOSS OF SUPPORT

GENERAL

Loss of profit occurs where patrimonial benefit obtained from an asset is reduced. Loss of income to an individual (typically from a personal injury

1 1997 SLT 626.
2 And, from the report, not wholly comprehensible. See 1997 SLT 626 at 627D–E, 629A–B and 629B–F.
3 1997 SLT 510.
4 Above, at 513E.
5 Above, at 513F.
6 Above, at 514I.
7 Above, at 513I–K.

action) and loss of support (necessarily from a fatal accident case) are usually treated separately from it, and from each other. However, they are all of essentially the same nature. The *damnum* is not part of a store of money already received either being lost (as with loss of assets) or expended (as with consequential expenditure). It is a flow of money expected but never received at all. All such losses are also examples of Atiyah's 'equivalent compensation' (except, perhaps, for the boundary case of loss of congeniality of employment, discussed below in relation to *solatium*), and all are subject to the limits on 'pure economic loss'[1].

A. LOSS OF PROFIT

Loss of profit is fundamental to certain intentional delict claims, for instance those concerned with intellectual property, interference with contractual or other economic relations and some claims of professional negligence.

Since there can be no physical damage to, or destruction of, an incorporeal asset, losses to them may in practice be regarded as losses of profit rather than losses of assets. It should also be noted that such claims may be contractual rather than delictual; that interdict or an account of profits are often preferred remedies; that the position is complicated by the fact that the legal regime is largely statutory and common to the whole United Kingdom; and that Scottish cases are rather rare.

B. LOSS OF INCOME

Loss of income might be part of any assault claim, might figure in a defamation or verbal injury claim, but is an important item in most negligence actions, and indeed forms a major head of damages in most personal injury actions (including those by mothers giving up work to care for children, as in *McLelland v Greater Glasgow Health Board*[2]).

What counts as income is not usually problematic, and can be treated as money paid for work done. Distinctions between contracts of service and contracts for services are of no consequence. However, specific issues necessary to consider are: 'fringe benefits'; the distinctions between income and share dividends and between income and the capital value of a company; and recently recognised claims related to loss of income, such as loss of employability, loss of pension rights, and loss of congeniality of employment.

Loss of income and fringe benefits

In general, 'fringe benefits' are part of income, but in any particular case the point may be arguable, as in *McMillan v McDowall*[3] where a question was whether board and lodging were part of a remuneration package or not.

---

1 Discussed in ch 3.
2 1999 SLT 543.
3 1993 SLT 311.

Loss of income and reduced share dividends

Remuneration from dividends as well as wages, salary or fees

Key employees may have a shareholding producing a significant part of their remuneration. Injury to them may reduce the profitability of the company, thus the share dividend, and thus their remuneration by this route. The position is even more common with directors, especially in 'one-man companies', and is necessarily the case with partners since, whether 'salaried' or 'full', they take a proportion of the firm's profits, in effect, a dividend on a share. In all cases, there is a related question of the effect on uninjured employees, directors and partners (and the company itself).

Share dividends distinguished from other income by remoteness

The difficulty in claiming such loss as loss of income is remoteness. It is a reflection of the loss of profitability of the company. That loss is the company's, not the employee's, and the company is a separate legal person. The company is, moreover, unlikely to be able to claim for this loss since, following *Allan v Barclay*[1] and *Reavis v Clan Line Steamers*[2], there is no claim for loss of services of employees. The shareholder's loss is therefore, in the words of Lord Mackay in *Young v Ormiston*[3], 'in a double sense remote'.

In that case, the pursuer held twelve-thirteenths of the shares in a company of which he was also director, manager and secretary. He was injured and, in an action for negligence, averred 'business loss', 'damage to his business' and other somewhat vague claims. Lord Mackay regarded this as suing for 'his proportion of the dividend', not 'his loss through failure of any remuneration as manager . . ., or as salaried or remunerated director'[4]. In a robust judgment, relying on *Reavis*, he decided against lifting the veil. Indeed, he wished the pursuer to realise that if he incorporated his business, he must take the consequences[5].

Implications and unfairness

The principle also seems to hold good for employees and partners who also, like shareholders, are separate legal persons from the company or firm. But it may operate extremely unfairly. It is not reasonable to expect this consideration to be taken into account in determining how a director or employee takes remuneration[6] or even, for 'one-man companies', in deciding whether to

---

1 (1864) 2 M 873.
2 1925 SC 725, 1925 SLT 538.
3 1936 SLT 79 at 81.
4 Above, at 80. Further facts were discovered by the Inner House in *Anthony v Brabbs* 1998 SLT 1137 at 1141C–J, 1998 SCLR 982.
5 These questions were considered earlier in English law, which decided that the veil might be pierced: see now *Lee v Sheard* [1956] 1 QB 192, [1955] 3 WLR 951, [1955] 3 All ER 777; *Ashcroft v Curtin* [1971] 1 WLR 1731; *Bellingham v Dhillon* [1973] 1 QB 304, [1972] 3 WLR 730, [1973] 1 All ER 20; and *Esso Petroleum v Mardon* [1976] QB 801, [1976] 2 WLR 583, [1976] 2 All ER 5.
6 Also taking a robust stance, in *Mackenzie v Sidgwick's Executor* 1978 SLT (Notes) 77, where a director's remuneration was reduced by an accident, at 78, Lord Stott declared that the pursuer had not averred any 'contract of employment [*sic*] entitling the pursuer to a salary and for aught that appeared, it might have been merely a way of distributing the profits of a private company'.

incorporate or not. It appears to deny partners prevented from working any possibility of compensation for loss of remuneration.

Modification of the application of remoteness

The unfairness in relation to partners emerged in *Vaughan v Greater Glasgow Passenger Transport Executive*[1]. The pursuer, one of two partners, was injured, and sued for 'loss of earnings'[2]. The Lord Ordinary (Grieve) simply applied the principle in *Young v Ormiston*.

However, on appeal, Lord President Emslie, in the leading judgment, decided the matter by looking back to the 'grand rule' of *Allan v Barclay*. Damages are payable for what may 'naturally and directly arise out of the wrong done; and such, therefore, as may reasonably be supposed to have been in the contemplation of the wrongdoer'[3]. A pursuer who was employed or 'self-employed'[4] could claim, so the question was whether a partner taking a percentage of the profits[5] was entitled to compensation for loss of that remuneration. Lord Emslie was satisfied that such loss did fall within *Allan v Barclay's* 'grand rule'. Loss of earnings was reasonably foreseeable, and the form in which they were received was irrelevant. The losses in question were not concerned with any 'secondary injuries done to the partnership', and the alternative principle simply left the losses uncompensated.

Indeed, on the facts both *Allan v Barclay* and *Reavis* could be distinguished, for they concerned employers suing for injury to employees[6]. *Young v Ormiston* itself was not overturned, but also distinguished (presumably because it concerned a shareholder not a partner, though this is not wholly clear)[7] and doubted in relation to managers whose income depended upon share dividends, though approved insofar as it related simply to shareholders.

The unfairness in relation to 'one-man companies' emerged in *Anthony v Brabbs*[8]. The pursuer ran an engineering design and drafting consultancy which was incorporated. He and his wife were the shareholders, and he was the sole director and employee. He received a salary but also a dividend on shares, determined by the company's profit. At the relevant time, the company had a profitable contract providing the pursuer's skills, which it was unable to fulfil properly because of the accident to the pursuer. This reduced the gross dividend and thus the pursuer's (although it appears his salary continued). His loss of dividend was also averred to be several times his salary.

---

1 1984 SC 32.
2 Condescendence 4, quoted at 33, and repeated by Lord Emslie at 40 and Lord Stott at 45.
3 For discussion of this rule, see ch 3.
4 In this context presumably meaning 'as sole trader'.
5 The pursuer was described in the pleadings, at 32, as entitled to a salary and a 55% share in the net profits. However, at 37, Lord Emslie stated that in the contract of co-partnery '[n]o provision is made for payment of a salary ... [but] it is provided that the pursuer's share in profits and losses is 55%'. The significance is not, of course, whether he was drawing a salary, but whether his loss of partnership profits was 'loss of earnings'.
6 So could *Quin v Greenock and Port Glasgow Tramways Co Ltd* 1926 SC 544, 1926 SLT 313 (the only other Inner House case) and Outer House cases such as *Gibson v Glasgow Corporation* 1963 SLT (Notes) 16 and *Fox v Caulfield & Co* 1975 SLT (Notes) 71.
7 1984 SC 32, per Lord Emslie at 43–44 and, more clearly, Lord Stott at 46. Given the pursuer's involvement in the business in *Young v Ormiston*, this seems a surprising distinction.
8 1998 SLT 1137, 1998 SCLR 982.

The Inner House carefully examined the authorities, doubted *Young v Ormiston* and approved *Vaughan*, and noted that such claims were recognised in England. It concluded that proof before answer should be allowed. Giving the opinion of the court, Lord President Rodger said '[t]he pursuer is seeking to recover a loss of income from his usual work, a loss which is alleged to be due to the defender's wrongful act. In our view such a loss is foreseeable and is not too remote. If the pursuer proves that loss, it should be recoverable'[1]. He added that 'the mere fact that the secondary claims of the company and the other shareholder would be irrelevant is not in itself a reason for holding that this element in the pursuer's claim is irrelevant'[2], and he observed that what dividend the company might declare was simply a matter of quantification.

A conclusion

Shareholders as such continue to have no claim, nor probably do employees or directors whose shareholding is incidental. However, where either take most of their income from dividends, they do have a claim, as do partners (presumably including 'salaried' and 'sleeping' ones). Sole traders are, of course, unaffected.

A remaining difficulty, however, is that people in the position of Vaughan's partner are also affected. They continue to have no claim, their losses being too remote, for there is no duty towards them not to injure their partners. Indeed, Vaughan's partner was trebly unfortunate. He took 45 per cent of a smaller profit. He had to do more than 45 per cent of the work to generate any profit. And he suffered from the reduced capital value of the firm which must have ensued.

Loss of income and loss of capital

Income and capital distinguished

Capital is a store of money held by its owners, not a flow of it received by them, like income. Partners own the capital of their firm, but employees and directors only have a direct interest in the capital of their company if they are shareholders. Nevertheless, particularly with 'one-man' companies, such persons may regard themselves as better off where there is an increase in such capital, and vice versa, regardless of whether the change is reflected in their remuneration.

Capital and remoteness

Thus, if reduction of capital results from injury to the employee or director the question of remoteness arises again. *Fox v Caulfield & Co*, well before *Vaughan*, had similar facts to *Young v Ormiston*, but the claim was expressed in part in terms of reduced capital[3]. The Lord Ordinary treated the case as at one with *Young v Ormiston*, and decided accordingly.

---

1 1998 SLT 1137 at 1140E.
2 Above, at 1142G–I.
3 1975 SLT (Notes) 71. It was asserted that on being taken over or wound up the shareholders would receive £16,000 less than they would have before the accident. A loss of £23,000 over two years was also averred, which may have been lost remuneration.

Vaughan itself did not alter the position. This was clearly shown in *Fullemann v McInnes's Executors*[1], with facts also similar to *Young v Ormiston*. Fullemann effectively wholly owned a company which owned a garage of which he was sole manager. He fixed his remuneration annually, varying it with profits. This sum was paid into a loan account with the company, and he drew on it from time to time. At the time of the accident, he was considering disposing of the company and acquiring a bigger one. In a negligence action, he claimed for (in Lord Cullen's words): '(i) loss of or diminution in the profits of the motor business (before allowance for [his] remuneration) which resulted from [his] incapacity; (ii) loss of benefits sustained by [him] as a result of that incapacity; and (iii) the loss of the goodwill of the motor business'[2].

Lord Cullen, applying *Vaughan*, concluded there was a clear distinction between 'loss of earnings' to those working for a company and loss of value to those owning that company[3]. The pursuer and the company were separate entities. The 'loss of benefits' was loss of income and damages were awarded, but 'loss of profits' and 'loss of goodwill' were not the pursuer's earnings (ie income) but the company's value (ie capital).

A conclusion

Following *Vaughan*, for some employees and directors, and for partners, while loss of share dividend may be regarded as loss of income, reduction in capital value as such will not.

Indeed, the income/capital distinction is important irrespective of the separate legal personality of the company. In *Owenson v Rennie's Lion and Comfort Coaches*[4] the pursuer owned and ran a shop as a sole trader. As a result of an accident, she could no longer do so, and sold the shop. She was awarded damages which effectively maintained her income. Had she continued to run the shop, but found its value as a going concern to have declined because of her inability to run it well, could she have claimed for this reduced capital value?

Loss of income and loss of employability claims

Loss of employability claims arise in practice in negligence cases. While on the face of it 'equivalent compensation', they are perhaps better seen as 'substitute or solace'.

Origins of 'loss of employability' claims

These are regarded as flowing from the English Court of Appeal case of *Smith v Manchester Corporation*[5], although it is clear that the phrase and general

---

1 1993 SLT 259.
2 Above, at 263.
3 Above, at 265G: 'loss of value to the corporator'. In fact this seems an exaggeration. *Vaughan* was only concerned with earnings and loss of value appeared tangentially. Admittedly, at 1984 SC 32, 43, Lord President Emslie described the claim for loss of value in *Fox v Caulfield & Co* as 'somewhat remarkable', and could have doubted, rather than distinguished, the case.
4 1976 SLT (Notes) 58.
5 [1974] 17 KIR 1.

concept were already in currency[1]. A woman, injured by a fall, was partly incapacitated. She was able to return to her former job, at the same wage, though at reduced efficiency. At first instance, she was awarded, inter alia, damages for 'possible loss of earning capacity'[2].

On appeal, without reference to precedent, Scarman LJ declared[3] that '[l]oss of future earnings or future earning capacity is usually compounded of two elements'. The first was actual 'loss of earnings'. He described the second as 'the weakening of the plaintiff's competitive position in the labour market', which would arise if she ever had to seek employment on the open market[4].

A narrow version of the *ratio*[5] is that if a plaintiff is still employed at the same job and suffers no wage loss, but has suffered a handicap and so might have to leave the job and accept lower wages or unemployment in future, then he or she may receive damages for any such contingent losses. A broader version is that if a plaintiff, whether still employed or not (and thus whether suffering a wage loss or not), has suffered a handicap and so might have to accept lower wages or continued unemployment in future, then he or she may receive damages for any such contingent losses, in addition to any damages for loss of earnings.

Neither version is, of course, binding in Scotland, but claims have been accepted for many years, extending well beyond the facts of *Smith v Manchester Corporation*.

'Loss of employability' in Scotland

The terms 'loss of employability', 'loss of the opportunity to work' and 'loss of earning capacity' and others have all been used for what appear to be the same sort of claim. Some cases fit readily within the narrow *ratio* of *Smith v Manchester* (though often without reference to it), such as *Whyte v University of Dundee*[6], where the pursuer was in no danger of losing his job, but was subject to permanent eye damage and so would 'be at a considerable disadvantage if he was in the position of having to compete for alternative employment'[7]. (This was later referred to as 'loss of future earning capacity').

Since then, the Outer House has accepted extensions (generally without reference to authority) to include situations where the pursuer: left for un-related reasons, but was in other employment at a lower wage (*Hoey v British Steel Corporation*[8]); received damages for lost earnings, left for related reasons, but might expect less earnings in future (*Kennedy v Lees of Scotland*[9]); received damages for loss of earnings, left for unrelated reasons, and was unemployed

1 See Edmund Davies LJ's opinion at [1974] 17 KIR 1, 6–7.
2 Above, per Scarman LJ at 7: Edmund Davies LJ, at 2, used the words 'possible loss of future earnings' and, at 6, 'future financial loss'.
3 Above, at 7.
4 Above, at 8.
5 In *Robertson's CB v Anderson* 1996 SC 217, at 224E, 1996 SLT 828 it was suggested that in England and Wales the principle is restricted to this narrower version by *Moeliker v A Reyrolle & Co Ltd* [1976] ICR 253. However, the Inner House does not seem to have adopted that position itself.
6 1990 SLT 545.
7 Above, at 547B–C.
8 1991 SLT 196.
9 1997 SLT 510.

(*Hodge v British Coal Corporation*[1]); and never had employment and might never have sought it (*McMenemy v Argyll Stores Ltd*[2]).

An Extra Division considered such claims in *Robertson's CB v Anderson*[3] and *Hill v Wilson*[4]. In *Robertson's CB* the *incapax* had been a disorderly youth, was unemployed, but was turning his life around, and was awarded a small lump sum for 'loss of employability'. On appeal, the Extra Division referred to some of the cases, without express approval or disapproval, and offered no definition. It did note that 'it appears that usually' the phrase 'loss of employ-ability' (alias 'loss of the opportunity to obtain work in the future') described a claim fitting the narrow version of the *ratio* in that case[5].

It drew attention to the inconsistent terminology employed[6], and summarised the analysis offered by an English commentary[7], seemingly placing some reliance upon it. Ultimately, however it decided that the relevant distinction was whether future lost earnings could reasonably be calculated because the pursuer was working or would shortly have obtained employment, or whether they could not because that was a 'remote possibility'[8]. On the facts it held that those averred were not 'speculative', and therefore the claim should be treated as one for loss of earnings[9].

Shortly thereafter, the First Division decided *Hill v Wilson*, where the pursuer had suffered the accident a year after being made redundant, and so was unemployed and would never be able to obtain employment requiring strength, agility or concentration. He sought damages for 'disadvantage on the labour market'. He argued that such claims were not restricted (as the defender argued) to where employment was probable, but included other cases where precise computation was difficult[10]. The First Division, without explicit reference to *Robertson's CB* added to ambiguity by offering further apparently synonymous phrases, including 'impairment to earning capacity', 'putting at a disadvantage in the labour market', 'market disadvantage', 'loss (or diminution) of opportunity', and 'loss of a chance', but concluded that past and future claims could be made, that employability might vary over time, and that it might be concerned with several separate failures to obtain employment[11]. The First Division also observed[12], that at least in relation to

1 1992 SLT 913.
2 1992 SLT 971, 1992 SCLR 576.
3 1996 SC 217.
4 1998 SC 81, 1998 SLT 69.
5 1996 SLT 217 at 224C–D.
6 Above, at 225B–E.
7 Kemp & Kemp *The Quantum of damages in personal injury and fatal accident claims* (1982) (4th edn, rev) vol 1 para 5–137, which is headed 'Handicap in the Labour Market' (with a footnote distinguishing this from 'future loss which can be calculated mathematically'), and subheaded 'Terminology: Handicap in the labour market at some future date: *Smith v Manchester* damages'. Relying on numerous English authorities, the text points out that 'damages for loss of earning capacity' is ambiguous, and prefers 'handicap in the labour market at some future date' for such cases, clearly seen as defined by a fairly narrow *ratio*. There is also English authority in *Moeliker v A Reyrolle & Co Ltd* [1976] ICR 253 that loss of employability awards are only available in respect of those in employment. As noted, presumably the Inner House was not persuaded by this or its reasoning would have been simpler.
8 1996 SLT 217 at 225B–C and 225E–G.
9 Above, at 223E–F and 225F–G.
10 1998 SC 81 at 84E–F.
11 Above, at 83H–84A.
12 Above, at 85G–I.

jury trials, separate heads of damages were simply a convenient way of discovering how a jury had made up its total, so that allotment to past earnings could be made for the purpose of calculating interest[1].

A conclusion

Thus, whatever the origins of such claims, and however they are described, if a pursuer cannot quantify a loss of earnings claim as a result of an injury, he or she may claim damages for reduced chances on the labour market which affected him or her between accident and trial, and which may affect him or her in the future. This is so whether the pursuer has remained in the same employment; changed employment (whether because of the accident or not); or has been unemployed (whether because of the accident or not).

Loss of income and loss of pension rights

The spread of occupational pension schemes has meant that this head of future lost income is very important. Where the accident has prevented employment temporarily or permanently, there may be fewer, or reduced, employer's contributions, resulting in a reduced pension at retirement, as in *Mitchell v Glenrothes Development Corporation*[2].

It is important to note the nature and characteristics of a claim for lost pension rights. Firstly, it concerns rights to a pension at some future time, not one payable immediately. Secondly, rights under a private pension scheme are irrelevant. Such pensions are simply a form of expenditure from income, and so compensated by a claim for loss of income (whether the pension is continued, modified, or discontinued). Thirdly, rights under occupational pensions are irrelevant to the extent that they reflect the employee's contribution, even though that may be compulsory, because again it is simply a form of expenditure of income. However, such schemes usually contain an employer's contribution[3]. This is a deferred wage[4], in that it is stored by the employer for payment, with interest, on retirement. It may be lost for any period when the pursuer cannot work as a result of injury, or if he or she changes jobs. Thus a claim may be made for a sum to represent such contributions.

Loss of income and loss of congeniality of employment

Conceptually separate from 'loss of employability' is 'loss of congeniality of employment', but this is not a matter of Atiyah's 'equivalent compensation' but rather his 'substitute or solace' and so is a matter of *solatium* and therefore discussed below in relation to that.

---

1 One reason for this issue seems to have been that in English law (on the basis of *Moeliker v A Reyrolle & Co Ltd*) [1976] ICR 253), 'loss of employability' is regarded as part of general damages, without an award of interest.
2 1991 SLT 284.
3 Indeed, they may be 'non-contributory', ie wholly paid for by the employer, as is the case with sheriffs and judges.
4 See eg the English House of Lords case *Smoker v London Fire and Civil Defence Authority* [1991] AC 502, [1991] 2 WLR 1052, [1991] 2 All ER 449.

Past and future loss of profit, loss of income and loss of support

All three forms can relate to the past or the future, and so may fall to be regarded as occasional or continuing future loss for the purposes of quantification and interest.

C. LOSS OF SUPPORT

The nature of 'loss of support' actions

The institutional writers[1], and the common law[2], accepted that dependent ascendants and descendants of a person wrongfully killed might maintain an action in respect of that dependency against the wrongdoer. In modern terms, this includes loss of support from earnings, or from occupational pensions.

Liability now flows from s 1(3) of the Damages (Scotland) Act 1976, read with s 1(1). The deceased requires to have died 'in consequence of personal injuries sustained by him as a result of an act or omission of another person ... giving rise to liability to pay damages'. The responsible person is obliged to pay to any defined relatives damages 'such as will compensate the relative for any loss of support suffered by him since the date of the deceased's death or likely to be suffered by him'. Support is a factual matter, which must be established. Section 1(6) provides that it is not essential for such a claim that the deceased had a legal obligation to support, but if that is so, it is to be taken into account in deciding if support is established.

The claim is not 'free-standing', in so far as liability to the relatives depends upon liability to the deceased, but does not depend upon an action by the deceased's executor[3].

Defined relatives

Relatives for this purpose are defined in Sch 1 of the 1976 Act[4], which is similar to, but generally wider than, that in s 13(1) of the Administration of Justice 1982 for 'notional consequential expenditure' under ss 8 and 9. They are: spouses; 'ascendants', 'descendants'[5]; siblings; uncles and aunts; nephews and nieces; and first cousins.

Again, the list is wider than might appear, as 'common law' spouses are included[6] (but not divorced spouses), as are also those treated as children of the family[7] and illegitimate children[8]. So again are stepchildren, and

---

1 Eg Stair I,9,4.
2 *Dick v Burgh of Falkirk* 1976 SC (HL) 1, per Lord Kilbrandon at 22–23, 1976 SLT 21.
3 *Dick v Burgh of Falkirk*, above.
4 As amended by the Administration of Justice Act 1982, s 14(4), and Law Reform (Parent and Child) (Scotland) Act 1986.
5 Damages (Scotland) Act 1976, s 10(1), Sch 1, paras 1(b) and (d) separate 'parent or child' from 'ascendant or descendant (other than a parent or child)', as a matter of drafting, but nothing turns on this.
6 D(S)A 1976, Sch 1, para 1(aa) (as inserted by the Administration of Justice Act 1982, s 14(4)).
7 D(S)A 1976, Sch 1, para 1(c).
8 D(S)A 1976, Sch 1, para 2(b) (as substituted by the Law Reform (Parent and Child) (Scotland) Act 1986, Sch 1, para 15).

since 'any relationship of the half blood shall be treated as a relationship of the whole blood', and 'any relationship of affinity shall be treated as a relationship by consanguinity'[1], presumably again, a variety of relationships such as half-siblings, uncles and aunts by marriage, 'grand-parents-in-law', and even 'half-nephews' and cousins by marriage are included.

Daughters-in-law and mothers-in-law are certainly included, as decided in *McAllister v Imperial Chemical Industries plc*[2] and *Monteith v Cape Insulation Ltd*[3], respectively.

Dependency and apportionment

However, such relatives can claim only if they were in fact dependent on the deceased.

Commonly, more than one relative will be dependent, for example a widow and children. In such cases, the sum awarded requires to be apportioned between them.

Past and future loss of support

Loss of support can relate to both the past and the future, so can and usually does extend into the future so falls to be regarded as occasional or continuing future loss for the purposes of quantification and interest.

4. PERSONAL LOSSES: *SOLATIUM* AND 'LOSS OF SOCIETY'

Intentional delicts to the person, such as assault, and some others such as defamation (assuming it to be an intentional delict), may cause *damnum* which is 'personal' rather than patrimonial loss. So may most negligence actions (including claims for 'loss of society' for the death of a relative[4]).

'Personal loss' is not a term of art, though the category is well recognised. Confusingly, it is sometimes referred to as *solatium*, that is, by the term for compensation for such loss. It can be distinguished from patrimonial loss on the ground that it concerns loss of things not on the market. This raises the question of what sorts of personal loss are recognised as *damnum*, which is dealt with here. It also raises the question of how the compensation is quantified in the absence of market prices. This is dealt with in chs 4 and 5, though it should be noted that this form of compensation is the principal example of Atiyah's 'substitute or solace compensation'.

---

1 D(S)A 1976, Sch 1, para 2(a).
2 1997 SLT 351.
3 1999 SLT 116.
4 That terminology is now, strictly speaking, inaccurate. However, early common law *solatium* cases are in fact 'loss of society' awards.

A. *SOLATIUM*

Origins and nature of *solatium*

Solatium is occasionally distinguished from damages[1]. Its origins are obscure[2]. There may have been a Roman law antecedent[3], and the concept figures in the institutional writings, although the term may not[4]. The first explicit mention may have been in the mid-eighteenth century, and the modern concept may have emerged from the action of assythment. In the course of the nineteenth century, as assythment became obsolete, *solatium* came to be used in the *actio injuriarum*[5], the action open to relatives of a deceased person wrongfully killed[6]. As negligence was not then well developed, descriptions of *solatium* tend to emerge from such actions. Lord President Inglis in *Eisten v North British Railway Co*[7], said a pursuer 'may sue...for *solatium* where he can quantify no real damage', and in *Black v North British Railway Co*, that *solatium* 'has come to mean reparation for feelings'[8]. In both cases it was distinguished from pecuniary loss.

Solatium has long been accepted as available in delictual actions generally[9]. In *Duffy v Kinneil Cannel & Coking Co*[10] (although again an *actio injuriarum*), Lord President Clyde approved the *Eisten* description, observing that '[s]*olatium* ... properly means reparation for the pain and suffering inflicted on anyone in consequence of the commission of a delict against him ... [which] is in contrast with patrimonial loss'.

The (English) Law Commission provided one of the few attempts to consider the justification of such 'non-pecuniary damages' by asking if they should be abolished[11]. It concluded against, on the grounds that there should be recognition of personal losses, and that there was overwhelming support for them[12].

---

1 See eg *Black v North British Railway Co* 1908 SC 440 per Lord President Dunedin at 444, 45 SLR 340, 15 SLT 840; *Dick v Burgh of Falkirk*, 1976 SC(HL) 1, at 25 and 26, per Lord Kilbrandon, 1976 SLT 21, and the Interest on Damages (Scotland) Act 1971, s 1(1): also *McKendrick v Sinclair* 1972 SC(HL) 25.

2 They were discussed in *Black v North British Railway Co*, above (a decision of a Court of Seven Judges which was to be appealed to the House of Lords) by Lord President Dunedin, and, along with assythment, at greater length in Walker 'Solatium' (1950) LXII *Juridical Review* 144–168. However, their conclusions are not universally accepted.

3 See *Digest* VIII.4.13 and XXVI.7.33.

4 See Walker 'Solatium' (1950) LXII *Judicial Review* 144 at 149, but the concept was recognised by Stair (see I.9.4), and is mentioned in notes to Erskine III, 1, 14.

5 The meaning of that phrase has been a matter of debate.

6 English common law had no equivalent, acquiring it only through the Fatal Accidents Acts. Paradoxically, it has also now been abolished by statute in Scotland, and replaced by the 'loss of society' claim.

7 (1870) 8M 980, at 984.

8 1908 SC 440, at 453.

9 That in actions concerning bereavement sometimes, confusingly, being referred to as 'pure *solatium*'.

10 1930 SC 596, at 597.

11 Consultation Paper no 140 *Damages for Personal Injury: non-pecuniary loss* (1995) paras 4.5–4.8: *Damages for Personal Injury: non-pecuniary loss* (Law Com no 257) (HC Paper 344 (1998–99)) para 2.1–2.3.

12 Cynically, it can be asked if it is surprising that when people are asked if other people should pay them money, they answer 'Yes!' As Atiyah has observed, there is little consideration of whether the money would be better spent on other things, such as accident prevention.

Types of loss covered

Viewing 'personal loss' as all non-patrimonial loss begs the question of what types of such loss courts will entertain as *damnum*.

Items within such a claim are commonly not fully listed, and there is strong authority for courts to regard it as an undifferentiated whole. The First Division in *Keith v Fraser*[1] criticised the Lord Ordinary for awarding separate sums for different heads of such loss. The approach:

'involved, in effect, a division of what is truly an indivisible head of damages into several parts which are no more than representative of certain of the elements which should properly be considered together in the assessment of the claim for *solatium*. As a general rule we are in no doubt that *solatium* should be considered and assessed as a single entity'.

This was repeated by the Second Division in *McManus v British Railways Board* with the words 'not only unconventional, but . . . unsound'[2].

The approach is very understandable in the light of the interpenetrating nature of the different aspects of personal loss, and a good example of this undifferentiated treatment is *Duffy v Mairs*[3]. In one paragraph Lord Hamilton listed together the pain and discomfort of the pursuer; his disfigurement through scarring; the embarrassment it occasioned; and the sporting activities he had to forgo. In another, he summarised them and awarded an undifferentiated £20,000 as *solatium*. (In practice, *solatium* may also be difficult to separate from other heads of damages such as loss of earnings or 'necessary services'.)

However, since claims for *solatium* appear in the majority of reported delict cases[4], and there is an increasing propensity to itemise claims, it is important to know what courts will accept as *damnum*.

Although no *catalogue raisonée* exists, illumination has been given in cases such as *Quin v Greenock and Port Glasgow Tramways Co*[5]; and *Duffy v Kinneil*[6]. Lord Justice Clerk Wheatley provided some conceptual and practical analysis in *Dalgleish v Glasgow Corporation*[7], and is often quoted. He roundly declared that '[t]here are three heads of damages in a *solatium* claim (a) pain and suffering; (b) loss of faculties and amenities; and (c) loss of expectation of life'. This handy formulation was more recently repeated by the Scottish Law Commission as an uncontentious statement of the law, and given greater detail[8].

---

1 (1973) unreported, but quoted by Lord Allanbridge in *Parke v Glasgow District Council* 1979 SLT 45, at 47.
2 1993 SC 553 at 558 F–G, 1994 SLT 496, 1993 SCLR 783. The Damages (Scotland) Act 1976, s 9A(3) specifically declares that a court making an award for loss of expectation of life need not specifically ascribe any part of a *solatium* award to that head. This appears to permit a court to do so if it wishes.
3 1998 SLT 433, at 434H–I, 1997 SCLR 590.
4 In the 1990s, the *Scots Law Times* reported 20–50 delictual damages cases per annum, the great majority of which were concerned wholly or partly with the amount of damages, and the majority of such claims included a claim for *solatium*.
5 1926 SC 544, at 547.
6 Ie *Duffy v Kinneal Cannel and Smoking Co Ltd* 1930 SC 596 at 597.
7 1976 SC 32, especially 53.
8 *Report on the Effect of Death on Damages* (Scot Law Com no 134) (Cm 1848 (1992)) para 2.3.

However, this does not go far enough. The formulation neither defines its terms (what is an 'amenity'?), nor reflects the range of cases in which *solatium* is in fact awarded (what of *solatium* for defamation?). It is suggested that the cases justify a categorisation of this fascinatingly amorphous concept, comprising:

(i)   physical pain and discomfort;
(ii)   physical injury and disfigurement;
(iii)   physical illness and disease;
(iv)   psychological suffering;
(v)   wounded feelings and affront;
(vi)   loss of faculties;
(vii)   loss of amenities;
(viii) loss of expectation of life.

(i) Physical pain and discomfort[1]

Physical pain is of the essence of actions based on accidents caused by negligence (though it may result otherwise than by negligence, for example from an assault, as in *Downie v Chief Constable, Strathclyde Police*[2] or even from a breach of a Convention right, such as that against torture, inhuman or degrading treatment[3]). Illustration is almost otiose, but *McLaurin v North British Railway Co*[4], provides a memorable example, and see also *McFarlane v Tayside Health Board*[5] and *McLelland v Greater Glasgow Health Board*[6], in both of which the physical consequences of pregnancy, as such, attracted *solatium*. Pain may be at the time of the accident and thereafter, temporarily or permanently. The wide variety of conditions producing pain, make useful the anatomical diagrams, lists, and glossaries readily available in some texts[7]. A wide interpretation covers medical procedures, as in *Allan v Greater Glasgow Health Board*[8], where a failed sterilisation operation involved a further operation.

Apparent physical causes for pain are normally described, as requirements of proof of loss and causation may necessitate. However, it is a subjective affective state, so proof of existence, intensity, and duration is sometimes difficult, as seen, for example, in *Fallan v Lanarkshire Health Board*[9].

If it is a subjective state, then a person in a coma or persistent vegetative state presumably suffers no pain, so no award under this head is appropriate,

1 'Physical pain' is used to refer to a subjective affective state, distinguished from 'injury', of which 'discomfort' is a lesser form. Although subjective, it is presumed to require a perceptible physical analogue ('injury') which caused it. It is possible to argue that pain is a form of psychological suffering. However 'psychological suffering' is here reserved for conditions not presumed to require a perceptible physical analogue.
2 1998 SLT 8, 1997 SCLR 603.
3 Human Rights Act 1998, s 1(3), Sch 1, Pt I the Convention, Rights and Freedoms, art 3.
4 (1892) 19R 346, at 346 and 348.
5 1998 SC 389, 1998 SLT 307 (IH), upheld to this extent by the House of Lords: (1999) Times, 26 November, HL.
6 1999 SLT 543.
7 Eg McEwan & Paton *McEwan and Patons The Law of Damages for Personal Injury in Scotland* (2nd edn, 1989) (looseleaf updated) 'Glossary' (including Glossary of medical terms and Glossary of medical abbreviations); Kemp and Kemp *The Quantum of damages in personal injury and fatal accident claims* (1982) (4th edn, rev) Vol 1 paras 0–001 to 0–089 (Diagrams of human body, Medico-legal matters, Glossary of medical terms); and the (English) Cherry & Judicial Studies Board *Guidelines for the assessment of general damages in personal injury cases* (4th edn, 1998).
8 1998 SLT 580.
9 1997 SLT 902, 1996 SCLR 110.

as concluded in *Dalgleish v Glasgow Corporation*[1]. However, Lord Justice-Clerk Wheatley distinguished between pain and suffering (including awareness of loss of faculties and amenities) and 'objective loss sustained' for which *solatium* could be awarded[2].

These remarks were all obiter, but this general interpretation was applied by the House of Lords in the English case of *Lim Poh Choo v Camden Area Health Authority*[3]. Authority permitting damages for 'loss of amenities' despite the plaintiff's unconsciousness was of long standing, and could not be overturned without causing injustice[4]. Nevertheless 'pain and suffering' were distinguished from loss of amenity, and depended not upon the fact of deprivation, but upon 'the plaintiff's personal awareness of pain, her capacity for suffering'[5].

Liability for precipitated or accelerated symptoms of existing conditions, as in *McCarvel v Strathclyde Fire Board*[6], is beyond the scope of this book, but should be noted, for they increase the *damnum*.

(ii) Physical injury and disfigurement

'Physical injury' is an objectively determinable damage, so *solatium* is presumably available for it. Indeed, analysis of 'pain and suffering' tends to consider injury (with loss of amenity in mind), ignoring pain and suffering as such. This accounts for the anatomical diagrams, lists etc, referred to above, and used to construct tariffs for *solatium* which make up so large a part of some texts on damages. Further, the coma and persistent vegetative state cases show that *solatium* is available for injury without pain and suffering.

However, such *damnum* is difficult to distinguish from 'loss of faculties', 'loss of amenities' and loss of expectation of life (as well as from physical pain). Thus, in *Dalgleish v Glasgow Corporation* it is not clear that Lord Justice-Clerk Wheatley distinguished between injury as such, and these losses. The same is true in *Lim Poh Choo*.

It is difficult to imagine injury without pain and suffering or loss of amenity. Disfigurement cases might provide examples. However, they seem to regard the *damnum* other than physical pain as psychological suffering, as in *McLaurin v North British Railway Co* (per Lord M'Laren)[7] and *McColl v Barnes* (per Lord Morison)[8].

Thus, there is surprisingly little authority for *solatium* for injury as such.

(iii) Physical disease or illness

Disease or illness may be *damnum*, as in *Donoghue v Stevenson*[9]. Many other well-known cases, such as *Wardlaw v Bonnington Castings*[10], and *McGhee v*

---

1 1976 SC 32.
2 Above, at 54.
3 [1980] AC 174, [1979] 3 WLR 440, [1979] 2 All ER 910.
4 *West & Sons v Shephard* [1964] AC 326. Interestingly, in *Dalgleish* the Inner House did not regard itself as bound by this precedent.
5 1980 AC 174 at 188G, per Lord Scarman.
6 1997 SLT 1015, 1997 SCLR 573.
7 1892 19R 346 at 350.
8 1992 SLT 1188 at 1189F–K, 1991 SCLR 907.
9 1932 SC(HL)31 [1932] AC 562, 1932 SLT 317.
10 1956 SC(HL) 26, [1956] AC 613, 1956 SLT 135.

National Coal Board[1] have concerned 'industrial diseases'. However, in *Moffat v Secretary of State for Scotland*[2], a pursuer had suffered 'injury to his health' in the form of pain and discomfort, but the Lord Ordinary (Kirkwood) said he would have awarded damages for the injury to health 'which resulted in significant physical discomfort and mental suffering'[3]. Thus, it is arguable that, as with physical injury, the *damnum* is really the physical pain and psychological suffering resulting from the disease or illness.

Accidents, or injuries resulting from accidents, may also cause later medical conditions rather than (or as well as) immediate ones, and they may not be regarded as too remote, as in *Dingley v Chief Constable, Strathclyde Police*[4]. These cases are essentially the same as the 'accelerated symptoms' ones, referred to above.

(iv) Psychological suffering and unhappiness

Conceptual difficulties

'Psychological suffering' is used in contradistinction to 'physical pain', and 'physical disease and illness'. It includes conditions popularly regarded as pathological and as mental equivalents of physical pain (such as anxiety, depression, etc)[5]. Thus, it encompasses 'psychiatric illness', 'psychiatric disorder', 'mental disorder' and the forensically most popular 'mental distress' or 'nervous shock'[6] (whether resulting from 'shock' or otherwise). However, this category also includes not only 'psychoses', but also 'neuroses', and 'unhappiness'[7] (seen, like discomfort, as an attenuated, non-pathological form of the condition), and merges, in different directions, into 'wounded feelings and affront', loss of expectation of life, and 'loss of society' (traditionally, and here, all treated separately), not to mention 'problem behaviour'[8], and 'normal emotional reactions' (for which there will not be liability). It is thus amorphous.

Practical difficulties

As well as conceptual difficulties, there are practical ones of proof, causation and remoteness, essentially similar to those for physical pain, but more

---

1   1973 SC(HL) 37, [1973] 1 WLR 1, 1973 SLT 14.
2   1994 SLT 729.
3   Above, at 733A–B.
4   1997 SLT 880.
5   This is, of course, psychologically naive: see eg *Diagnostic and Statistical Manual of Mental Disorders (International Version)* (4th edn, 1995) American Psychiatric Association ('DSM IV') p xxi. But, at p xvi, it is acknowledged that 'mental disorders' are ill-understood in terms of phenomenology, aetiology, and even defining characteristics. Thus the efflorescence of terminology. Psychological conditions are commonly simply descriptions of behaviour with no explicative value: but NB *'angina pectoris'* only means 'pain in the chest'.
6   A term apparently coined by the English Court of Appeal in *Dulieu v White & Sons* [1901] 2 KB 669, but which does not coincide with any recognised medical category. 'Psychiatric injury' or 'mental injury' are not popular terms, but see Napier & Wheat *Recovering Damages for Psychiatric Injury* (1995).
7   In *McManus v British Railways Board* 1994 SLT 496, at 497H–K, the Inner House was in principle prepared to accept *solatium* for irrational guilt and loss of libido.
8   See Kesey *One Flew Over the Cuckoo's Nest* (1962) *passim*.

intractable as, for example, in *Lenaghan v Ayrshire and Arran Health Board*[1] ('psychological overlay' and exaggeration), and *Burns v Harper Collins Ltd*[2] ('chronic pain disorder'). Remoteness does not seem to have been raised as a problem in the reported cases.

Doctrinal difficulties

There might also be doctrinal difficulties, whereby some forms of psychological suffering attract no damages. Although a matter of liability, this requires attention. These problems arise where the suffering does not flow from physical pain etc and the delict is negligence or breach of statutory duty, that is typically, in 'nervous shock' cases. If they arise, it is because, on the one hand, recent disaster cases mean that claims for psychological suffering are more readily entertained even where there is no physical injury, while, on the other, judges have sought to limit liability for such claims for fear of opening the floodgates to the common phenomena of anxiety, fear, grief and shock.

'Nervous shock' cases have been much discussed[3], but discussion has been wrapped up in the related but separate issue of damages for bereavement, and driven by a number of English cases. Until recently, the principal authority in both Scotland and England and Wales was *Bourhill v Young*[4]. However, a series of English cases, principally *McLoughlin v O'Brian*[5], *Alcock v Chief Constable of South Yorkshire Police*[6], and *Page v Smith*[7], have altered the law somewhat, probably on both sides of the border. Most of the implications of these decisions are presently irrelevant. However, one which is not is the apparent requirement that, to recover damages, there must be a 'positive psychiatric illness'. This appears most readily, albeit obiter, in Lord Bridge's opinion in *McLoughlin*[8], as an implication of the principle of English law that no damages are awarded for normal emotional distress from bereavement[9].

Positive psychiatric illnesses

The requirement of a positive psychiatric illness predicates a test of such conditions. As indicated above, it is arguable whether such a test can exist. In practice, there has been heavy reliance upon the *Diagnostic and Statistical Manual of Mental Disorders* ('DSM IV'[10]). This fascinating work includes 17 coded broad (and not discrete) categories of 'disorder', each divided into

---

1 1994 SC 365, 1994 SLT 765 (IH). 1993 SLT 544, 1994 SCLR 158 (OH).
2 1997 SLT 607, 1996 SCLR 1135.
3 See, eg, Mullany and Hadford *Tort Liability for Psychiatric Damage* (1993), Napier and Kay *Recovering Damages for Psychiatric Injury* (1995), and Wells *Negotiating Tragedy: law and disasters* (1995), and an enormous literature in the periodicals.
4 1942 (SC) HL 78, [1943] AC 92, 1943 SLT 105.
5 [1983] AC 410, [1982] 2 WLR 982, [1982] 2 All ER 298.
6 [1992] 1 AC 310, [1991] 3 WLR 1057, [1991] 4 All ER 907.
7 [1996] 1 AC 155, [1995] 2 WLR 644, [1995] 2 All ER 736.
8 [1983] AC 410 at 431–432.
9 Whether such difficulties would apply in respect of a claim for psychological suffering as a result of a breach of the Convention right against torture, inhuman or degrading treatment (or indeed otherwise) must be a matter for discussion: see the Human Rights Act 1998, s 1(3), the Convention, Rights and Freedoms, art 3, *et passim*.
10 Noted above: DSM IV replaced DSM III. The *'International Version'* of DSM IV is correlated with another system, the *International Classification of Mental and Behaviourial Disorders: clinical descriptions and diagnostic guidelines* (1992) World Health Organisation ('ICD 10').

several coded (and not discrete) syndromes. Each syndrome has a description of 'Features', and a list of 'Criteria', and may also have lists of 'Associated Features and Disorders' etc. DSM has had considerable influence in the popularisation of 'Post-Traumatic Stress Disorder' ('PTSD')[1] among litigants[2], and its acceptance by the courts[3]. However, not all medical authorities accept that such a condition exists; other such conditions may be involved in any case[4]; and DSM is designed for clinical practice and research, so there are 'significant risks that diagnostic information will be misused or misunderstood' if used for forensic purposes[5].

The Scottish position

However, although academic and judicial opinion frequently appear to assume it, and although there may be a minimum threshold of 'normal emotional distress' to surmount, most quotably described as the 'customary phlegm test'[6], authority for Lord Bridge's requirement applying in Scotland is thin.

The principal case after *McLoughlin* was *Simpson v Imperial Chemical Industries*[7], and the majority in the Inner House explicitly imposed Lord Bridge's requirement, and denied remedies to pursuers who had suffered the 'normal emotional reaction' of fright after an explosion. This was followed, for example, in *Mallon v Monklands District Council*[8] where the Lord Ordinary (Jauncey) considered self-mutilation, anger, irrationality and withdrawal as a 'minor psychiatric illness'.

On the other hand, Lord Bridge concluded that the requirement followed from the principle that there are no damages for bereavement at English common law, which is not the case in Scots law. Indeed, *solatium* may have emerged from the *actio injuriarum*. Further, in *Simpson* the Inner House considered that the case had been badly dealt with in the Outer House[9], and Lord Justice-Clerk Wheatley expressly reserved his position on whether mere fright could not attract damages. And in *Mallon*, Lord Jauncey gave the impression of regarding the requirement of psychiatric illness an unwelcome hurdle, and took his decision on the basis of the opinion of two social workers[10].

Further, in a series of subsequent cases, reference to the requirement evaporated, and damages were given for conditions less than psychiatric

---

1 DSM IV pp 432–440, coded 'F43.1'.
2 It has been observed cynically that PTSD is the only medical condition where patients see their lawyers before their doctors.
3 Eg *Stark v Lothian and Borders Fire Board* 1993 SLT 652, 1993 SCLR 186.
4 The (English) Law Commission noted that English courts had accepted 'morbid depression', 'hysterical personality disorder', 'post traumatic stress disorder', and 'chronic fatigue syndrome' (not all of which are accepted by DSM IV): *Liability for Psychiatric Illness* (Law Com no 249) (HC Paper no 525 (1997–98)) para 2.3.
5 DSM IV p xxxiii: see also p i *et passim*, especially the 'Cautionary Statement' at p xxvii, and the multi-axial system for diagnosis described at pp 25–35. See also Lord Bridge on problems of proof in *McLoughlin v O'Brien* [1983] AC 410 at 432.
6 Per Lord Porter in *Bourhill v Young* 1942 SC (HL) 78 at 98, echoing Lord Mackay in the Inner House (1941 SC 385 at 413).
7 1983 SLT 601.
8 1986 SLT 347.
9 It was not clear, for example, what injuries the pursuers had in fact suffered.
10 It does not appear that there was any medical evidence.

illness although there was no physical pain etc, nor any intentional delict[1] (and no mention of 'customary phlegm' was made). Thus in *Martin v Bell-Ingram*[2], the *damnum* was 'worry and inconvenience'[3]; in *George Buchanan v Newington Property Centre*[4], it was 'discomfort, anxiety and distress'[5]; and in both cases the pursuers alleged negligence, and recovered damages. *Palmer v Beck*[6] and *Quin v Monklands District Council*[7] are similar, relying on misrepresentation and breach of statutory duty respectively[8]. This was most clear in *McLelland v Greater Glasgow Health Board*[9], in which both parents of a child born handicapped were awarded *solatium* for the shock and distress undergone upon discovery of the handicap, and long term stress in bringing him up. Lord Macfadyen expressly followed *McFarlane v Tayside Health Board*[10] and implicitly doubted or distinguished *McLoughlin* and *Simpson*[11]. Such cases merge into the disappointment, distress and annoyance, dealt with below.

Reported cases in Scotland involving psychological suffering without physical pain etc resulting from negligence or breach of statutory duty are rare, and among those which are reported, it is difficult to find ones in which the requirement of a 'positive psychological illness' has been applied. Indeed, it does not seem that the requirement of a 'positive psychiatric illness' has been much discussed at all. Thus it is possible that damages are recoverable for any psychiatric suffering (perhaps only subject to a 'customary phlegm' test).

(v) Wounded feelings and affront

Wounded feelings, affront, and psychological suffering

Wounded feelings and affront are here distinguished from psychological suffering. The *damnum* is seen as a form of insult, rather than as an analogue to physical illness[12]. It is possible that references to 'aggravated damages' are to be seen as references to this form of *solatium*, as suggested in ch 3. *Solatium* for wounded feelings and affront is taken to include that awarded in actions for defamation and verbal injury, disappointment, distress and annoyance, wrongful arrest and detention, and malicious prosecution.

---

1 None are 'nervous shock' cases, but the question is whether the requirement of a 'positive psychological illness' applies where there is no physical pain, etc, and no intentional delict, not whether the case is a 'nervous shock' one.
2 1986 SC 208, 1986 SLT 575.
3 1986 SLT 575 at 585I–J.
4 1992 SCLR 583.
5 Above, at 584D–F: in the passage quoted, the sheriff does not mention the word '*solatium*', but the learned editor of SCLR had no doubt that this is what it was.
6 1993 SLT 485.
7 1995 SCLR 393.
8 See also *Moffat v Secretary of State for Scotland* 1994 SLT 729, and *Kennedy v Steinberg* 1997 SLT 1204, 1997 SCLR 595.
9 1999 SLT 543.
10 1998 SC 389, 1998 SLT 307, 1998 SCLR 126 (in part overturned by the House of Lords (1999) Times, 26 November, HL).
11 1999 SLT 543, at 548C–D and 549B–I.
12 The distinction bears some relationship to the difference in Roman law between the *actio injuriarum* and Aquilian liability; the results of breach of Convention rights might be understood in this sense also, see the Human Rights Act 1998, s 1(3), Sch 1, Pt I, the Convention, Rights and Freedoms, art 6 (right to a fair trial), art 7 (no punishment without law), art 8 (respect for private and family life), etc.

Defamation and *solatium*

Almost invariably, a major part of the damages in a defamation action is *solatium*. Only where the pursuer is not a natural person, but a corporation, might *solatium* be inappropriate.

The *solatium* element is in practice not necessarily distinguished from any other such as an element for damage to career prospects, which is fairly clearly patrimonial. No particular loss has to be proved, for loss of reputation is of the essence of what is proved in a defamation action.

Verbal injury and *solatium*

Verbal injury includes statements which are not defamatory, but nevertheless bring a person into hatred, ridicule and contempt. It also includes 'slander of title', 'slander of business' and 'slander of property'. There are few precedents, but no doubt that damages awarded fall to be considered as *solatium* in respect of the first example. (It has been suggested[1] that it does not in the others, because in such cases there is no intention to injure character or reputation, only to cause patrimonial loss.)

Disappointment, distress and annoyance and *solatium*

A variety of miscellaneous losses have been accepted by the courts, usually without comment and involving small awards, which might be collectively regarded as 'disappointment, distress and annoyance', and are not defamation or verbal injury but are attenuated forms of 'wounded feelings and affront', perhaps merging into psychological suffering.

Thus in *Taylor v Marshalls Food Group*[2], where the principal *damnum* was pain and loss of amenities, the pursuer was prevented from engaging in his pursuits of caravanning for holidays and car maintenance as a hobby, and obtained *solatium* for that too. (This was also an 'accelerated symptom' case.)

Two particular statutory forms of damages deserve mention. Section 97(2) of the Copyright, Designs and Patents Act 1988 allows a court to award 'additional damages' where (inter alia), there is 'flagrant' breach of copyright. As 'additional', this can only be awarded where other damages are also, as was held by the House of Lords in *Redrow Homes Ltd v Bett Brothers plc*[3]. Their Lordships reserved their position on the precise nature of such 'additional damages', but they appear at least closely related to *solatium* for disappointment, distress and annoyance.

Also at least closely related to such *solatium* are the 'moral rights' under ss 77–89 of the same Act. These include rights to be identified as author or director of a work; to object to derogatory treatment of it; against false attribution of other works; and to privacy of certain photographs and films. Section 103(1) expressly declares infringement of a moral right to be 'actionable as a breach of duty' which presumably means (inter alia) that damages are available, and these would seem to be a form of *solatium* again clearly related to disappointment, distress and annoyance.

---

1 Thomson *Delictual Liability* (2nd edn, 1999) p 260.
2 1998 SLT 869, 1997 SCLR 815.
3 1998 SC (HL) 64, [1998] 2 WLR 198, 1998 SLT 648, 1998 SCLR 325.

Wrongful arrest and detention and *solatium*

Reported wrongful arrest and detention cases are rare and, as with assault and defamation, the damages sought fall to be considered as *solatium*, although the *damnum* is not easy to pin down[1].

The classic case is the complicated *McKenzie v Cluny Hill Hydropathic Co*[2]. In brief, a guest at a 'hydropathic'[3] averred that she was detained in the manager's room. She sued the company on the grounds of illegal and improper detention which had permitted assault and defamation, by means of which she suffered in her feelings and health and been subjected to great indignity. The Inner House found these averments relevant.

More recently, there have been reported cases involving the police. In *Munro v Morrison*[4] a bus driver tried to prevent police from entering his bus, was arrested and thus detained in a cell. Lord Cowie called this 'very distressing', and would have awarded damages, but his remarks were obiter, as he held arrest justified. In *Henderson v Chief Constable, Fife Police*[5], scientific officers participating in a 'work-in' in a medical laboratory were arrested and detained in cells, one handcuffed (later conceded to have been unnecessary), and both weeping and professing to be very upset. Lord Jauncey agreed it had been 'not a particularly pleasant experience', and awarded damages, increased in respect of one to 'reflect the invasion of privacy and liberty which [she] suffered as a result of having to remove her brassiere'. The *damnum* in both cases appears to straddle psychological damage and 'wounded feelings and affront'.

Malicious prosecution and *solatium*

Malicious prosecution is, of course, conceptually entirely separate, but again, reported cases are rare[6]. *Downie v Chief Constable, Strathclyde Police* provides an example, and it seems sensible to regard the *solatium* sought as for 'wounded feelings and affront', although the reasoning is not expressed at length.

(vi) Loss of faculties

An action concerning a physical injury may involve the *damnum* of 'loss of faculties'. It is central to the idea of 'substitute or solace' compensation, allowing 'a new pleasure for an old'. Typically, it follows physical injury, though such is its potential breadth, it might follow any delict.

Although a common phrase, it is ill-defined. It is often coupled with 'loss of amenities', but it is not clear if they are separate categories, or synonyms. Although judicial statements may use the terms interchangeably, for the purpose of the present classification, 'loss of faculties' is confined to loss of physical functions and impairment of bodily powers, leaving 'loss of

---

1 Cf the Convention right to liberty and security: the Human Rights Act 1998, s 1(3), Sch I, the Convention Rights and Freedoms, art 5.
2 1908 SC 200, 15 SLT 518.
3 The modern equivalent would probably be a health farm.
4 1980 SLT (Notes) 87.
5 1988 SLT 361, 1988 SCLR 77.
6 Cf the Convention right against punishment without law: HRA 1998, s 1(3), Sch 1, Pt I, the Convention Rights and Freedoms, art 7.

amenities' for other losses of ability or opportunity. Commonly, losses of faculties will involve consequential losses of amenities[1].

The Scottish Law Commission distinguished impairment of bodily powers or senses from loss of faculties[2], but this distinction is difficult to make, and the categories are treated as variations on the same theme.

Types of loss of physical function and impairment of bodily powers

Illustration is almost otiose but such a wide range of such losses have been accepted by the courts, it is useful to give some examples[3]. In *McLaurin v North British Railway Co*[4] the pursuer lost his sense of smell and taste. Lord President Robertson noted that 'loss of smell is not only a loss of all pleasures connected with that sense, but of a certain safeguard against familiar dangers'[5].

In *Kennedy v Lees of Scotland*[6], the pursuer injured her wrist, and Lord Gill noted '[s]he finds it necessary to wear clothes without buttons . . . wears skirts with elastic waists rather than with zips . . . cannot hold heavy objects in her right hand . . . has difficulty in writing her signature . . . finds it painful to hold a book and turn the pages with her right hand . . . can no longer prepare a meal without help . . . cannot wash, comb or brush her hair without difficulty . . . has difficulty in washing herself . . .'[7], and so on.

In *Dalgleish v Glasgow Corporation* the Lord Ordinary recorded[8], that the child was 'blind and doubly incontinent and has no voluntary movement of limbs. She requires to be fed by tube. Except for occasional moaning sounds her responses are negative'[9].

Causes, proof, objectivity and coma or persistent vegetative state pursuers

A reasonable degree of detail is required in description, but as loss of faculty is relatively objective, proof is relatively simpler than that of pain or psychological suffering.

This objectivity has a particular effect where the pursuer is in a coma or persistent vegetative state. As noted above, on the basis of *Dalgleish*, while such a pursuer is regarded as not undergoing pain and suffering, he or she is regarded as having suffered loss of faculties (or amenities)[10]. Lord Justice-Clerk Wheatley quoted the Lord Ordinary as noting the injured child 'has, of course, suffered a total loss of amenities of life. She is left with the fact of phys-

---

1 For instance, amputation of a leg (loss of faculty) with consequential loss of the ability to play football (loss of amenity).
2 *Report on the Effect of Death on Damages* (Scot Law Com no 134) (Cm 1848 (1992)) para 2.3.
3 For list of examples, see Walker *The Law of Civil Remedies in Scotland* pp 891–895.
4 (1892) 19 R 346.
5 Above, at 346.
6 1997 SLT 510.
7 Above, at 512A–D.
8 1976 SC 32, at 39–40.
9 That is, presumably, 'non-existent'.
10 Lord Justice-Clerk Wheatley's words are confusing. He said that 'the fact that the victim was throughout *unaware of the loss of faculties and amenities* was a matter which *fell properly for consideration under the head of pain and suffering*, and ex concessu no award falls to be made at all under *this head*' (emphases added). Presumably he meant that pain and suffering is subjective, loss of faculty or amenity is objective, but actual awareness of loss of faculty or amenity is a form of suffering.

ical existence and nothing more', and added that 'the actual mutilation of the body seems to me to call for damages on a scale commensurate with the nature of the injuries and not simply on a conventional scale'[1].

Also as noted, the same conclusion was arrived at in an English case before the House of Lords, *Lim Poh Choo*[2]. Lord Scarman observed, albeit with some reluctance, that it would be wrong to reverse the rule that 'the fact of unconsciousness does not eliminate the actuality of deprivation of the ordinary experiences and amenities of life'[3].

As with pain and suffering, it is possible that an existing or potential condition is precipitated or accelerated, in which case, the same issues arise as with pain and suffering.

(vii) Loss of amenities

As noted, it is difficult to distinguish clearly between 'loss of faculties' and 'loss of amenities', but the latter is taken here to refer to losses of ability or opportunity other than those constituted by loss of physical function or impairment of bodily powers, including those consequential upon such loss or impairment.

These may include such obvious losses as the ability to play games or to pursue hobbies. In *Currie v Kilmarnock & Loudon District Council*[4] the serious injuries resulting in amputation produced claims for, inter alia, termination of a career as an amateur athlete. Similarly, in *Girvan v Inverness Farmers Dairy (No 2)*[5], injuries prevented the pursuer from clay pigeon-shooting, a specific head of damages claimed.

The potential range of such losses is however, in principle, much wider and need not be consequential upon loss of faculties[6]. In *George Porteous Arts Ltd v Regal Motors*[7], Lord Fraser made a 'token award' for the inconvenience of not having a car, and a class of loss of amenity which has emerged in recent years is loss of congeniality of employment. Separate awards are not made, as has been the case in England, but it has been encompassed within *solatium*. Temporary Judge Horsburgh was invited to make such an award in *Stark v Lothian and Borders Fire Board*[8] under reference to *Blamey v London Fire and Civil Defence Authority*[9] in England. He declined concluding that *solatium* is not restricted to pain and suffering, and that the reasoning in the English case was not persuasive[10]. However, he awarded a global sum expressed as being for pain and suffering, post-traumatic stress disorder and loss of job satisfaction[11].

---

1 1976 SC 32, at 54.
2 [1980] AC 174, [1979] 3 WLR 44, [1979] 2 All ER 910.
3 [1980] AC 174, at 188.
4 1996 SC 55, 1996 SLT 481.
5 1998 SC (HL) 1, 1998 SLT 21, 1998 SCLR 72.
6 It might be possible to classify some 'wounded feelings' cases as 'loss of amenities'.
7 1970 SLT (Notes) 75, at 76.
8 1993 SLT 652n, 1993 SCLR 186.
9 16 December 1988, unreported.
10 1993 SLT 652n, at 654C–D.
11 See also *Lenaghan v Ayrshire and Arran Health Board* 1993 SLT 544 and *MacLean v Lothian & Borders Fire Brigade* 1999 SLT 702.

(viii) Loss of expectation of life

This is a traditional category of *solatium*, and was one of the three heads of *solatium* in Lord Justice-Clerk Wheatley's formulation in *Dalgleish v Glasgow Corporation*. Cases have been common.

A fundamental difficulty is whether the *damnum* is objective or subjective. If the former, it is really one aspect of 'loss of amenity'. If the latter, it is really one example of 'psychological suffering', flowing from the awareness of the loss. In either case, separate judicial reference to it is really otiose. However, as classic expositions of *solatium* mention it separately, it requires separate analysis.

Traditionally, the law regarded it as an objective loss. Thus in *Dalgleish* itself, damages awarded to an unconscious victim were expressed as reflecting this as well as loss of faculty or amenity. However, the law was changed to reflect a subjective view by the Damages (Scotland) Act 1976, s 9A, as inserted by s 5 of the Damages (Scotland) Act 1993 (incidentally thus overturning the relevant part of the decision in *Dalgleish*)[1]. This declares that where a pursuer has suffered a reduction of expectation of life as a result of personal injury, and 'was, at any time, or is likely to become, aware of that reduction', then a court assessing damages 'shall ... have regard to the extent that, in consequence of that awareness, he has suffered or is likely to suffer'. Thus such claims would better now be referred to as 'awareness of loss of expectation of life' claims.

The implications require some unpacking. Firstly, the provision as a whole prevents a court from awarding damages to an unaware pursuer[2]. Secondly, it does not oblige a court to award such damages to an aware pursuer; merely to consider the suffering undergone if it is assessing damages for the personal injury[3]. However, thirdly, if there is an aware pursuer, by analogy with pain and suffering, it would be an unusual case in which a court considered that there had been no suffering at all in consequence of the loss of expectation of life, and fourthly, this conclusion is reinforced by the fact that the briefest awareness presumably suffices, and the likelihood of future awareness certainly does[4]. Thus, it seems possible to regard unequivocally as 'unaware' only very young children not likely to live long, and those in a coma or persistent vegetative state. Nevertheless, fifthly, there might be room for debate as to what constitutes 'awareness', and even (where the pursuer has received no unequivocal prognosis) of the difference between awareness of the reduction, and mere awareness of its possibility. Lastly, strictly speaking, the pursuer must prove his loss. However, in practice, this has not been required, nor is likely to be in future.

1 This change emulated the law in England and Wales where a similar outcome is achieved by a different route through s 1(1) of the Administration of Justice Act 1982 (see *Report on the Effect of Death on Damages* (Scot Law Com no 134) (Cm 1848 (1992)). This provision abolished the loss of expectation of life claim, as such, but entitles a court to take into account 'suffering caused or likely to be caused to [a plaintiff] by awareness that his expectation of life has been so reduced'.
2 Damages (Scotland) Act 1976, s 9A(1) merely refers to a court taking into account the awareness of an aware pursuer. However, s 9A(2) says that '[s]ubject to subsection (1), no damages by way of *solatium* shall be recoverable in respect of loss of expectation of life'.
3 The provision opens with the words 'In assessing ...', but it cannot be thought that this means a court must assess.
4 See *Wells v Hay's Exr* (25 November 1998, unreported but discussed in Hajducki 'Death Payments – a new approach' 1999 SLT (News) 77–79).

Past and future solatium

Solatium can be both past and future, so may fall to be regarded as future loss for the purposes of quantification and interest. However, if so, it is so treated as being something between a single sum and a continuing one.

B. 'LOSS OF SOCIETY'

Common law provision

As noted, *solatium* may have commenced life as part of assythment, entering delict via the *actio injuriarum*. If this is so, *solatium* for the relatives of a deceased person is more fundamental than the usual sort (although any justification of it has been described as 'a forlorn hope'[1]).

Eisten v North British Railway Co[2] is the classic statement of the common law and, at least from *Black v North British Railway Co*[3] (a decision of a Court of Seven Judges), it accepted that the immediate family of a person killed by delictual act (in addition to any claim for support) could claim *solatium* for their grief and sorrow at the death, and for their distress in contemplating the suffering of the deceased before death. Further, that grief and sorrow was held by the Inner House in *Kelly v Glasgow Corporation*[4], to include 'not only the immediate personal grief felt, but also the continuing sense of loss arising from the deprivation . . . of a mother's care and affection (*quoad*[5] the children) and a wife's society and companionship (*quoad* the husband)'. Thus, some three types of such *solatium* existed: distress in contemplation of the death, grief and sorrow at the death, and sense of loss after the death.

Initial statutory provisions

Section 1(4) of the Damages (Scotland) Act 1976, read with s 1(1), and s 1(7), replaced *solatium* by 'loss of society awards'[6].

The original form of s 1(4) permitted (without prejudice to claims for loss of support or funeral expenses) awards of damages as 'compensation for loss of such non-patrimonial benefit as [members of the 'immediate family'] might have been expected to derive from the deceased's society and guidance if he had not died'. These were to be referred to as 'loss of society' awards.

'Members of the immediate family'

'Immediate family' is defined by s 10(2) as specified 'relatives' from the list in Sch 1 (as amended), that is, the inclusively defined spouses, parents and children[7]. It

1 Per Lord President Cooper in *McKay v Scottish Airways Ltd* 1948 SC 254, at 263, 1948 SLT 402.
2 (1870) 8 M 980, 45 SLR 304.
3 1908 SC 440, 15 SLT 840.
4 1949 SC 496 at 501, per Lord Russell, confirmed by the House of Lords at 1951 SC (HL) 15.
5 Ie 'towards'.
6 Following Scottish Law Commission *The Law Relating to Damages for Injury Causing Death* (Scot Law Com no 31) (HC Paper 393 (1972–3)). A consideration was that 'loss of society' awards would duplicate any *solatium* recovered by the executor, which *Darling v Gray & Sons* (1892) 19 R(HL) 31 hitherto prevented. However, *Darling* was in fact overturned by *Dick v Burgh of Falkirk* 1976 SC 1 before the 1976 Act came into force.
7 Damages (Scotland) Act 1976, Schedule 1 defines relatives generally for the purposes of 'loss of support' claims, and the inclusive nature of the definition is discussed above in that context.

includes both daughter-in-law and mother-in-law, as decided in *McAllister v Imperial Chemical Industries plc*[1] and *Monteith v Cape Insulation Ltd*[2].

Interpretation of the initial statutory provision

The provision, flowing from the Scottish Law Commission recommendation, was not intended simply to reproduce the common law, but to encourage larger awards[3]. The drafting clearly covered the third type of *solatium* for the 'sense of loss after the death'. As well as the explicitly mentioned 'guidance', it was reasonably apt to include the common law 'care and affection, society and companionship'. However, it was inapt to include distress in contemplation of the death, or grief and sorrow at the death, the two other types recognised by the common law[4].

Dingwall v Walter Alexander & Sons (Midland) Ltd[5] became authority on the matter, although the decision was obiter[6]. It is still relevant to quantification, but it is not necessary to consider it in detail here, nor *Donald v Strathclyde Passenger Transport Executive*[7], because they have been otherwise overtaken by amendment of s 1(4) of the Damages (Scotland) Act 1976. However, in the light of subsequent events, it is useful to look at them briefly. In *Dingwall*, argument turned largely upon the word 'compensation'. All three judges rejected the argument that it excluded grief and sorrow at the death. Lords Robertson and Kissen considered that *solatium* had expanded from the traditional grief and sorrow at the death to include loss of care and affection, society and companionship after the death as well, and that s 1(4) did not expand it further. Lord Justice-Clerk Wheatley thought *solatium* had not expanded from grief and sorrow at the death, but that s 1(4) had expanded to include not only that but also loss of care and affection, society and companionship after the death. Lord Wheatley's conclusions were expressly doubted by the First Division in *Donald v Strathclyde Passenger Transport Executive*[8]. Further, the court said that it would be 'very strange' if grief and sorrow at the death were excluded and effectively confirmed Lord Robertson's analysis in *Dingwall*[9]. (It also accepted that loss of a business relationship between father and son might be part of a 'loss of society' award.)

Amendment to the statutory provision

Following a further Scottish Law Commission Report[10], amendment by the Damages (Scotland) Act 1993 intended to redraft s 1(4) to accord with the way it had been interpreted in *Dingwall* and *Donald*.

1 1997 SLT 351.
2 1998 SCLR 940.
3 *The Law Relating to Damages for Injury Causing Death* (Scot Law Com no 31) (HC Paper no 393 (1972–3)), paras 105–112.
4 *Report on the Effect of Death on Damages* (Scot Law Com no 134) (Cm 1848 (1992)), para 2.7: 'we doubt whether such compensation, in particular compensation for pre-death distress, can be justified on a strict reading of the 1976 Act ... [The loss of society] award looks to the future not the past'.
5 1981 SLT 313.
6 The Inner House overturning the Lord Ordinary on the question of liability: confirmed by the House of Lords at 1982 SC(HL) 179.
7 1986 SLT 625.
8 Above.
9 Above, at 628.
10 *Report on the Effect of Death on Damages* (Scot Law Com no 134) (Cm 1848 (1992)): see paras 2.19–2.33, 3.20–3.25 and 4.38–4.40.

The term 'loss of society' was deleted (though it remains a useful shorthand title), and the original provision prefaced by two others to allow a claim for:

'all or any of the following—
(a) distress and anxiety endured by the relative in contemplation of the suffering of the deceased before his death;
(b) grief and sorrow of the relative caused by the deceased's death;
(c) the loss of such non-patrimonial benefit as the relative might have been expected to derive from the deceased's society and guidance had he not died'.

There appear to be no reported cases on the extended provision, but it can be expected that the line of thought reflected in *Dingwall* and *Donald*, and indeed at common law, will continue to apply. All three types of common law *solatium* seem clearly covered.

Past and future loss of society etc awards

Even before the 1993 amendment, loss of society awards were (like *solatium*) attributed to both past and future, as in *Davidson v Upper Clyde Shipbuilders*[1] and *Campbell v Gillespie*[2]. Clearly, since 1993, s 1(4)(a) relates to the past, while s 1(4)(b) and (c) can relate to both past and future.

Thus, it seems appropriate (as with *solatium*) to treat the award as relating to a continuing loss (like loss of support), rather than one-off loss (like funeral expenses). However, the cases treat it, like *solatium*, as something between the two. The reasoning is not clear, but is no doubt the same as for *solatium*.

5. WHO MAY CLAIM DAMAGES?

GENERAL

In general, it is clearly the injured person who can claim. The law of delictual liability determines who has suffered *damnum* by means of *injuria*, and thus determines who can be a pursuer[3].

However, there are four claims which require special mention: for funeral expenses; for losses under the Administration of Justice Act 1982, ss 8 or 9; for loss of support and loss of society; and by representatives in succession, typically, executors[4].

---

1 1990 SLT 329.
2 1996 SLT 503.
3 In respect of breach of Convention rights under the Human Rights Act 1998, the person who can sue must be a 'victim', as defined in s 7(7) by reference to art 34 of the European Convention on Human Rights. This is a question of liability, and therefore not dealt with further here.
4 Representatives in bankruptcy, and tutors and curators, or assignees, are beyond the scope of this work.

CLAIMS FOR FUNERAL EXPENSES

These are claims by persons on their own behalf and not on behalf of the deceased. They have suffered the *damnum* of consequential expenses upon the *injuria* causing the deceased's death, and can sue in a personal capacity.

The claim, in s 1(3) of the Damages (Scotland) Act 1976, is restricted to relatives, defined in the same way as for loss of support claims.

CLAIMS UNDER SS 8 AND 9 OF THE ADMINISTRATION OF JUSTICE ACT 1982

These are claims on behalf of the person suffering *damnum*, not by them. The *damnum* is providing 'necessary services' or being deprived of 'personal services' under ss 8 or 9 of the Administration of Justice Act 1982, through *injuria* to the injured person.

Those suffering *damnum* must be 'relatives' (as defined by s 13(1) of the Act), but cannot sue, and must rely on the injured person doing so.

McLelland v Greater Glasgow Health Board[1] illustrates a surprising feature of the legislation. The mother of a child *in utero* was negligently not offered an amniocentesis test. It would have shown the child to suffer Down's syndrome, which would have caused her to abort him. The child was not the victim of the negligence, and so was not an 'injured person', and indeed, could sue for nothing. The parents, who were the victims of the negligence, obtained damages for various costs of bringing up the child, but could not claim damages under s 8, even though they were rendering relevant services, because it is 'the injured person' who sues, and the child was not an 'injured person'.

CLAIMS FOR LOSS OF SUPPORT AND LOSS OF SOCIETY

These are again claims by persons on their own behalf, and not on behalf of the deceased. They have suffered the *damnum* of loss of support or loss of society, through the *injuria* of the deceased's death, and can sue in a personal capacity[2].

The claims are, respectively, under s 1(3) of the Damages (Scotland) Act 1976 (brought by a relative as defined in s 10(1) and Sch 1, as amended); and under s 1(4), brought by immediate family (as defined in s 10(2) and Sch 1, as amended). These definitions are discussed above in relation to those claims.

CLAIMS BY EXECUTORS

These are claims by the executor acting in place of a deceased person, who suffered the *damnum* by means of *injuria* to him or her. They sue in a representative capacity[3].

It is important to note that the deceased may have been:

1 1999 SLT 543.
2 Nor is this action debarred by one commenced by the deceased, and continued by the executor: *Dick v Burgh of Falkirk* 1976 SC 1.
3 Therefore do not debar a claim by immediate family for loss of support: *Dick v Burgh of Falkirk* 1976 SC 1.

(i)   killed instantly in an accident;
(ii)   injured in an accident and later have died of those injuries (but did so before the claims arising out of the accident were disposed of);
(iii)   injured in an accident and later have died for some other reason (but did so before the claims arising out of the accident were disposed of);
(iv)   not injured in any accident and later have died for some other reason, incidentally having a claim for funeral expenses, loss of support or loss of society in relation to some third party who was killed in an accident (but did so before the claims for funeral expenses etc were disposed of);
(v)   not injured in any accident, and later have died for some other reason, incidentally having some other delictual claim (but did so before the claims arising out of the delict were disposed of).

It is equally important to note that the same principles apply to all these five types, *mutatis mutandis*.

The general principle

Where a person holding a right of action dies from any cause, that right is incorporeal moveable property and can be vindicated by an executor[1] (unless the claim was disposed of before death, or is otherwise excluded[2]). Thus (subject to a limitation and an exception) delictual damages which would have been awarded to a now-deceased person could be sought by an executor and awarded to the estate. This principle applied to all five types of claim outlined above[3].

The limitation related to future loss. There is surprisingly little authority on this, but in *Dick v Burgh of Falkirk*[4] Lord Kilbrandon noted in passing that '[t]he executrix could recover no more than the damages for the personal injury and the amount of patrimonial loss suffered ... up to the [now-deceased's] death ... '. This principle would prevent potentially massive windfalls to heirs and successors where there might have been large claims for future consequential expenditure and future loss of earnings[5]. It also prevents any double compensation where dependent relatives sue for loss of support, and immediate family for loss of society.

There is a dearth of authority perhaps because the issue was concealed by the exception. This exception was that (although an executor could continue an action actually started[6]) any claim by the now-deceased for *solatium*, past and future, was extinguished by death[7] since the *damnum* was personal to the

1   *Auld v Shairp* (1874) 2 R 191; *Bern's Exor v Montrose Asylum* (1893) 20 R 859; *Smith v Stewart & Co* 1961 SC 91, 1961 SLT 67.
2   See eg *McKay v Scottish Airways* 1948 SC 265.
3   Though, in the first, there would only be a claim arising out of the accident for losses of assets.
4   1976 SC 1 at 21.
5   This can still occur where the pursuer dies after decree. In 1997, Nottingham Health Authority settled a medical negligence claim in respect of a catastrophically injured child with a predicted life-span of some years for £700,000, containing a large element for future care costs. The child died a week later. The Health Authority considered seeking return of the care costs. The parents successfully resisted this. See (1997) Scotsman, 13 June.
6   *Neilson v Rodger* (1853) 16 D 325; *Darling v Gray & Sons* (1892) 19 R(HL) 31; *Bern's Exor v Montrose Asylum*; *Smith v Stewart & Co.*
7   *Bern's Exor v Montrose Asylum*; *Stewart v London, Midland and Scottish Railway Co* 1943 SC (HL) 19; *Smith v Stewart & Co.*

deceased ('substitute or solace' in Atiyah's terminology), and designed to alleviate his or her pain and suffering etc, which died with him or her. This exception applied to any delictual action. Therefore, any claim to *solatium* in the second and third types of claim by executor outlined above would be subject to it, as would any claim by a relative in the fourth type for 'loss of society' *solatium*[1], or by any other person in the fifth type suing for *solatium* as part of a defamation action, etc.

Modification of the general principle by statute

Remaining claims under common law

The changes wrought by statute appear to cover all possible damages claims, so there are no probably claims to which the common law, as such, applies.

Personal injury claims

For personal injury claims, the common law is now replaced by ss 2 and 2A of the Damages (Scotland) Act 1976 (as substituted by ss 3 and 4, respectively, of the Damages (Scotland) Act 1993).

Originally, s 2 prevented the executor from even continuing an action for *solatium*, or for any patrimonial loss after the date of death. However, this provision gave rise to the fear that defenders were encouraged to delay settlement in cases of the second type outlined above, in the hope that death would intervene and reduce damages payable. The matter was referred to the Scottish Law Commission[2] which found no hard evidence of this, but observed delay to be endemic; the effect of the provision to be capricious; and the view of *solatium* as 'personal' overstated; and recommended legislation.

Thus, by the current form of s 2(1), 'the like rights to damages in relation to personal injury (including a right to damages by way of *solatium*) . . . as were vested in the deceased immediately before his death' are transmitted to the executor. However, this is subject to s 2(2) and (3) which now limit both patrimonial loss and *solatium* to the period before death[3]. This removes any incentive to delay.

Section 2A permits the executor to bring or continue an action to enforce such a right. Thus an executor may claim damages for the benefit of the estate in relation to the period until death for all or any of: losses of assets; consequential expenditure (actual, or notional); loss of profit or loss of income; and *solatium*[4].

Defamation and other solatium *claims*

The arguments on personal injury claims did not persuade the Scottish Law Commission in relation to other claims.

---

1 On which see *Fraser v Livermore Bros* (1900) 7 SLT 450; *Kelly v Glasgow Corporation* 1944 SC 496 (IH), 1951 SC (HL) 15.
2 See *Report on the Effect of Death on Damages* (Scot Law Com no 134) (Cm 1848 (1992)). The original provision flowed from *The Law Relating to Damages for Injuries Causing Death* (Scot Law Com no 31) (1973).
3 For observations on the transmission of *solatium*, see *Beggs v Motherwell Bridge Fabricators Ltd* 1998 SLT 1216 at 1123I–1224B, 1997 SCLR 1019.
4 Though where the deceased was killed instantly, there would only be a claim for loss of assets.

For 'defamation, or any other verbal injury, or other injury to reputation', s 2(4) maintains the common law principle. Non-patrimonial claims may be continued by executors, but not initiated by them. However, because such claims are defined as 'personal injury' ones for the purposes of the Act[1], s 2(2) and (3) apply, and no claim is possible except for the period before the death.

Depending upon interpretation of s 2(4), this provision covers all *solatium* claims which are not 'real' personal injury ones[2], except those for loss of society etc.

Loss of society claims

As originally drafted, loss of society claims were specifically prevented by s 3 of the Damages (Scotland) Act 1976 from transmitting to executors, paralleling the position taken in respect of *solatium*. However, when the Damages (Scotland) Act 1993 changed the law in relation to *solatium*, it also did so in relation to loss of society claims. Thus s 3 was repealed, and s 1A applies that principle. Section 2A entitles an executor to bring or continue an action to enforce such rights.

Effects of extinction or limitation of the deceased's rights to damages

Section 1(2) of the Damages (Scotland) Act 1976 maintains the common law position, subject (by virtue of s 1(5A)) to the possibility of provisional damages. Thus, no liability rises under s 1 of that Act if liability 'has been excluded or discharged . . . by the deceased before his death', or 'is excluded by virtue of any enactment'. Also, s 6 provides that where damages are limited by agreement (as in many transport contracts), that limit is not removed, and where there are two or more pursuers, their damages will be reduced pro rata.

Reciprocal effect of claims by relatives and executors

By s 4, claims by executors and claims by relatives arising out of the same events do not preclude each other[3].

---

1 Damages (Scotland) Act 1976, s 10(1), as amended by the Administration of Justice Act 1982, s 7(2) and Sch, para 3.
2 See previous note and associated text.
3 This effects *Dick v Burgh of Falkirk* 1976 SC (HL) 1, confirming the overturning of *Darling v Gray & Sons* (1892) 19R (HL) 31.

3. Principles of damages—*Restitutio in integrum* and limitations upon it

THE SIGNIFICANCE AND MEANING OF *RESTITUTIO IN INTEGRUM*

It is axiomatic that damages are reparation for *damnum* suffered. As noted in ch 1, the aim of such reparation is commonly expressed in the principle *restitutio in integrum*[1]. Literally translated, this means something like 'complete compensation', but usually it is freely translated[2] in words such as Stair's 'putting [the pursuer] in as good a condition as he was in before the injury'[3]. Damages under the Human Rights Act 1998, ss 6–8 (not in force at the time of writing) are designed to afford 'just satisfaction' in conformity with the European Convention on Human Rights. It will be a matter of interpretation how far this accords with traditional notions of *restitio in integrum*.

IMPLICATIONS OF *RESTITUTIO IN INTEGRUM*

RESTITUTIO IN INTEGRUM, THE PURSUER'S NEEDS AND THE DEFENDER'S MEANS[4]

The chief implication of *restitutio in integrum* is that the central issue is the pursuer's needs. Quantification is calculation of the pursuer's *damnum*. The point is expressed in the maxim 'you take your victim as you find him'[5], and in particular, in 'thin skull' cases. Thus, at least in relation to physical injury resulting from negligence, vulnerable pursuers get more damages than robust ones because they have suffered greater *damnum* by virtue of that

---

1 The actual phrase was used in, for instance, *Pomphrey v James A Cuthbertson* 1951 SC 147, at 161, per Lord Jamieson (and the English House of Lords case *British Transport Commission v Gourley* [1956] AC 185, at 197, per Earl Jowitt).

2 As in *Livingstone v Rawyards Coal Co Ltd* (1880) 7 R (HL) 1, at 7, per Lord Blackburn ('you should as nearly as possible get at the sum of money which will put the party who has been injured ... in the same position as he would have been if he had not sustained the wrong'), approved by the House of Lords in *British Transport Commission v Gourley*, at 197; or *O'Brien's CB v British Steel plc* 1991 SC 315, at 319, per Lord President Hope ('to place the pursuer as near as may be in the same financial position as he would have been if the accident had not occurred').

3 I, 9, 2.

4 The analysis in this and the next section owes much to Cane (ed) *Atiyah's Accidents, Compensation and the Law* (6th edn, 1999) ch 7.

5 Eg *McKillen v Barclay Curle & Co* 1967 SLT 41, per Lord Guthrie, at 44, (citing Lord Justice-Clerk Thomson in *Malcolm v Dickson* 1951 SC 542 at 548, 1951 SLT 357), *Burke v Royal Infirmary of Edinburgh NHS Trust Ltd* 1999 SLT 359, at 543B–C, per Lord Eassie.

vulnerability. Conversely, pursuers who lose little, receive little[1]. Incidental advantages to the pursuer are, however, likely to be ignored[2].

By the same token, the defender's means are irrelevant. Thus, the rich defender is not required to pay more, but also the poor defender does not escape through poverty. It is, of course, only worth suing a rich defender, but in certain important areas, the requirement of third party insurance means that, effectively, all defenders are rich.

RESTITUTIO IN INTEGRUM AND 'PUNITIVE', 'EXEMPLARY' AND 'AGGRAVATED' DAMAGES

By the same token again, *restitutio in integrum* limits damages to compensation by indicating that they are not designed to punish the defender. This is what distinguishes compensation from punishment[3], and there is no reason (save coincidence) why the size of damages should reflect the degree of blameworthiness of the defender. In *Black v North British Railway Co*[4], Lord President Dunedin explicitly observed that '[c]ertain judges [had] countenanced the idea that damages are partly *in poenam*[5], and that consequently if the fault is gross the penalty ought to be great . . . [but] I do not think this view will bear a moment's examination'[6]. Great carelessness may produce no loss; minor errors produce catastrophic results[7].

Thus, there should be no 'punitive' or 'exemplary' damages, increased to impose retribution, express disapprobation, provide deterrence, or otherwise punish (although, interestingly, the position was different in Roman law and is different in English law[8], and possibly this accounts

1 See eg *United Horse Shoe & Nail Co Ltd v John Stewart & Co* (1888) 15 R(HL) 45, 13 App Cas 401, 25 SLR 447, where a patent was infringed, but few lost sales resulted so damages were small.
2 In *McFarlane v Tayside Health Board* 1999 SC 389, 1998 SCLR 126, 1998 SLT 307, at 312 F–G, Lord Justice-Clerk Cullen observed '[i]t is not uncommon to encounter cases in which the occurrence of an accident has brought in train not only loss of earnings for the pursuer but also incidental improvement in his enjoyment of life, but the latter is not treated as deductible from that loss', and at 316G–I, Lord McCluskey memorably exemplified the point. The House of Lords overturned the decision in part, largely on other grounds: (1999) Times, 26 November, HL. The principle was specifically reaffirmed by Lord Slynn of Hadley and (at least in relation to *solatium*) Lord Hope of Craighead. Other judges were more equivocal, at least on the facts of that case.
3 The Criminal Procedure (Scotland) Act 1995, s 211(7) specifically provides that in fixing the level of a fine a sentencer must take into consideration 'the means of the offender so far as known to the court'. In *McMillan v McDowall* 1993 SLT 312, at 313D, Temporary Judge Coutts observed that '. . . the Scots approach is not to look at whether the wrongdoer gains or is penalised but only at whether the sufferer requires to be compensated or recompensed for loss'.
4 1908 SLT 840, at 842.
5 Ie 'by way of punishment'.
6 And as noted above, in *United Horse Shoe & Nail Co Ltd*, the pursuer had lost little, so was entitled to little, and damages were not to be used to punish the wrongdoer.
7 But see the reasoning of Lords Steyn and Clyde in *McFarlane v Tayside Health Board* noted above.
8 The issue was examined by the (English) Law Commission in *Aggravated, Exemplary and Restitutionary Damages* (Law Com no 247) (HC Paper 346 (1997–98)). It concluded that they should continue, and were appropriate (even with vicarious liability) where the defendant deliberately and outrageously disregarded the plaintiff's rights, irrespective of his or her means, the amount being fixed by the judge, not a jury. This could be seen as a reference to *solatium* for wounded feelings and affront.

for the existence of 'additional damages' for 'flagrant' breaches of copyright[1]).

It has been suggested that there are 'aggravated damages', conceptually separate from punitive or exemplary damages. Walker asserts that '. . . in cases of deliberate wrongs damages may sometimes be aggravated by the outrageous nature of the conduct complained of and in all cases, damages are aggravated by the greater gravity of the loss suffered'[2]. However, he offers no authority, and such situations are perhaps best explained as ones where the 'outrageous behaviour' is part of the *damnum*[3], and in any case, where compensation is 'substitute or solace' rather than 'equivalent'[4], there is no clear test as to what in fact constitutes *restitutio in integrum.*

Also, 'violent profits' (damages covering profits on assets lost through wrongful occupation by another) may be greater than the rightful possessor has in fact lost. However, possibly 'violent profits' should not be regarded as delictual damages at all, but as some form of restitution[5].

In any case, when damages are assessed by a jury, it is not possible to tell if they have abandoned *restitutio in integrum* in favour of a penalty, as must be suspected in some cases[6].

RESTITUTIO IN INTEGRUM AND 'NOMINAL' AND 'CONVENTIONAL' DAMAGES

'Nominal damages' is not a term of art. If taken to mean that the pursuer, even though successful, was not awarded full compensation for the *damnum* actually suffered, then such damages are clearly inconsistent with *restitutio in integrum.*

However, *restitutio in integrum* is consistent with very small damages reflecting insignificant *damnum*, as in *Morrison v Forsyth*[7], where the Lord Ordinary observed that 'a nominal sum' would be appropriate for the pursuers.

The position may sometimes be confused in relation to *solatium* (as with 'aggravated damages') as it is 'substitute or solace', rather than 'equivalent', compensation, with no clear test of what is *restitutio in integrum.*

---

1 Copyright, Designs and Patents Act 1988, s 97(2) (also s 229(3)). In *Redrow Homes Ltd v Bett Brothers plc* 1998 SC (HL) 64, at 69C–D, Lord Jauncey of Tullichettle expressly reserved his position as to whether these damages were 'by nature punitive or purely compensatory', and at 71A–B, Lord Clyde considered them 'exemplary damages, or more probably aggravated damages'. Lord Hope of Craighead and two English judges merely concurred. Perhaps they are a form of *solatium.*
2 *The Law of Civil Remedies in Scotland* (1974) p 815.
3 Echoing the Roman *actio injuriarum*, compensating for insult. As noted above, in *Redrow Homes Ltd*, Lord Clyde considered 'additional damages' for 'flagrant' breach of copyright to be probably 'aggravated damages'.
4 For the meaning of 'substitute or solace' and 'equivalent' compensation, see ch 1.
5 See eg Stewart *Delict* (3rd edn, 1998) pp 251–252. 'Additional damages' in copyright (noted above) are also possible 'having regard to . . . any benefit accruing to the defendant by reason of the infringement'. Perhaps this form should be regarded as 'violent profits'.
6 Such as *Winter v News Scotland Ltd* 1991 SLT 828.
7 1995 SLT 539, at 540. See also *United Horse Shoe & Nail Co Ltd v John Stewart & Co* (1888) 15 R (HL) 95.

'Conventional damages' is not a term of art either, but is used to describe awards which are mere acknowledgments or token payments in cases where equivalent compensation appears impossible[1]. At common law, for example, awards for loss of expectation of life and *solatium* as 'loss of society' were conventional. Neither now is, because of the enactment of ss 9A and 1(4) (as amended), of the Damages (Scotland) Act 1976, respectively.

RESTITUTIO IN INTEGRUM AND 'ONCE AND FOR ALL' LUMP SUM PAYMENTS

Damages are traditionally paid in a 'once and for all' lump sum, as *restitutio in integrum* seems to require. A number of devices now exist to circumvent some of the unfortunate results for the defender which flow from that, including interim damages, provisional and further damages, and structured settlements. These are discussed in ch 4.

RESTITUTIO IN INTEGRUM AND TAXATION ETC

It has been accepted that *restitutio in integrum* for income losses implies a sum net of tax since the English House of Lords case of *British Transport Commission v Gourley*[2], although the point had been uncertain until then, and it was only a majority decision[3].

The position is the same in relation to national insurance contributions, which are effectively another tax. These questions are considered in ch 5.

COMPENSATION FROM OTHER SOURCES AND *RESTITUTIO IN INTEGRUM*

It might be thought that where compensation for the same *damnum* is received from other sources as well as damages, *restitutio in integrum* would imply that damages should be reduced accordingly.

This is true in relation to some social security and other benefits, by virtue of the Administration of Justice Act 1982 and related legislation. Strangely, this is not true in relation to first party insurance (by virtue of the Damages (Scotland) Act 1976, s 1(5)), nor of contractual pensions or benefits (by virtue of the Administration of Justice Act 1982, s 10(a)). Likewise, charitable and similar payments are not deducted. In such cases, there would seem to be clear double compensation. These issues are considered more fully in ch 6.

---

1 In *McFarlane v Tayside Health Board* (1999) Times, 26 November, HL, Lord Millett would disallow damages for the extra expenditure of bringing up a healthy child, but would award up to £5,000 as a 'conventional sum' for that loss as 'general damages'. This appears to be *solatium*, although he also refused *solatium* to the mother for the pain and suffering of pregnancy and childbirth.
2 [1956] AC 185, [1956] 2 WLR 41, [1955] 3 All ER 769.
3 The position is in fact more complicated. If the damages are invested, the interest is taxed (*Gourley* in reverse) or even, if an annuity is purchased, taxed twice: see (English) Law Commission *Structured Settlements . . . [etc]* (Law Com 224) (Cm 2646) (1994) paras 2.45–2.46.

LIMITATIONS UPON *RESTITUTIO IN INTEGRUM*

TYPES OF LIMITATION UPON *RESTITUTIO IN INTEGRUM*

There are limitations to *restitutio in integrum*. Firstly, it is a principle, not a rule. As a principle, it must be concretised into something approaching rules of quantification[1]. Secondly, any principle or rule may fail to achieve its aim. Invocations of the principle in major authorities may be hedged by qualifications. The consequences these two limitations imply are most obvious in relation to *solatium*, that is, 'substitute or solace compensation'. What sort of rules determine the sum of money which constitutes *restitutio in integrum* for, say, a broken arm?[2] However, they also apply to 'equivalent compensation'. For example, there is more than one possible rule for quantifying damages for *damnum* to corporeal property. The concretising of the principle into rules of quantification, including limitations on 'once and for all' lump sum damages (as noted above) is dealt with in chs 4 and 5.

Thirdly, *restitutio in integrum* must be reconciled with other principles. Thus, primarily, it is limited by the requirement of *culpa*. There is no compensation without decree against a defender, for that would be *damnum absque injuria*. This is a matter of liability, and therefore not further dealt with here, but it does constitute the most significant limitation to *restitutio in integrum*, and some other limitations, on examination, resolve themselves into questions of liability.

Thus, the principle must be reconciled with various other principles revolving around causation and remoteness (including the doctrines of *novus actus interveniens*, joint fault, contributory negligence, *volenti non fit injuria* and vicarious liability). These also principally concern liability, but remoteness of damages is dealt with in this chapter, and related doctrines mentioned so far as relevant.

Further, *restitutio in integrum* must be reconciled with the principle that the defender must minimise the *damnum* he or she suffers. Yet further, for various reasons, courts have been loath to compensate for 'pure' economic losses. The principle this represents must also be reconciled with *restitutio in integrum*. Still yet further, there is the question of whether there are thresholds or ceilings imposed by the common law or statute which limit *restitutio in integrum* by limiting the minimum and maximum amounts that may be claimed. Finally, the principle of 'just satisfaction' and related limits on the award of damages under the Human Rights Act 1998 must be reconciled with *restitutio in integrum*. These reconciliations are also dealt with in the chapter.

---

1 Though it is noteworthy that judges often assert there to be no rules, only guidelines.
2 An example of this difficulty in conjunction with an invocation of the principle is *British Transport Commission v Gourley* [1956] AC 185, at 197, where Earl Jowitt continued 'but it is manifest that no award of money can possibly compensate a man for such grievous injuries as the respondent in this case has suffered'. In such cases 'the judge can do no more than endeavour to arrive at a fair estimate, taking into account all the relevant considerations'. At 208, Lord Goddard doubted if '*restitutio in integrum* has any application to general damages' (a concept roughly equating to *solatium*) and, at 212, Lord Reid did not think it 'a very helpful or accurate way of stating his right'.

CAUSATION, RELATED DOCTRINES AND REMOTENESS OF DAMAGES AS LIMITATIONS ON *RESTITUTIO IN INTEGRUM*

Causation and related doctrines

Causation and related doctrines are a limitation upon *restitutio in integrum*. Unless the causal connection between *culpa* and *damnum* is made out, the defender is not liable to make *restitutio in integrum*. Thus, it is essentially a question of liability, and as such, not discussed here. *Volenti non fit injuria* is a related doctrine, as is *novus actus interveniens*, which remove liability from the defender.

Joint fault is somewhat different[1]. Where there is a single *damnum*, there may nevertheless be several defenders who contributed to it (which is a question of liability and causation). The pursuer is entitled to *restitutio in integrum*, and may sue all or any of the defenders for it as they are jointly and severally liable. Defenders are obliged to pay the damages 'in such proportions as the jury or the court may deem just' by virtue of the Law Reform (Miscellaneous Provisions) (Scotland) Act 1940, s 3(1), and by s 3(2), any defender found liable is entitled in a separate action to recover 'such contribution, if any, as the court may deem just' from others who could have been defenders. (These situations are to be distinguished from vicarious liability, where a person without *culpa* is liable because of the relationship with a person with *culpa*).

Contributory negligence is also different, although at common law it was regarded as an example of *novus actus interveniens* or of *volenti non fit injuria*. The Law Reform (Contributory Negligence) Act 1945, s 1(1) now requires a court to reduce damages 'to such an extent as [it] thinks just and equitable' where a pursuer's *damnum* is 'the result partly of his own fault'. (Fault and causation must be proved.) This applies to all delict actions, including personal injury and fatal accident cases.

There is no guidance in the statute as to the principles according to which reduction is to be made. In such cases, judges inevitably declare the pursuer to be liable to a certain percentage, attempting to reflect the relative importance of the actions of defender and pursuer, and award damages reduced by that percentage. A wide variety of percentages, sometimes greater than 50 per cent, has been deducted[2]. No doubt because this is an epistemologically doubtful proceeding, it is treated like a matter of fact, and '[t]he appeal court will not readily upset the assessment of apportionment ... by the trial judge ... unless ... [he] has manifestly and to a substantial degree gone wrong'[3]. By the same token, where there is a jury '[a]pportionment of fault for contributory negligence is essentially a question for the jury, who saw and heard the witnesses, who were entitled to give such weight as was thought proper to such evidence as was

---

1 Thomson *Delictual Liability* (2nd ed, 1999) p 146 distinguishes two varieties: 'joint liability' in negligence cases, and 'joint wrongdoing' in others.

2 In one English case, *Uddin v Associated Portland Cement Manufacturers Ltd* [1965] 2 QB 582, [1965] 2 WLR 1183, [1965] 1 All ER 213, 80% was deducted.

3 Even if 'the Lord Ordinary's conclusion on this matter occasions surprise': per Lord Robertson in *McCusker v Saveheat Cavity Wall Insulation Ltd* 1987 SLT 24, at 31.

accepted and who were entitled to draw such inferences as they thought proper from the acceptable evidence'[1].

The requirements the defender must fulfil in order to persuade the court are treated as questions of liability and causation, and therefore not dealt with here.

Remoteness of damages

Remoteness of damages[2] and remoteness of injury distinguished

'Remoteness of damages' and 'remoteness of injury' are separate, if ill-distinguished, concepts[3] designed as 'threshold devices' to limit how much a defender must pay, because to consequences, there is no end[4]. The former is a doctrine requiring that where there is undoubted *damnum*, undoubtedly causally connected with an act, which is undoubtedly *injuria*, nevertheless, damages are not payable where the *damnum* is in some sense 'too remote' from the *injuria*. The latter is a doctrine requiring that where there is undoubted *damnum*, causally connected with an act which would otherwise be regarded as *injuria*, nevertheless, it is not regarded as *injuria* where the *damnum* is in some sense 'too remote' from the act.

Two possible tests: 'Polemis' *and* 'Wagon Mound'

In practice two possible tests of remoteness of damages have been argued for. Either a defender is liable for all the *damnum* 'directly caused' by the *injuria*, or he or she is liable for only the *damnum* which was 'reasonably foreseeable'. Commonly, the tests will produce the same result, so the question is which is to be preferred when they do not. The alternatives are conventionally named respectively after the curiously factually similar, but legally contrasting, *Polemis* and *Wagon Mound* cases[5], around which debate has tended to weave ever since[6].

1 *Kirkland v British Railways Board* 1978 SC 71, at 74, per Lord Kissen, giving the opinion of the Second Division.
2 'Remoteness of damage' is the orthodox phrase. 'Remoteness of damages', proposed by Thomson *Delictual Liability* pp 265ff, is used here the better to distinguish it from 'remoteness of injury'.
3 The learned author of the subsection 'remoteness of damage' (*sic*) in the section on 'Fault' in vol 15 ('Obligations') of the *Stair Memorial Encyclopaedia*, at para 379, while accepting the distinction 'for presentational purposes', considers it has no practical purpose and lacks House of Lords authority (but Lord Clyde seemed specifically to support it in *McFarlane v Tayside Health Board* (1999) Times, 26 November, HL). Arguably, 'remoteness of injury' has, since *Donoghue v Stevenson* 1932 SC(HL) 31, [1932] AC 62, 1932 SLT 317, been abandoned by the courts which now use 'duty of care' to achieve the same result: see eg Thomson *Delictual Liability* pp 126–127.
4 The point was colourfully put by Lord Wright in the English case of *Owners of the Dredger Liesbosch v Owners of the Steamship Edison* [1933] AC 449, at 460: '. . . the loss of a ship by collision, due to the other ship's sole fault, may force the shipowner into bankruptcy and that again may involve his family in suffering, loss of education and opportunities in life, but no such loss can be recovered from the wrongdoer. In the varied web of affairs, the law must abstract some consequences as relevant, not perhaps on the ground of pure logic, but for practical reasons'.
5 *In Re an Arbitration between Polemis and Furness Withy and Co Ltd* [1921] 3 KB 560, CA, and *Overseas Tankship (UK) Ltd v Morts Dock and Engineering Co Ltd (the Wagon Mound) (No 1)* [1961] AC 388, [1961] 2 WLR 126, [1961] 1 All ER 404, PC.
6 Thomson *Delictual Liability* p 268, however, submits that 'in Scots law, it is too simplistic to see the question . . . in terms of reasonable foreseeability on the one hand and direct consequences on the other'.

In *Polemis*, tins of petrol in the hold of a ship had leaked during a voyage. In port, while stevedores were moving the cargo, there was a fire which destroyed the ship. The stevedores were found by arbitrators to have negligently knocked a plank into the hold which event, it was inferred, had produced a spark, in turn resulting in an explosion and the fire. Before the English Court of Appeal were questions as to who was liable, and whether for all the loss, or only that which was reasonably foreseeable. On the authorities, it unequivocally rejected foreseeability as the test of remoteness in favour of 'direct' consequences (though without supplying a clear test of when consequences became 'indirect').

In *Wagon Mound*, heavy furnace oil was negligently spilled from a ship in Sydney Harbour. Some of it, floating on the water, drifted under a wharf. People were working on the wharf with oxy-acetylene torches, and molten metal fell on to cotton waste also floating on the water. This caught fire, and in turn either set fire to the floating furnace oil directly, or to the wooden piles of the wharf which then set fire to the furnace oil. A major fire resulted, which destroyed the wharf and associated installations. The trial judge found the loss which occurred was not a reasonably foreseeable result of the act of negligence. In the appeal to the Privy Council (for whom *Polemis* was only a potentially persuasive precedent), the single opinion, delivered by Lord Warrington, asserted that the *Polemis* rule was difficult to apply because it was not clear what 'direct' meant, and proceeded from a doubtful reading of weak precedents. Moreover, it had not been popular with courts. Further, since liability does not exist in the abstract but only when loss has occurred, there was a logical difficulty in discounting unforeseeable loss for the purpose of determining liability, but then resurrecting it for the purpose of assessing compensation.

The position in Scots law

The *Polemis* proposition appears to be required by *restitutio in integrum*, and the idea that 'the wrong-doer must take his victim as he finds him'. On the other hand, the *Wagon Mound* proposition appears to be required by the principle that liability in negligence depends on reasonable foreseeability. Given this contradiction, and the fact that commonly both propositions produce the same result, it is perhaps unsurprising that, despite references to a 'grand rule', it is not clear which alternative represents the law, and both continue to be argued.

Intentional and unintentional delicts

Debate has been almost entirely in relation to negligence, and there is very little authority in relation to intentional delicts.

It has been argued that, irrespective of what rule applies in relation to unintentional delicts[1], there is liability for all losses directly caused by

---

1 Eg Thomson *Delictual Liability* p 53 and pp 268, 269, who sees it as a consequence of the intention necessary to such delicts, but offers no authority. The learned authors of 15 *Stair Memorial Encyclopaedia of the Laws of Scotland*, paras 391 and 907–908 respectively doubt the proposition, and do not mention it.

intentional delicts. *Quinn v Leathem*[1] has been cited as authority[2]. However, although a House of Lords decision, it dealt with English law, was primarily concerned with liability, and concerned an area of law which has changed a lot in a century.

The 'grand rule'

ORIGIN

The traditional starting point is *Allan v Barclay*[3]. A carter, employed by the pursuer, came upon a warning fire left by the defender. His horse shied at the sight, tipping over the cart. This damaged the cart and its load, and badly injured the horse and the carter. The pursuer sought damages for, inter alia, loss of the carter's services, arguing that there was no rule against consequential damages. The case is remembered for Lord Kinloch's dictum on remoteness of damages, which has become a standard statement of the law:

'The grand rule on the subject of damages is, that none can be claimed except such as naturally and directly arise out of the wrong done; and such therefore, as may reasonably be supposed to have been in the view of the wrongdoer'[4].

However, there are two sorts of problem with Lord Kinloch's dictum: as to authority; and as to meaning.

AUTHORITY

The dictum was uttered in the Outer House and was not referred to by the Inner House which upheld the Lord Ordinary's decision that the claim was irrelevant, on the adequacy of the pleadings, not on the ground of 'remoteness of damages'[5]. Further, during the first century of its life it was little referred to[6], and 'remoteness of damages' was little distinguished from 'remoteness of injury'.

Though cited approvingly in the Inner House in *Bourhill v Young*[7] (though not in the House of Lords), it seems first to have received strong approval in

---

1 [1901] AC 495.
2 15 *Stair Memorial Encyclopaedia*, para 391.
3 (1864) 2 M 873. *Robertson v Connolly* (1851) 13 D 779 is sometimes referred to. There, the Inner House was unanimous, but described consequences as 'direct', 'natural', 'common', 'probable', and 'immediate' without much analysis, and apparently interchangeably, and the decision may be confined to the facts. See particularly Lord Mackenzie's opinion at 781.
4 (1864) 2 M 873, at 874.
5 Above, at 875, Lord President McNeill said, obiter, of the claim that it 'appears to be a new proposal in the law of Scotland'; Lord Deas went slightly further, saying '[t]here is no instance of an action of this kind'; Lords Curriehill and Ardmillan merely concurred.
6 In *Reavis v Clan Line Steamers* 1925 SC 725, at 739, Lord President Clyde noted that Lord Fraser's *Master and Servant* did not mention it and asserted a contradictory principle. It was not even mentioned in *Kelvin Shipping Co (Owners of the SS Baron Vernon) v Canadian Pacific Railway Co (Owners of the SS Metagama)* 1928 SC (HL) 21, 1928 SLT 117, or *Muir v Glasgow Corporation* 1943 SC (HL) 3, [1943] AC 448, 1944 SLT 60. See also *Green's Encyclopaedia* (2nd edn, 1910) vol 4 p 185 and (3rd edn, 1928) vol 5 p 388 and vol 12 (1931).
7 1941 SC 395.

Steel v Glasgow Iron & Steel[1], but this was a majority decision, approval was not necessarily as a 'remoteness of damages' case, and it was noted that the dictum had been 'reformulated'[2], with 'different adjectives, adverbs and phrases'[3]. Only in *McKillen v Barclay Curle & Co Ltd*[4], when it was a century old, could it be said to be explicitly approved in relation to remoteness of damages. Lord President Clyde declared that Lord Kinloch's 'statement of the law has never . . . been controverted'; Lords Guthrie, Migdale and Cameron heartily agreed[5].

This appears exaggerated, and perhaps enthusiasm for the 'grand rule' is related to the variety of views of what it actually means.

MEANING

The basic problem is the compound sentence. Lord Kinloch actually uttered two distinct sentences conjoined by a semi-colon. The first said that only losses 'such as naturally and directly arise' can be claimed, and the second that only losses 'such . . . as may reasonably be supposed to have been in the view of the wrongdoer' can be claimed[6].

This looks remarkably like a prefiguring of both *Polemis* and *Wagon Mound* doctrines, now regarded as alternatives, but then seen as synonymous. Lord Kinloch linked the two sentences with the words 'and such, therefore', so the second sentence is an explanation of the first. Thus 'naturally and directly' means 'what may be reasonably supposed to have been in the view of the wrongdoer', and the following sentences indicate the same conclusion. He would therefore presumably have agreed with Viscount Simonds in *Wagon Mound* that usually the two tests produce the same result, and that if they did not, what is now the *Wagon Mound* approach was preferable.

However, Lord Kinloch's words have sometimes been taken to mean that he rejected foreseeability as the test. If so, the phrase 'naturally and directly' must be considered. But the two adverbs are joined by the conjunction 'and', which leaves it unclear whether they are synonyms[7] (effectively a *Polemis* approach), or cumulative[8] (perhaps another approach yet).

Such *explication de texte* is tedious, but important. It draws attention to the unfortunate effects of judicial promiscuity with adverbs and adjectives (usually paired)[9]. It also shows that the 'grand rule' does not answer all questions. Thus it remains to see how the courts deal with 'remoteness of damages' in practice.

1 1944 SC 237.
2 Per Lord President Cooper 1944 SC 237, at 247.
3 Per Lord Jamieson 1944 SC 237, at 267.
4 1967 SLT 41.
5 Above, at 42, 43, 45 and 46 respectively.
6 Strictly speaking, Lord Kinloch spoke of 'damages', rather than losses.
7 'Naturally' = 'directly'.
8 Thus 'natural' losses which are not 'direct' are not recoverable, nor 'direct' losses which are not 'natural'. (It is assumed that 'and' did not mean 'and/or', in which case, 'natural' and 'direct' would not be cumulative, but alternative tests, requiring either *Wagon Mound*, or *Polemis* to be fulfilled.)
9 Walker's *Delict* (2nd edn, 1981) pp 276–277, lists a dozen different formulations including, in addition to the *Allan v Barclay* version, 'common and natural', 'natural and probable', 'direct and immediate', and 'direct and natural'. This tendency was forcefully criticised by Scrutton LJ in *Polemis* itself, at [1921] 3 KB 560, at 576, but appears ineradicable.

Practice inferred from the cases

Practice has been neither clear nor consistent, and examination of the cases is necessary.

Between *Allan v Barclay* and *Polemis*, there was one reported House of Lords case in which remoteness of damages arose, *Kelvin Shipping Co (Owners of the SS Baron Vernon) v Canadian Pacific Railway Co (Owners of the SS Metagama)*[1]. The SS Baron Vernon was rammed by the SS Metagama in the Clyde, and was beached on the north shore to prevent it sinking. However, it slipped off, and beached itself on the south shore, slipped off again, sinking and becoming a total loss. The defenders admitted liability for the ramming but alleged much of the damage resulted from the pursuer's negligence in failing properly to secure the boat when beached on the north shore, or again when beached on the south.

The matter was argued before the House of Lords in terms of *novus actus interveniens*, and opinions concerned burden of proof. Precedents cited were generally concerned with maritime accidents, and did not include *Allan v Barclay*. Remoteness of damages arose only because the majority found there was no *novus actus interveniens*, and thus effectively had to pronounce on the issue. The Lord Chancellor, Viscount Haldane, in the leading judgment noted a basic principle in collision cases that:

'the damage is recoverable . . . if it is the natural and reasonable result of the negligent act, and it will assume this character if it can be shown to be such a consequence as in the ordinary course of things would flow from the situation which the [wrongdoer] had created'[2].

He thus failed to avoid the two-adjective trap ('natural and reasonable'), but close reading suggests that he was proposing a single test, described in different ways and, coupled with the fact that he found for the pursuers, makes it tolerably clear that he took a *Polemis* line before *Polemis*.

Between *Polemis* and *Wagon Mound*, cases of relevance included *Bourhill v Young*[3], *Steel v Glasgow Iron & Steel*[4], and *Malcolm v Dickson*[5]. *Polemis* might be thought to constitute a benchmark.

In *Bourhill v Young*, the most famous case, a man on a motorcycle overtook a tram on the inside[6], and crashed into a car coming from the opposite direction which was turning right in front of the tram. Although there was

---

1 1928 SC (HL) 21.
2 Above, at 25.
3 1941 SC 395 (OH and IH), 1942 SC (HL) 78, [1943] AC 92, 1943 SLT 105.
4 1944 SC 237, 1945 SLT 70.
5 1951 SC 542, 1951 SLT 357. *Muir v Glasgow Corporation* 1943 SC (HL) 3 also deserves passing mention, and *Hutchinson v Davidson* 1945 SC 395, 1946 SLT 11, *Pomphrey v Cuthbertson* 1951 SC 147, 1951 SLT 191 and *Cowan v National Coal Board* 1958 SLT (Notes) 19 are other examples.
6 Tram lines usually ran along the centre of roadways. Overtaking on the inside was thus almost unavoidable.

some doubt as to the facts, it seems that Mrs Bourhill, heavily pregnant at the time, was getting her creel from the off-side of the tram. She had her back to the accident, but heard the crash and thereafter saw some of the effects. She sued the executors of the fatally injured motorcyclist for nervous shock, and claimed that her baby was stillborn as a result of the shock.

These facts interwove several issues of duty of care, liability for nervous shock, causation, and 'remoteness'. 'Remoteness' was used in the Inner House both in terms of causation (something which had no recognised causal connection would be 'remote'), and to describe the ambit of the group to whom a duty of care was owed (a person outside that group would be 'remote'). *Allan v Barclay* was cited approvingly, though it may be wondered for what proposition. No less significantly, *Polemis* was doubted and distinguished, apparently representing a change of views from *Kelvin Shipping Co* on 'remoteness of damages', albeit obiter.

In the House of Lords the matter was firmly considered as one of duty of care, and other issues therefore obiter. *Allan v Barclay* was not even mentioned, but the Scottish judges at least seem to have agreed with their brethren in the Inner House in rejecting the *Polemis* approach[1].

Steel v Glasgow Iron & Steel was decided shortly thereafter. Steel was a railway guard. During shunting operations he became aware that (because of admitted negligence by another railwayman) a row of trucks was rolling down upon his train. He gave a warning to the driver and tried to uncouple some of the trucks to minimise the damage, but was unsuccessful and died in the resulting collision. Again, the case was not concerned directly with 'remoteness of damages', being argued in terms of *novus actus interveniens* and whether it amounted to a 'rescue case'.

The decision was a majority one. Lord President Cooper decided the case on the basis of the 'grand rule' of *Allan v Barclay* which he considered firmly established although reformulated by the House of Lords in *Bourhill v Young* and *Muir v Glasgow Corporation*[2]. However, it is clear from his reference to 'reformulation', and from his illustrations of Lord Thankerton's and Lord Macmillan's dicta, that he regarded *Allan v Barclay* as primarily concerning duty of care rather than remoteness of damages. Interestingly, nevertheless, he did mention in passing its application to remoteness of damages, clearly regarding it as expressing what would become the *Wagon Mound* test, and confirming the change of views in *Bourhill*. Lord Jamieson agreed with the Lord President, but it is not clear what he thought about what *Allan v Barclay* said on remoteness of damages. Lord Mackay, dissenting, also strongly approved *Allan v Barclay*, and may have regarded it as supporting the *Polemis* line, but did not regard it as concerning remoteness of damages, but rather causation where *novus actus interveniens* was pled.

In *Malcolm v Dickson*, a few years later, a painter inadvertently set fire to a house with his blow torch. The fire was not at first dangerous, and a guest returned into the house several times to remove papers, personal effects and furniture. His exertions caused him to collapse and die of a stroke. His widow sued the painter's employer. The decision did not mention *Allan v Barclay*, relying chiefly upon *Bourhill*, *Muir* and *Steel*. *Polemis* was mentioned, and the

---

1 See Lord Thankerton, 1942 SC (HL) 78, at 84; Lord Macmillan, at 89; but, however, Lord Wright, at 92.
2 1944 SC 237 at 247–248.

case as a whole was looked at variously as concerning remoteness of injury or duty of care, *novus actus interveniens* and rescuers, remoteness of damages, and even straight causation.

Lord Justice-Clerk Thomson, in the appeal to the Inner House, delivered his well-known dictum on remoteness[1], although this conflates remoteness of damages with remoteness of injury[2]. Nevertheless, insofar as he was concerned with remoteness of damages, he clearly supported a *Wagon Mound* view. The leading judgment is that of Lord Mackay (who gave the dissenting judgement in *Steel*) who regarded *Malcolm v Dickson* as essentially a case of *novus actus interveniens*. He was, however, concerned to reject *Polemis* and found his remoteness of damages standard in *Muir* and *Bourhill*, thus not necessarily distinguishing between remoteness of damages and remoteness of injury.

Thus, in so far as a conclusion can be drawn, the courts seem to have changed to what would become the *Wagon Mound* line before *Wagon Mound*.

CASES SINCE *WAGON MOUND*

It might be expected that, since *Wagon Mound*, opinions on remoteness of damages would be focused upon it, although the waters are somewhat muddied by criticisms of the reasoning in the decision. The cases requiring attention are *Hughes v Lord Advocate*[3], *McKillen v Barclay Curle & Co*[4] and *Margrie Holdings Ltd v City of Edinburgh District Council*[5].

Hughes v Lord Advocate, decided shortly after *Wagon Mound*, has facts in some ways remarkably similar, although the precise sequence of events was not established. Workmen left a hole in the ground unattended, but with paraffin lamps and other equipment around it. It appears that two boys then climbed in and out of the hole, and at some point, a lamp fell or was put into the hole, and broke open. This allowed the escape of paraffin, which vapourised and then exploded, causing one boy to fall into the hole and suffer injuries including severe burns and consequent scarring and disabilities. Such an explosion was a very unlikely event.

The case was argued in terms of liability rather than remoteness of damages. The Lord Ordinary (Wheatley) held that the explosion was not

1 1951 SC 542, at 547: 'A wrongdoer is not responsible for all the results which flow from his negligent act. Practical considerations dictate, and the law accepts, that there comes a point in the sequence of events when liability can no longer be enforced. The rule of convenience and common sense is enshrined in the maxim *causa proxima non remota spectatur* ['proximate causes, not remote ones, are looked at']. It is for this court to say whether as a matter of law, the pursuer's claim falls to be classified as proximate or remote.'

2 He observed, for instance, that 'if a court is satisfied that something which flowed from the original act is "remote" in the sense in which I have set out, a pursuer's case must be dismissed. The reason for this is that no legal ground of action exists . . .'.

3 1961 SC 310 (OH and IH), 1963 SC (HL) 31, [1963] 2 WLR 779, 1963 SLT 150.

4 1967 SLT 41.

5 1994 SLT 971, 1993 SCLR 570n. *McKew v Holland & Hannen & Cubitts (Scotland) Ltd* 1969 SC 14, 1969 SLT 101 (IH) upheld at 1970 SLT 68 and *Campbell v F & F Moffat (Transport)* 1992 SLT 962 also deserve mention. In the former, at 31, Lord Walker in the Inner House suggested application of a *Polemis* rule to personal injury actions, and a *Wagon Mound* one to other actions. In the latter, Lord Cameron of Lochbroom in the Outer House seemed to favour a *Polemis* line.

reasonably foreseeable and thus, on a standard application of principle[1], there was no liability. The Inner House, by a majority, upheld this[2]. Although the idea of a 'chain of circumstances' was remarked upon, there was no explicit suggestion that, although there had been *injuria* on the part of the workmen, the *damnum* complained of was too remote because the chain was foreseeable so far as some injuries were concerned, but not as far as the vapourising of the paraffin, the ignition of the vapour, and the consequent explosion.

The House of Lords, however, reversed the decision, accepting the argument that because some burning accident was foreseeable, this particular burning accident was. Again, however, this was not expressly treated as a question of remoteness of damages (although Lord Reid did refer to observations by Lord Thankerton in *Muir*[3], Lord Guest to the 'chain of causation'[4], and Lord Morris of Borth-y-Gest to 'concatenation of circumstances') and the case could be viewed as affirmation of the *Polemis* doctrine.

McKillen v Barclay Curle Ltd concerned a plumber working in a shipyard who slipped, breaking a rib. His slip was admitted to be the result of negligence by his employer. However, his loss was not merely the broken rib, for the fracture was argued to have caused congestion in the lung, which in turn re-activated tuberculosis from which the pursuer had suffered a decade earlier, but which had apparently cleared up.

The Lord Ordinary found for the pursuer and awarded damages for both the fracture and the tuberculosis. One ground of appeal was that the tuberculosis was not reasonably foreseeable and was therefore too remote. The Inner House held that the causal connection between fracture and congestion, and congestion and tuberculosis, was not made out. Therefore, any observations on remoteness of damage were obiter. Their Lordships were enthusiastically unanimous in their support for *Allan v Barclay* (and their belief that the English cases were irrelevant because the rule in Scots law was so well settled), but examination of the opinions shows that the enthusiasm betrays the weakness of the 'grand rule'.

Lord President Clyde declared that 'reasonable foreseeability ... has no relevance once liability has been established', distinguishing *Bourhill* and *Muir* as concerning only liability. This clearly takes a *Polemis* line. Equally, Lord Cameron said 'I cannot see at what point you can draw the line and say for damage beyond this point there shall be no reparation', taking a similar line. Lord Guthrie said '[t]here is ... no justification for limiting an award in [the pursuer's] favour to the amount which would have been due to another person with a stronger constitution' and that 'the wrongdoer must take his victim as he finds him', and relied on *Malcolm v Dickson*[5]. This may indicate a *Polemis* line, but seems rather to treat the case as a 'thin skull' case rather than to deal with remoteness of damages.

However Lord Migdale said that 'there is a formidable body of opinion to

---

1 Including reference to *Wagon Mound*, at 1961 SC 310, at 323, which was treated as going to liability, and to *Bourhill* and *Muir* as well as *Donoghue v Stevenson* and *Bolton v Stone* [1951] AC 850, [1951] 1 All ER 1078.

2 Mentioning *Wagon Mound* only by way of quotation from Lord Wheatley.

3 1963 SC (HL) 31, at 39: 'In my opinion, it has long been held in Scotland that all that a person can be held bound to foresee are the reasonable and probable consequences of the failure to take care ...'. Arguably, Lord Reid regarded this as going to remoteness of damages.

4 Above, at 46 and 47.

5 Above, at 42, 46 and 44 respectively.

support the view that the rule laid down in *In re Polemis* was not and is not the law of Scotland'. He continued that he knew of 'no case of personal injury where damages have been refused where they flow directly from the injury but could not be reasonably foreseen', but added 'I prefer the view that the doctrine of reasonable foreseeability does extend to the measure of damage and can be invoked by a defender if the damages are too remote but not in a case of personal injuries'. Nevertheless, he continued that in such a case the test of directness was foreseeability on the basis of the 'thin skull' principle[1]. Effectively, then, he came down in favour of *Wagon Mound*, but with personal injuries an exception, though one in which *Wagon Mound* foreseeability becomes the test of *Polemis* liability[2].

More recently, *Margrie Holdings Ltd v City of Edinburgh District Council* came before the Inner House[3]. The pursuer had applied for an improvement grant from the defender, and been told that the housing committee had approved it in principle, following which he commenced work. Some months later, the defender intimated that it was no longer processing the applications. The pursuer therefore had to borrow money to tide him over. After sundry procedure, the matter was largely settled out of court, the defender agreeing to pay the pursuer the capital sum of the improvement grant and interest on it at judicial rates. The pursuer then sued, however, for losses suffered, that is, the extra financial outlay he had had to make because of the delays, and because real rates were higher than judicial rates. The case raised several presently irrelevant issues, but also including whether the losses claimed for were too remote.

The Inner House specifically, although probably obiter, declared them too remote. It did so without reference to *Allan v Barclay*, and applied a test of foreseeability, declaring that it was a matter of fact and circumstance whether any particular loss was reasonably foreseeable. Lord President Hope, giving the opinion of the Inner House observed[4] that '. . . in order to be recoverable as damages, the loss claimed in the present action must satisfy the test that it was foreseeable. Otherwise the claim must be restricted to legal interest which, according to the general rule, is the measure of liability where a sum of money has not been paid when it ought to have been paid'.

This conclusion was reached largely following an English Court of Appeal case, *Dodd Properties (Kent) Ltd v Canterbury City Council*[5], which was said to be 'consistent with the modern authorities', though also seeking fortification from *Chanthall Investments Ltd v FG Minter*[6], not previously reported on this aspect. In any case the Inner House concluded that the losses claimed for were not foreseeable.

Reference was made to the *Liesbosch* case[7], and part of the argument was in terms of whether the extra costs the pursuer incurred were the result of his

---

1 1963 SC (HL) 31, at 44.
2 Thus the entire First Division applauded the 'grand rule' and asserted its widespread use, but did so obiter, without any examples, with two of their Lordships viewing it as representing a *Polemis* line, one considering it concerned with liability, and one considering it represented a *Wagon Mound* line.
3 1994 SC 1, 1994 SLT 971, 1993 SCLR 570n.
4 1994 SC 1, at 11A–B.
5 [1980] 1 WLR 433.
6 1976 SC 73.
7 *Owners of the Dredger Liesbosch v Owners of the Steamship Edison* [1933] AC 449, especially Lord Wright at 468.

impecuniosity, which it appears is not now to be regarded as a too remote cause. It may be that the *ratio* should be seen as restricted to cases where the loss is financial.

Conclusions on remoteness of damages as a limitation on *restitutio in integrum*

Restitutio in integrum is the chief principle underlying delictual damages. Remoteness of damages operates as a limit because the 'chain of causation' metaphor, central to the idea of causation, admits of no end to consequences. Thus a rule is required to identify those consequences which in practical terms a court cannot be concerned with and in moral terms are regarded as too diluted by other causes.

The doctrine of remoteness of damages, while uncontroversial in itself, is not easy to apply. A limit to 'direct consequences' may be appropriate, but entirely begs the question of how 'direct' and 'indirect' are to be distinguished. Alternatively, a limit to 'reasonably foreseeable' consequences may be sensible, but less well fulfils the requirements of *restitutio in integrum*.

The courts have not taken a clear line, and debate has not been assisted by appeal to *Allan v Barclay*, for it is not clear what that case decided, and in any case, the distinction between remoteness of damages and remoteness of injury postdates it.

It can be said that, although there is authority for a *Polemis* line before *Polemis* itself, for a generation before *Wagon Mound*, the courts favoured a test including an element of 'foreseeability', or at least, fairly explicitly rejected *Polemis* reasoning. However, curiously, the practice has been less consistent in the generation since *Wagon Mound*, when a more *Polemis*-like approach was favoured in *Hughes* (where the issue of remoteness of damages was not in fact raised) and *McKillen* (where it was), though not in *Margrie* (where it also was)[1].

It may be that what the courts are doing is seeking to apply a test that includes unequivocally caused losses generally, while reserving the right to exclude some which seem unfair to transfer to the defender. Such exclusion is described as 'remoteness'. Sometimes it is justified by reference to 'directness' and sometimes to 'reasonable foreseeability', but above all, the courts do not wish to be tied to a formula as explicit and limiting as *Polemis*, but also not to a case considered so ill-argued and decided as *Wagon Mound*. The infinite variety of factual circumstance (not to mention the inadequacy of underlying explanations of notions of 'causation') make it difficult to do otherwise and the function of *Allan v Barclay* has been to express this difficulty[2].

Minimisation of *damnum* as a limitation on *restitutio in integrum*

There is an obligation upon the pursuer, sometimes referred to as 'mitigation of damages', to minimise the *damnum* suffered, and thus the damages payable. Lord Justice-Clerk Thomson explicitly stated in *Pomphrey v James A*

---

1 In *McFarlane v Tayside Health Board* (1999) Times, 26 November, HL, Lord Hope of Craighead seemed, in passing, to consider the test was one of reasonable foreseeability.

2 Thomson *Delictual Liability* p 268 reaches a similar conclusion, adding that 'it is clear . . . that in a case of personal injuries, the defender takes her victim as she finds him . . . [and where death results] reasonable foreseeability of death is treated as irrelevant or, alternatively, the defender is deemed to have reasonably foreseen that the pursuer could have been an ill, as opposed to a healthy, person'.

Cuthbert Ltd[1], that '[i]t is a pursuer's duty to take reasonable steps to minimise the defender's loss'[2]. It is only reasonable steps which are required, however[3], and it may be that the pursuer's inability to take steps to mitigate cannot be pled against him or her[4]. The onus of proving *damnum* was not minimised lies upon the defender[5].

This clearly is a limitation upon *restitutio in integrum* in that the pursuer may receive less than he or she has actually lost[6]. The principle touches upon contributory negligence, in that the pursuer clearly cannot claim damages for loss aggravated by his or her actions. On the other hand, equally clearly, the pursuer cannot be expected to take much action to limit the defender's obligation of *restitutio in integrum*[7].

There are rather few delict cases specifically concerning minimisation (save in relation to defamation), and the English cases cited are also commonly breach of contract ones (though it is not argued that different principles apply in contract). The question in relation to defamation is dealt with in ch 5. However, explicitly or implicitly, as ch 4 shows, the issue hovers behind every example of quantification as, for instance, cases on alternative methods of quantifying losses of assets exemplify[8], and it may be that those cases where a 'reasonableness' test seems to have been applied should be seen in this light[9].

The various rules concerning deduction from damages of certain social security benefits and charitable payments (dealt with in ch 6) are not examples of minimisation because no one is required to claim such benefits or receive such payments (although their effect is to encourage the pursuer to claim them).

1 1951 SC 147 at 152, 1951 SLT 191.
2 Ie 'liability for damages'. In *Pomphrey*, the pursuer claimed for the replacement price of a vehicle plus conversion costs, which was cheaper than repair costs plus interim replacement hire costs (though they were unspecified). However, the court considered that pre-accident price minus post-accident price would have been cheaper than either for the defender, and therefore the appropriate sum.
3 In *Gunter & Co v Lauritzen* (1894) 31 SLR 359 (a contract case), at 360, the Lord Ordinary (Stormonth Darling) noted 'I think there was no duty on the purchaser to make extraordinary exertions to supply himself with goods [alternative to those not supplied] elsewhere'. See also *Clippens Oil Co Ltd v Edinburgh & District Water Trustees* 1907 SC (HL) 9, 1907 AC 291, 44 SLR 669, 15 SLT 92. See also the remarks of Lord Clyde in *McFarlane v Tayside Health Board* (1999) Times, 26 November, HL.
4 *Clippens Oil Co Ltd v Edinburgh & District Water Trustees* 1907 SC (HL) 9 at 14, per Lord Collins. However, this seems difficult to reconcile with the decision in *Liesbosch*. If actions to mitigate the *damnum* in fact remove it entirely, or produce a profit, there is no loss: see the English case of *British Westinghouse Electric and Manufacturing Co Ltd v Underground Electric Railways Co of London Ltd* [1912] AC 673.
5 In *Connal, Cotton & Co v Fisher, Renwick & Co* (1883) 10 R 824 (a contract case), at 829, the Lord President observed that 'it lay on the defenders, if they meant to allege [minimisation] in defence, to prove that it could be done more cheaply'.
6 As has been observed, the sanction for breaching the obligation is bearing the difference between minimised and unminimised loss.
7 The principle was described in an English House of Lords case, *Admiralty Commissioners v SS Chekiang* [1926] AC 637, at 646, by Lord Sumner who said it was designed 'to prevent a tort-sufferer from recovering for damages, which is really self-inflicted, because with reasonable effort he could have avoided it', but this did not 'extend to investing the tortfeasor with a right to call on [the tort-sufferer] to do things which do not follow from [the action complained of] in order to diminish liability for the wrong'.
8 Eg *Pomphrey v James A Cuthbertson Ltd* 1951 SC 147, 1951 SLT 91.
9 Eg *McMillan v McDowall* 1993 SLT 311, and cf the restriction on funeral costs to 'any reasonable expense' in the Damages (Scotland) Act 1975, s 1(3).

Restrictions on compensation for 'pure' economic loss as a limitation on *restitutio in integrum*

'Economic loss' and delict

Claims for damages for economic loss have caused difficulties over many years. 'Economic loss' is not a closely defined term, but refers to financial, non-physical, *damnum*. It is of the essence of some delicts, most obviously fraud, but also of 'economic delicts' such as 'inducing breach of contract'[1]. These are intentional delicts. The 'economic delicts' represent a compromise between regarding economic harm in trading as no wrong (but simply competition in the free market) on the one hand, and some notion of 'fair trading' on the other. This resolves itself into a matter of liability, and requires no further mention.

The position is more complicated in relation to economic loss resulting from negligence, and does require further mention[2]. A distinction has to be drawn between what may be called 'pure' and 'consequential' economic losses[3]. The former are such losses as occur as a direct result of the delict; the latter are such losses as are consequential upon physical loss such as personal injury. In brief, damages are not awarded for 'pure' economic loss resulting from negligence (even if undoubtedly caused by it, and not too remote), but they are for 'consequential' economic loss (assuming caused by it, and not too remote). The notion of 'pure' economic loss therefore operates in negligence as a further limitation upon *restitutio in integrum*[4].

Negligence and 'consequential' economic loss

Negligence may cause injuries and thus physical *damnum* with any consequential economic loss, for example loss of wages after injury. This has long been accepted and requires no illustration since it is the substance of a large proportion of all reported cases on delict.

Negligence and 'pure' economic loss

There may or may not be good institutional and civilian reasons for the limitation on pure economic loss[5]. However, (quite apart from the need to balance free trade against fair trading) the great growth in the use of negligence since *Donoghue v Stevenson*[6] provided it with a governing principle, allowed expansion to include, for instance, negligent misstatements[7] and other negligent actions not involving physical *damnum*[8]. Moreover, the pure

---

1 See eg *British Motor Trade Association v Gray* 1951 SC 586, 1951 SLT 247.
2 The analysis which follows owes much to the seminal Wilkinson and Forte 'Pure Economic Loss — a Scottish perspective' (1985) 30 JR 1.
3 But see *McFarlane v Tayside Health Board* (1999) Times, 26 November, HL.
4 This seems paradoxical, given that with intentional delicts such as fraud, for which *restitutio in integrum* is available, the economic loss is in these terms 'pure'.
5 Wilkinson and Forte 'Pure Economic Loss — a Scottish perspective; (1985) 30 JR 1 at pp 3–8.
6 1932 SC(HL) 31.
7 As in the classic English case *Hedley Byrne & Co Ltd v Heller & Partners* [1964] AC 465, [1963] 3 WLR 101, [1963] 2 All ER 575.
8 Such as *Junior Books v The Veitchi Co*, 1982 SC (HL) 244, 1982 SLT 492, [1982] 3 WLR 477.

economic loss may be 'primary' (or 'non-derivative'), in the sense that it is suffered by the 'primary victim', the person against whom the *injuria* was primarily committed (for instance the recipient of a negligent mis-statement). But it may also be 'secondary' (or 'derivative'), in the sense that a 'secondary victim', against whom no *injuria* was committed directly, is adversely affected as a further consequence of the effect on that primary victim. For instance, the primary victim may be, as a result of the delict, unable to fulfil a contract with the secondary victim, who thereby suffers *damnum*[1].

A particular difficulty with any economic loss resulting from all this is that such *injuriae* may entail literally incalculable *damnum*[2]. This has caused judges to seek 'threshold devices' in addition to remoteness of damages in order to keep potential liability within bounds. Thus the principal result is that, subject to exceptions, there is no *restitutio in integrum* for 'pure' economic loss caused by negligence. Put in terms of liability, there is no duty not to cause pure economic loss, however foreseeable, unless certain additional specific factors operate.

Most of the cases on these factors are English[3], but there is little doubt that the principles have been applied by Scottish courts[4]. They also, in essence, are treated as concerning liability, and are therefore outwith the scope of this work. Nevertheless, certain special cases do require mention. Principally, claims by relatives of a negligently killed person for loss of support, and claims on behalf of relatives under ss 8 and 9 of the Administration of Justice Act 1982, are both clearly 'secondary (or derivative) pure economic loss' claims, and so form exceptions[5]. Another possible example arose out of 'wrongful birth' cases. Some Scottish and English authorities held that there might be damages for the extra expenditure of maintaining a healthy child born through another's negligence. However this was firmly rejected by the House of Lords in *McFarlane v Tayside Health*

---

1 Both *Allan v Barclay* and *Reavis v Clan Line Steamers* were 'secondary' pure economic loss cases. Both involved physical injury, and no doubt consequential economic loss, to the primary victim, but pure economic loss to the actual pursuer.
2 In a major English case, *Candlewood Navigation Corporation Ltd v Mitsui OSK Lines Ltd* [1986] 1 AC 1, at 12, [1985] 3 WLR 381, [1985] 2 All ER 935, Lord Brandon of Oakwood said quite explicitly 'the policy reason for the rule was to avoid opening the floodgates so as to expose a person guilty of want of care to unlimited liability to an indefinite number of other persons . . .'. A clear example is another major English case, *Caparo Industries plc v Dickman* [1990] AC 605, [1990] 2 WLR 358, [1990] 1 All ER 568, in which a negligent audit inaccurately showed a company's financial health to be sound, as a result of which many people bought shares, and existing shareholders bought more shares. This reasoning was clearly influential in *McFarlane v Tayside Health Board* (1999) Times, 26 November, HL.
3 Such as *Hedley Byrne & Co Ltd v Heller & Partners* [1964] AC 465, [1963] 3 WLR 101, [1963] 2 All ER 575, *Anns v Merton London Borough Council* [1978] AC 728, [1977] 2 WLR 1024, [1977] 2 All ER 492, *Caparo Industries plc v Dickman*, *Murphy v Brentwood District Council* [1991] AC 398, [1990] 3 WLR 414, [1990] 2 All ER 908 and *Spring v Guardian Assurance plc* [1995] AC 296, [1994] 3 WLR 354, [1994] 3 All ER 129.
4 See eg *Martin v Bell-Ingram* 1986 1 SC 208, 1986 SLT 575, *Donlon v Colonial Mutual Group (UK Holdings) Ltd* 1997 SCLR 1088 and also *P&O Scottish Ferries v The Braer Corporation* 1999 SCLR 540 and *Skerries Salmon Ltd v The Braer Corporation* 1999 SCLR 225.
5 There may be others: see Wilkinson and Forte 'Pure Economic Loss — a Scottish Perspective' (1985) 30 JR 1 at pp 1–3.

Board[1] (thus overturning cases such as *Anderson v Forth Valley Health Board*[2]. Although a unanimous decision, five separate opinions were delivered, with reasoning which varied somewhat, and cross-referred little. Nevertheless, three of their Lordships relied on considering the expenditure to be 'pure economic loss'[3], although another roundly rejected the very distinction between 'pure' and 'consequential'[4].

Thresholds and ceilings for damages as a limitation on *restitutio in integrum*

At common law, subject to the principle *de minimis non curat lex*, there is no general limitation upon *restitutio in integrum* through some requirement for a minimum sum of damages to be claimed, such as legislation imposes in some other countries. It is for the pursuer (or more commonly, his or her insurance company or the Scottish Legal Aid Board) to decide if the game is worth the candle[5]. (There is, of course, in practice a general threshold in the United Kingdom for most social security benefits and first party commercial insurance claims. The Defamation Act 1952, s 4 allows an innocent publisher to make an offer of amends, which is a related provision.)

Equally, at common law, there is no general limitation of a maximum sum of damages, such as legislation also imposes in some other countries. Sums awarded may be 'conventional', and the effects of large claims upon commercial insurers or 'self-insurers' like the national health service are often remarked upon, but have no formal effect on awards[6]. On the other hand, a variety of statutory provisions limit damages in specific circumstances. For example, the Hotel Proprietors Act 1956, s 2 allows a hotel proprietor, within certain constraints, to limit liability for losses by guests to £50 for any one article and £100 overall. The Consumer Protection Act 1987, s 5 limits damages recoverable to those for personal injury or for damage to property intended for private use to a maximum of £275.

'Just satisfaction' and related limits on awarding damages under the Human Rights Act 1998 as a limit on *restitutio in integrum*

The Human Rights Act 1998 allows damages for a breach of a 'Convention right' to the extent that it is 'just and appropriate'. However that power is limited, for the court must be 'satisfied that the award is necessary to afford just satisfaction'[7].

---

1 (1999) Times, 26 November, HL.
2 1999 SLT 588.
3 Lord Slynn of Hadley (who thought it not 'fair, just and reasonable' to impose such costs on a doctor); Lord Steyn (who also relied on an argument of 'distributive justice'), and Lord Hope of Craighead (who thought the potentially very large claims 'disproportionate' to the defender's duty). None discussed 'economic loss', as such, in detail.
4 Lord Millett found it 'technical and artificial' and on the facts 'suspect' and 'irrelevant'. Lord Clyde rejected the argument that the benefits of a healthy child offset the detriments, but nevertheless, concluded that such damages would be unreasonable.
5 The (English) Law Commission considered thresholds in its Consultation Paper and Report *Damages for Personal Injury: non-pecuniary loss* (Consultation Paper 140 (1995)) paras 4.23–4.26; and Law Com No 257 (HC Paper 334 (1998–99)) paras 2.25–2.28, but rejected the idea.
6 Atiyah does suggest that the level of damages awards is influenced by the fact that they are usually paid by an insurance company: see ch 6.
7 Human Rights Act 1998, s 8(1), (2).

In so deciding, it must take account of 'all the circumstances of the case' including any other remedy available, and 'the consequences of any [judicial] decision' concerning the act in question. Also, in taking that decision and any decision on the amount of damages, it must 'take into account the principles applied by the European Court of Human Rights in relation to an award of compensation under article 41'[1]. Further, damages may not be awarded 'in respect of a judicial act done in good faith', save for a breach of the right to liberty and security of the person[2].

In fact while numerous reported European Court of Human Rights cases include references to article 50[3], typically very little time is spent discussing damages. Although it has been said that the aim is to put the victim 'so far as possible . . . in the position he would have been in had the requirements of [the Convention] not been disregarded'[4], often, they are simply assessed 'on an equitable basis'. Commonly, this means that no damages, or only token awards, are made for non-pecuniary losses. The court does commonly award legal expenses and interest on damages.

---

1 HRA 1998, s 8(3), (4). Art 41 of the European Convention on Human Rights entitles the court to 'afford just satisfaction', and is a recently renumbered redraft of art 50.
2 HRA 1998, s 9(3).
3 See note 1 above and generally European Human Rights Reports, also Kempees *A Systematic Guide to the Case Law of the European Court of Human Rights* 1960–1994 (1995).
4 *Piersack v Belgium (Compensation)* (1985) 7 EHRR 251, para 12.

4. Effecting *restitutio in integrum*—lump sums and quantification

SIGNIFICANCE OF LUMP SUMS

'ONCE AND FOR ALL' LUMP SUM PAYMENTS

Damages are paid (subject to exceptions discussed below), as a once and for all lump sum. Settlements are too (subject to the growth of 'structured settlements', discussed below). This feature has tended to be regarded as axiomatic. However, variations, including devices permitting periodic payments, have emerged although they are exceptional in practice.

The strong preference for lump sums arises from viewing compensation as 'redressing the balance'. As noted in ch 1, this metaphor appeals to that fundamental symbol of the law, the scales of justice. A court finding the scales tipped one way must restore equilibrium by specifically fixing an appropriate weight to the other side. In short, *restitutio in integrum* implies it.

Further, once quantified, damages take on the nature of a debt, and in any case, litigation is designed to produce a final interlocutor (which settlements mimic). In a decision of a Court of Seven Judges, *Rieley v Kingslaw Riding School*[1], it was observed that the need for 'finality in litigation' produced the requirement that 'damages have to be assessed once and for all' which was so 'whether they relate to reparation for loss already incurred and capable of accurate computation or to prospective loss where assessment may necessarily include an element of speculation'[2].

It has also been noted that any other arrangements require systems to operate them for which the courts are ill-equipped, and imply a certain sophistication in quantification which the delict action cannot achieve.

LUMP SUMS AND PERIODIC PAYMENTS

However, it has been long argued that at least for future losses (which, though relatively unusual, almost by definition involve large damages) periodic payments are to be preferred. The (English) Law Commission considered the

---

1 1975 SLT 61, at 64.
2 The principle was enunciated explicitly in respect of personal injury actions, but clearly applies generally. The Lord Ordinary had concluded that the pursuer would not suffer amputation. However, after proof, but before appeal was concluded, she did. The court accepted that normally the date of proof was the cut-off point, but the Rules of Court permitted amendment of the pleadings 'at any time before final judgment', and in this case, exceptionally, it allowed amendment. See also the more complicated, but better reasoned, *Balfour v Baird* 1959 SC 64, 1959 SLT 273, especially per Lord Patrick, at 75.

matter in a Working Paper in 1973[1], but rejected change. The Pearson Commission returned to the subject a few years later and, by a majority, favoured periodic payments in certain limited circumstances[2].

The (English) Law Commission reconsidered its views in the 1990s with a Consultation Paper[3] (in which the arguments are more fully outlined) and Report[4]. In favour of lump sums, it rehearsed the familiar arguments of finality and simplicity, but also argued that the practice created freedom of choice (the plaintiff can deal with the compensation as he or she wishes, and takes responsibility for the future) and flexibility (the lump sum can be invested, but partly liquidated for special needs in case of change of circumstance). Also, it argued, focusing on their entitlement makes plaintiffs aware of their bargaining strength.

Nevertheless, disadvantages remained. The system promised *restitutio in integrum*, but might not deliver it. Thus it was inaccurate, indeed, hypocritical, especially in relation to future damages. The traditional multiplier/multiplicand system, for example, was very inept at achieving *restitutio in integrum*, and lump sums might be dissipated, throwing the plaintiff back on other compensation systems, typically social security. Cost, delay and retarded rehabilitation might also be introduced because the plaintiff's condition has to stabilise and an accurate prognosis produced. Also, on the one hand, the plaintiff knew that rapid recovery would reduce damages and on the other delay could produce illness in itself. Further, while *British Transport Commission v Gourley*[5] meant that damages for loss of earnings are calculated net of tax, if the lump sum were invested, tax would be paid upon the interest, or if an annuity were purchased it would be taxed twice ('*Gourley*' in reverse'). Finally, the treatment of inflation was open to question.

CONSEQUENCES OF THE USE OF LUMP SUMS

The effectiveness of *restitutio in integrum* through once and for all lump sum damages

Despite continuing discussion on the advantages and disadvantages of once and for all lump sum damages, there has been little consideration of their effectiveness in actually achieving *restitutio in integrum*[6]. However, in parallel with the Report on structured settlements, the (English) Law Commission commissioned research on this question[7], which does not give a strong endorsement.

1 Law Commission *Personal Injury Litigation — assessment of damages* (Working Paper 41) paras 226–252.
2 *Royal Commission on Civil Liability and Compensation for Personal Injury* (Cmnd 7054–I (1978)) ch 14. The minority opinion was Lord Cameron's.
3 Law Commission *Structured Settlements and Interim and Provisional Damages* (Consultation Paper 125) (undated).
4 Law Commission *Structured Settlements and Interim and Provisional Damages* (Law Com no 224) (Cm 2646 (1994)).
5 [1956] AC 185, [1956] 2 WLR 41, [1955] 3 All ER 796.
6 See, however, Harris *et al Compensation and Support for Illness and Injury* (1984), and the reference in Cane (ed) *Atiyah's Accidents Compensation and the Law* (6th edn, 1999)) p 133 to *Thurston v Todd* (1966–67) WN (NSW) (Pt 1) 231.
7 (English) Law Commission Report *Personal Injury Compensation: How Much Is Enough? — a study of the compensation experiences of victims of personal injury* (Law Com no 225) (HC Paper 666 (1993–94)).

The Report surveyed a large number of people who had received damages for personal injuries or bereavement. The former had suffered a wide variety of injuries, including serious ones. They had in some cases suffered considerable losses of earnings (nearly half did not go back to work at all) and other losses (typically for extra travelling and heating and general living expenses). Some had family members who had to stop work to give unpaid care, and many had used up savings. Almost all were compensated through a settlement, but most had to wait years.

On the question of adequacy, victims got less than they expected. Of those unlikely to return to work, it appeared that the sums received did not cover all past losses, nor all future loss of earnings and future expenditure. Most importantly, many had not seemed to realise at the time of settlement how much assistance they would need (particularly in relation to unpaid care). Most thought their standard of living had suffered, and there was fear that day-to-day expenditure would not be covered. Nearly all had claimed state benefits.

As to disposal of the money, most seemed to have saved at least some, usually in building society or bank accounts, preferring safety over return. Those who had not saved had often done so because they had spent money on a big capital purchase, rather than because of the need to pay off debts.

The Law Commission also considered whether 'non-pecuniary damages' were too low, concluding (partly on the basis of the views of the public) that they were, and recommended accordingly, including how they might be raised[1].

Quantification of damages

This chapter, therefore, having considered the nature of lump sum damages, examines the devices used to mitigate its adverse effects. These are interim damages, provisional and further damages, and structured settlements. Then, in terms of three different approaches to quantifying the lump sum, it looks at the rules, such as they are, which concretise the principle *restitutio in integrum*, and the question of interest on damages. Chapter 5 looks at how the conclusions apply to the various types of damages identified in ch 2.

MITIGATION OF THE ADVERSE EFFECTS OF ONCE AND FOR ALL LUMP SUM DAMAGES

INTERIM DAMAGES

Interim damages are a payment on account in a personal injury or fatal accident case where it is sufficiently certain that full damages are going to be awarded.

---

1 Law Commission Consultation Paper and Report *Damages for Personal Injury: non-pecuniary loss* (Consultation Paper no 140 (1995)) paras 4.27–4.81, also 4.82–4.104; Law Com no 257 (HC Paper 344 (1998–9)) paras 3.1–3.205, also 4.1–4.32. As observed, if you ask people if other people should pay them money, no cynicism is required to conclude they are likely to say 'Yes!'.

The provision[1]

The power is in the effectively identically worded Court of Session Rules of Court 43.8–43.10[2] and Sheriff Court Ordinary Cause Rules 36.8–36.10[3]. The requirements are that:

'(i)   the court is satisfied that:
    (a)   the defender has admitted liability . . ., or;
    (b)   if the action proceeded to proof, the pursuer would succeed . . . on the question of liability without any substantial finding of contributory negligence . . ., and would obtain decree for damages against the defender, and

(ii)   [the defender] is insured . . ., or is a public authority, or [has] means and resources . . . such as to enable him to make the interim payment'.

If the requirements are fulfilled, the court may make an order 'in one lump sum or otherwise as [it] thinks fit'[4], for 'such amount as it thinks fit, not exceeding a reasonable proportion of the damages which . . . are likely to be recovered . . .'. More than one application can be made if there is a change of circumstance, and interim damages can be ordered on counterclaims.

No provision deals with apportionment between defenders (save on final decree), but in *McNicol v Buko Ltd*[5], Lord McCluskey felt able to decide that liability was joint and several where one or other of two defenders would be found liable. When final decree is pronounced, the court takes account of the interim payment 'as it thinks fit' and may, inter alia, order repayment to the defender and payments between defenders and third parties by way of contribution or indemnity (as, for example, in *Mitchell v HAT Contracting Services Ltd (No 3)*[6]).

The test for interim damages

In *Cowie v Atlantic Drilling Co Ltd*[7], the Inner House decided that the test meant that, in the absence of an admission, success at proof must be more likely than a 'high probability' (or must be 'practically certain' or 'almost certain'[8]) but need not be a 'complete certainty'[9].

In relation to the contributory negligence proviso, the court held that 'substantial' meant 'of real importance to . . . the assessment of the extent of the defender's liability', and was not a simple *de minimis* provision[10]. It did

---

1 Similar provisions exist in England and Wales under the Rules of the Supreme Court, Order 29, Pt II, r 11 and County Court Rules, Order 13, r 12. They are seemingly little used, and criticism is found in Law Commission Consultation Paper and Report on structured settlements (noted above) Pt IV.
2 Act of Sederunt (Rules of the Court of Session) 1994, SI 1994/1443. Some of the cases were under its effectively identical predecessor, SI 1965/321, r 89A.
3 Act of Sederunt (Sheriff Court Ordinary Cause Rules) 1993, SI 1993/1956.
4 This possibility of periodic payments appeared in the earlier legislation, and does not simply reflect the Damages Act 1996, s 2, for which, see below.
5 1986 SLT 12.
6 1993 SLT 1199.
7 1995 SC 228, at 292D–G, 1995 SLT 1151, 1995 SCLR 335.
8 Per Lord Grieve in *Nelson v Duraplex Industries Ltd* 1975 SLT (Notes) 31.
9 Per Lord Maxwell in *Douglas's CB v Douglas* 1974 SLT (Notes) 67.
10 1995 SC 288, at 294D–G.

not express this as a percentage, but noted without comment the observation[1] that a finding of contributory negligence of one third was not 'substantial'.

The requirement of a 'change of circumstances' before a second or subsequent motion for an interim award does not appear exiguous. It was seemingly fulfilled in *Thompson's CB v Burnett*[2] where the *curator bonis* concluded that purchase of the house for the injured person was required, and simply provided information as to what the award would be spent on, even though it was conceded that the earlier interim award had not been spent and the intended use of the further *tranche* was not chiefly a loss for which damages were being sought.

'Public authority' and 'in one lump sum or otherwise' do not appear to have been discussed in the reported cases. In *Martin v McKinsley*[3], the Motor Insurers' Bureau would satisfy any unsatisfied judgment in respect of the uninsured defender. Lord Ross concluded in relation to 'insured' and 'means and resources' that this fact did not mean that the defender was 'insured', nor that he had sufficient 'means and resources'.

The decision whether to make an order

The court is not obliged to make an order when the requirements are fulfilled, but no catalogue of matters to consider in such a decision has been laid down, and a variety of matters has been taken into account. Conviction of the defender of an offence was relevant as increasing the likelihood of proving liability in *McNicol v Buko Ltd*[4]. Numerous defenders, not all admitting liability, not all having lodged defences, and not all likely to be found liable, was a sufficient condition to preclude an order in *McCann v Miller Insulation & Engineering Ltd*[5]. It does not seem that hardship is a requirement, though it may be relevant[6].

Also, while in *McCann*, Lord Allanbridge considered that he was only entitled to look at the pleadings, and not at productions, medical reports or precognitions, in *Stone v Mountford*[7], Lord Johnston considered that *McCann* did not lay down a general rule, and was willing to look at other material such as photographs. Lord Cullen made it plain in *Bhatia v Tribax*[8], that how interim payments were to be applied was a matter for the court.

The size of an interim payment

In a merely noted, but often quoted, *dictum* in *Littlejohn v Clancy*[9], Lord Robertson said that the court:

1 Per Lord Ross in *Reid v Planet Welding Equipment Ltd* 1980 SLT (Notes) 7.
2 1989 SLT 264, 1989 SCLR 178.
3 1980 SLT (Notes) 15.
4 1986 SLT 12.
5 1986 SLT 147.
6 See *Nisbet v The Marley Roof Tile Co Ltd* 1988 SC 29 at 32, per Lord Clyde, 1988 SLT 608, 1988 SCLR 56.
7 1995 SLT 1279.
8 1994 SLT 1201, at 1205G.
9 1974 SLT 68.

'must take the broadest of axes. In my view it is inappropriate that there should be anything in the nature of a proof, with detailed *ex parte* statements and close scrutiny of detailed documents produced by each side. Nor can there be at this stage any concluded view on the medical aspects of the case, as these may in the end of the day look different. I do not regard an award of interim damages at any date as an attempt by the court to make an accurate and realistic estimate at that date of the fraction of the total sum of damages which may eventually be awarded'.

Clearly some estimate of the final figure has to be made in order to arrive at a 'reasonable proportion' of it[1], but courts have tended to adopt 'a conservative and moderate approach'[2], for instance taking the lowest figure the defender concedes likely, excluding heads of damages which are contentious, and reducing the figure if there are possible deductions (such as for state benefits[3]), as Lord McCluskey did in *McNicol*[4].

However, the interim payment does not have to be for losses already suffered, and could exceed such losses, as Lord Clyde expressly decided in *Nisbet v The Marley Roof Tile Co*[5], although Lord Cullen considered that they should normally be so in *Bhatia v Tribax*[6]. Indeed, from *Thompson's CB*, it appears that the award does not have to be employed on expenditure which falls under any of the heads of damages[7]. Nevertheless, the cases indicate that these are factors which may be significant. It is also clear from such cases that although the pursuer's hardship is not a precondition of an interim payment, it can be a factor in the size of award. Interestingly, in *McNicol*, Lord McCluskey was also prepared to consider hardship to the defender[8]. Another factor which the cases have taken into account is the stage of the proceedings.

The 'reasonable proportion' requirement thus imposes a ceiling, rather than expresses an appropriate level. Where interim payment orders have been made in reported cases, they have often been in the order of 60 per cent of the expected final award.

PROVISIONAL AND FURTHER DAMAGES

Provisional and further damages are designed to deal with personal injury actions where liability is certain, but prognosis is not[9].

---

1 In *McNicol v Buko Ltd* 1986 SLT 12, Lord McCluskey thought disclosure of the Lord Ordinary's estimate 'would be unfortunate'.
2 Per Lord Clyde in *Nisbet v The Marley Roof Tile Co Ltd* 1988 SC 29, 1988 SLT 608, 1988 SCLR 56.
3 See *Mitchell v Laing* 1998 SC 342, 1998 SLT 203, 1998 SCLR 266.
4 Decided under the previous legislation which included the additional requirement that the sum be 'just'.
5 1988 SC 29, 1988 SLT 608, 1988 SCLR 56, disapproving Lord McCluskey in *McNicol* on that point.
6 1994 SLT 1201 at 1205H.
7 This is, of course, conform to the lack of obligation to spend damages on repairing the loss suffered.
8 Although in that case he was insured and the insurer would suffer no hardship (though that must surely be irrelevant, as the insurer's liability to the defender is contractual).
9 In *Potter v McCulloch* 1987 SLT 308, at 310, Lord Weir suggested that the procedure still awarded one single sum, but in two stages.

The provision[1]

They are payable by virtue of the Administration of Justice Act 1982 s 12 (supplemented by the effectively identical Court of Session Rules of Court 43.11–43.13 and Sheriff Court Ordinary Cause Rules 36.11–36.13[2]). The conditions required are that:

(i)   there is proved or admitted to be 'a risk that at some definite or indefinite time in the future the injured person will, as a result of the [*injuria*] develop some serious disease, or suffer some serious deterioration in his physical or mental condition';

(iii)   the defender is 'a public authority or public corporation or is insured or otherwise indemnified in respect of the claim'.

In such a case, the pursuer may apply to the court to order that damages be 'assessed on the assumption that the [pursuer] will not develop the disease or suffer the deterioration in his condition', and may later apply again for 'further damages if he develops the disease or suffers the deterioration', provided that the application is within any period specified by the court. Periods specified are often lengthy. In *White v Inveresk Paper Co Ltd (No 2)*[3], Lord Murray would have fixed it at 20 years.

The various requirements of assessing 'risk'; concluding if it is of a 'serious disease' or 'deterioration' etc, clearly mean that such cases are peculiarly inappropriate for jury trial[4].

The test for provisional damages

In *White v Inveresk Paper Co Ltd (No 2)*[5], Lord Murray considered that 'risk' should have the ordinary or dictionary meaning and observed that 'serious' qualified 'deterioration', not the effects of deterioration. Perhaps this distinguishes a medical assessment of the condition from the activities the pursuer might or might not be able to continue, but in *Robertson v British Bakeries Ltd*[6], Lord Osborne regarded this as a distinction without a difference. He did observe that what is required is a proved or admitted risk, not a disagreement as to whether there is a risk at all.

'Public authority' and 'public corporation' and 'otherwise indemnified' do not appear to have been discussed in the reported cases.

The decision whether to make an order

The courts have required some future threshold event. Onset of disease is no doubt sufficient, but deterioration is more problematic. Thus, while in

---

1 Similar provisions exist in England and Wales, introduced by s 6 of the Administration of Justice Act 1982 which also introduced Supreme Court Act 1981, s 32A. The Law Commission Consultation Paper and Report *Damages for Personal Injury: non-pecuniary loss* also criticised this provision.
2 SI 1994/1443 and SI 1993/1956.
3 1987 SC 143, 1988 SLT 2.
4 See eg Lord Weir's observations in *Potter v McCulloch* 1987 SLT 308.
5 1987 SC 143, at 147.
6 1991 SLT 434.

Robertson v British Bakeries[1], Lord Osborne was content to see the possible onset of post-traumatic osteo-arthritis as such a threshold, in *White v Inveresk Paper Co Ltd (No 2)*, Lord Murray concluded there was a lack of a 'clear cut and severable threshold' where existing damage to a knee might simply deteriorate by development of osteo-arthritis[2]. Lord Gill observed in *Bonar v Trafalgar House Offshore Fabrication Ltd*[3], 'the court should not impose upon the defender or his insurers a contingent liability for final damages unless the nature and the extent of that liability are clear'.

The risk of disease or deterioration must be significant. In *White v Inveresk Paper Co Ltd*, Lord Murray regarded a 5–10 per cent risk of deterioration of osteo-arthritis as insufficient (and alternatively, a fortiori, a less than 1 per cent risk of joint replacement surgery). It must also be caused by the *injuria*, as Lord Davidson noted in *Paterson v Costain Mining Ltd*[4], although distinguishing that case, Lord Prosser considered sufficient 'an interaction between the condition produced by the original act and some future triggering event or other change in the pursuer's circumstances or environment', in *Meek v Burton's Gold Medal Biscuits Ltd*[5].

The courts have always been able to consider that the risk is so great that it may be taken into account in ordinary future damages instead, as occurred in fact in *White v Inveresk Paper Co Ltd*.

Further damages

There do not appear to be reported cases on actual applications for further damages.

'STRUCTURED SETTLEMENTS' AND 'PUBLIC SECTOR SETTLEMENTS'

Structured settlements have been developed in recent years, with Inland Revenue assistance, as a contractual device to overcome some of the disadvantages of lump sum awards[6]. Atiyah suggests they may achieve four ends: safe investment; periodic payments; inflation proofing; and tax avoidance[7]. 'Public sector settlements' are a development of the device for 'self-insuring' public bodies such national health service entities.

'Structured settlements' in the legislation

The 'structured settlement' is now explicitly recognised in legislation in the Damages Act 1996. This defines it in s 5(1)[8] as:

---

1 1991 SLT 434.
2 1987 SC 143 at 149–150.
3 1996 SLT 548, at 550J.
4 1988 SLT 413, 1988 SCLR 70.
5 1989 SLT 338, at 339.
6 For which see eg Law Commission Consultation Paper no 125 and Report no 224 (especially paras 3.10–3.22). See also Lewis *Structured Settlements: the law and practice* (1995).
7 Cane (ed) *Atiyah's Accidents, Compensation and the Law* (6th edn, 1999) p 118.
8 A previous definition was found in the Finance Act 1995, s 142.

'an agreement settling a claim or action for damages for personal injury whereby—

(a)   the damages are to consist wholly or partly of periodic payments; and
(b)   the person to whom the payments are made is to receive them as an annuitant under one or more annuities purchased for him by the person against whom the claim or action is brought or, if he is insured against the claim, by his insurer'[1].

The periodic payments 'may be for the life of the claimant, for a specified period or for a specified number or minimum number or include payments of more than one of those descriptions'. Also, the amounts paid may be 'specified in the agreement, with or without provision for increases of specified amounts or percentages' or 'subject to adjustment ... to preserve their real value' or both.

The nature of 'structured settlements'

In a structured settlement, the court awards damages in once and for all lump sum form, or the parties agree to such a sum in a settlement. The defender's insurer[2], instead of handing over the whole sum to the pursuer, agrees to hand it over in instalments. The Inland Revenue regards this as payment of the capital lump sum, not as income from it, so no income tax is paid. The insurance company finances these payments by using the whole, unpaid, lump sum to buy from another insurance company an annuity designed to pay out the agreed sums. Tax is paid on the annuity payments, but this can be deducted from the corporation tax the defender's insurance company would otherwise have to pay. Thus the pursuer receives periodic payments, and the defender's insurer pays less because, effectively, no tax is paid by anybody[3]. (Thus the taxpayer subsidises the settlement).

The device is very flexible, and various structures can be devised, including (as the legislation specifically reflects) inflation-proofing, payment of instalments for a fixed period, or for life, and payment of larger capital sums initially or at fixed future times. (The British Association of Insurers has produced Model Agreements, and a guidance note on Methods of Payment, to fit various circumstances[4], but structured settlements must be approved by the Inland Revenue to avoid tax.) It has been argued that settlements are made easier and earlier, and that the pursuer is relieved of the burden of investing a large sum wisely. However, structured settlements still require a lump sum to be arrived at; the parties are locked into any agreement they reach; and there is still no guarantee that the payments will be enough. Certainly, structured settlements are complicated and require expert advice, and are only useful for very large claims.

---

1   The Damages Act 1996, s 5(6) and (7) permits the Secretary of State to specify a body which is not an insurer, as an insurer for this purpose.
2   Or in the case of a 'self-insuring' public body, the defender itself.
3   See Income and Capital Taxes Act 1988, ss 329AA and 329AB (added by the Finance Act 1996, s 150, replacing ss 329A and 329B, as added by the Finance Act 1995, s 142).
4   'Basic Terms', 'Indexed Terms', 'Term for Life' and 'Indexed Terms for Life': reproduced in McEwan and Paton *McEwan & Paton's Damages for Personal Injury in Scotland* (2nd edn, 1982, looseleaf, updated) App VII and Bennett *Personal Injury Damages in Scotland* (1999) App III.

Incorporation and protection of 'structured settlements'

The principal object of the legislation on 'structured settlements' is found in s 2 of the 1996 Act which permits a court in a personal injury action, by consent, to make an order incorporating a structured settlement[1]. Section 4 enhances the existing protection of the claimant under the Policyholders Protection Act 1975 against insolvency of the insurer[2]. Section 6 provides a government guarantee for 'public sector settlements'.

Structured settlements have not figured much in reported cases yet, but *Bell's CB, Noter*[3], provides a useful illustration.

QUANTIFICATION IN GENERAL

PAST AND FUTURE LOSSES

In *Hill v Wilson*[4], the opinion of the Inner House recounted that '. . . allocation of certain heads of damages between the past and the future has come to be seen as appropriate, and normal'. It was conceded that this was not because of any distinction in principle, so the basic approaches to quantification are the same for both. However, the distinction is made for at least two reasons.

Firstly, as noted in *Hill v Wilson* itself, 'damage already suffered, when translated into pecuniary damages, will normally, according to our law and practice, bear interest for the period up to the date of decree, whereas damage yet to come, after the date of decree, will not, of course, require to do so'. Secondly, past losses may be in principle precisely quantifiable, whereas future losses have not yet happened, so always involve prediction and estimation, and are always a 'loss of chance', involving assessment of contingencies and opportunities. This is particularly important in that future losses usually only arise where losses are considerable, as with catastrophic injuries.

The point is made most clear by noting the comparisons that *restitutio in integrum* implies. As noted in ch 1, with past losses, comparison is between the claimant's actual present position and his or her hypothetical present position (inferred from his or her actual past position) had the event in question not occurred. With future losses, it is between the claimant's predicted future position (inferred from his or her actual present position) and a hypothetical future position (inferred from his or her hypothetical present position). Thus, in a personal injury action involving future losses, the future date and degree of recovery (if any) of the pursuer have to be predicted, and whether he or she would have otherwise suffered various contingencies (for instance become redundant for an unrelated reason) or obtained opportunities (for instance for promotion) has to be estimated, and this must be very speculative over a long period.

---

1 The Damages Act 1996, s 2 is not explicitly confined to structured settlements.
2 Including the Motor Insurers' Bureau and a Domestic Regulations Insurer: see ch 6.
3 1998 SC 365.
4 1998 SC 81 at 82H, 1998 SLT 69.

Further, the distinction flows into the nature of the lump sum. Where losses are all past, it is for *damnum* which has occurred. Where losses extend into the future, and the *damnum* has not all yet occurred, it is a capitalised sum for losses which may be suffered over a continuing future period, year by year or even week by week[1]. However, practice has been inconsistent and changed over time[2].

APPROACHES TO QUANTIFICATION PAST AND FUTURE

Although no judge has expressly so stated, examination of the cases suggests that there are three broad approaches to quantification past and future, though they are not entirely discrete. They are the 'precedential' or tariff approach, the 'reasonable sum' or jury approach and the 'calculational' or market approach.

The 'precedential' or tariff approach

One approach concludes *restitutio in integrum* is best sought by giving the same lump sum as was given for similar losses in the past. In a sense, a precedential approach is inevitable, as formal justice requires consistency. Like cases must be treated alike. However, this approach achieves consistency somewhat unsubtly by using what are in effect tariffs.

This approach is possible in the case of patrimonial losses, even if all such losses require 'equivalent' compensation, for 'equivalent' is hardly a term of exact meaning. On the other hand, tariffs are peculiarly apt for personal losses, as consistency is an obvious measure of justifiability of 'substitute or solace' compensation. Related areas in which tariffs are explicitly and most obviously used are industrial injuries benefits and criminal injuries compensation (which now has a tariff based on common law damages). All examples necessarily suffer from the unasked question of why one arbitrary sum is better than another[3].

The Inner House has said that a judge ought to give reasons for arriving at the figure selected although in some cases it 'may properly be truly arbitrary and not open to precise analysis'[4]. Clearly, even where figures are truly arbitrary, as in *solatium* awards, reference to precedent, especially to a tariff, is likely to be sufficient to explain the award, and indeed appeal against *quantum* in *solatium* cases must rely on asserting the award is out of tune with those in comparable cases.

A typical example of a broad tariff approach is Lord Grieve's opinion in *Gardner v Howard Doris*[5] (where he expressly determined an award by reference to two comparable earlier cases). Interesting and more subtle is Lord Milligan's in *Davidson v Upper Clyde Shipbuilders*[6] (where he carefully compared seven

1 See *Pearson Commission* (Cmnd 7054 (1978)) vol 1 paras 555 and 556, and Lord Diplock's careful examination of the issues under the Fatal Accidents Acts (paralleling loss of support claims) in English law, in *Cookson v Knowles* [1979] AC 556, at 569, [1978] 2 WLR 978, [1978] 2 All ER 604.
2 Lord President Hope in *O'Brien's CB v British Steel plc* 1991 SLT 477, 1991 SCLR 831, reviewed the history of the subject and observed, at 480D, that he had 'the strong impression from the Scottish cases to which we have been referred that the principles which should be applied have not always been appreciated' and, at 480J, that 'it can be seen that in practice the assessment of damages for a loss to be incurred in the future has been a developing art'.
3 Though there seems to be a rarely challenged assumption that more is better.
4 *Robertson's CB v Anderson* 1996 SC 217, at 220E–F, 1996 SLT 828.
5 1983 SLT 672.
6 1990 SLT 329.

characteristics of nine comparable earlier cases in respect of one head of damages, and two of five earlier cases in respect of another). More subtly still, the traditional use of multipliers for future damages for patrimonial loss (discussed below) effectively expresses a tariff of such multipliers. Allotment of *solatium* to past and future is readily done on such an approach on a percentage basis, which might ultimately reflect conventional views on how long the pain and suffering etc are thought likely to last.

The importance of tariffs has produced a special form of law report, devoted to briefly recording *solatium* claims and awards[1]. In addition, there is now in England a semi-official published version in the 'Judicial Studies Board Guidelines'[2], (though it remains a summary of earlier decisions, not a legislative instrument)[3]. One result is reference to (commonly higher) English tariffs, held permissible by the Second Division (without the Lord Justice-Clerk) in *Allan v Scott*[4]. Despite argument that they rest on rather different principles, *solatium* is in Lord Walker's words[5] 'strictly equivalent' to 'general damages', and the Judicial Studies Board Guidelines themselves were specifically noted in *Girvan v Inverness Farmers Dairy (No 2)*[6], by Lord Abernethy in the Inner House[7].

Nevertheless, the Inner House has eschewed formal tariffs. This view was most forcefully declared by Lord Guthrie in *McCallum v Paterson*[8], where he exclaimed 'There can be no tariff for *solatium*'. It took the view in *Girvan v Inverness Farmers Dairy*[9] that such published tariffs constitute only a rough guide, a view which can only be said to be reinforced by the House of Lords decision in *Girvan v Inverness Farmers Dairy (No 2)*[10] which emphasised the role of juries (discussed below). This provides an interesting contrast with England and Wales, where the Court of Appeal has taken a strong lead in indicating what is often explicitly referred to as 'the judicial tariff system', and juries are almost unknown[11].

1 Most obviously, in Scotland, in McEwan and Paton *McEwan & Paton's Damages for Personal Injury in Scotland* (2nd edn, 1982, looseleaf, updated) 'Case Notes' pp 401–610, and in England, Kemp and Kemp *The Quantum of Damages in Personal Injury and Fatal Accident Cases* (rev 4th edn, looseleaf updated) vols 2 and 3, and see also *Current Law*.

2 Cherry and Judicial Studies Board *Guidelines for the Assessment of General Damages in Personal Injury Cases* (4th edn, 1998), reproduced in Bennett *Personal Injury Damages in Scotland* (1999) App VII.

3 The (English) Law Commission Consultation Paper and Report *Damages for Personal Injury: non-pecuniary losses* (Consultation Paper no 140 (1995)), paras 4.53–4.67, and 4.68–4.81; (Law Com no 257 (HC Paper 344 (1998–9)), paras 3.124–3.130, 3.177–3.188, and 3.111–3.129, 3.171–3.176, 3.189–3.205 considered legislative tariffs of various types, and other means of assisting judges in fixing awards, such as a 'Compensation Advisory Board', but rejected them, save as a fall-back position.

4 1972 SLT 45.

5 Above, at 48.

6 1996 SC 134 at 149, 1996 SLT 631.

7 See also the reference in the opinion of Lord Hope of Craighead in the House of Lords, 1998 SC (HL) 1, at 19H–I.

8 1969 SC 85, at 90.

9 1995 SLT 735.

10 1998 SC (HL) 1, 1998 SCLR 72, 1998 SLT 21.

11 The (English) Law Commission *Damages for Personal Injury: non-pecuniary loss* (Law Com no 257) (HC Paper 344 (1998–99)), paras 3.140–3.170, also 3.171–3.176, concluded that awards were generally too low, requiring to be raised by a factor of 1.5 to 2 in respect of awards over £3,000 with tapered increases below that (paras 3.107–3.110). It considered they would be best raised, at least initially, by the Court of Appeal and House of Lords giving a lead.

In any case, notoriously, inflation has been significant in recent decades, reaching double figures per annum on occasion[1]. This means that any award which is treated precedentially requires to be increased to give a current value. Usually, resort is had to the Government-produced Retail Price Inflation Index[2], which produces a multiplier[3]. Thus an award from some 50 years ago may require to be multiplied by a factor of 20 to give a current equivalent sum.

The 'reasonable sum' or jury approach

A second approach considers that to seek *restitutio in integrum*, 'reasonable people' should be asked what is a 'reasonable sum'. The jury is the standard means of determining this[4], although there is authority to suggest that a 'reasonable sum' may be less than *restitutio in integrum*[5].

The use of the jury approach

Civil juries are regarded as fundamental. They are available, indeed required, for personal injury and most other delict actions in the Court of Session, unless special cause is shown[6]. Indeed, an often enunciated principle is that (subject to limitations) damages are traditionally a matter for the jury, as, for instance, Lord Hope declared in *O'Brien's CB v British Steel plc*[7] and reiterated in *Girvan (No 2)*. Moreover, this approach is thus frequently employed when there is no jury, and although judges are enjoined normally to give reasons[8], there are numerous examples of them taking a rough and ready approach to the quantification of damages which might be described as employing 'the reasonable judgment of an ordinary man'[9].

Juries provide another interesting contrast with England and Wales, mirroring that on tariffs. Although now firmly, and perhaps increasingly strongly, rooted in Scotland, civil juries are an import from English law[10]. Yet paradoxically, they have long been dying out there, and in *Ward v James*[11], the

---

1 In *Cookson v Knowles* [1979] AC 556, an English House of Lords case, it was noted that following inflation of some 10% p a, average wages had nominally risen by 27% over the two-and-a-half years between the death in question and the trial.
2 Published, inter alia, in McEwan and Paton *Damages* and Kemp & Kemp *Quantum*.
3 Not to be confused with the those of the 'multiplicand/multiplier' method of calculating *future* damages, discussed below.
4 It is interesting that juries are used in delict actions to determine a verdict, and to assess damages, while in major criminal trials they are used to determine a verdict, but not to assess any fine or other punishment. On Civil jury trials generally, see Hajducki *Civil Jury Trials* (1998).
5 Lord Hope, in *O'Brien's CB v British Steel plc* 1981 SLT 477 drew attention to Lord Kinnear's observation in *Casey v United Collieries* 1907 SC 690, at 693, that a jury 'ought not to fix damages at the full amount of compensation for the injury that a man has suffered but that they should take a reasonable view of the case and give what they consider in the circumstances to be fair compensation'.
6 Court of Session Act 1988, ss 9 and 11.
7 1991 SLT 477, at 481H, 1991 SCLR 831.
8 *Robertson's CB v Anderson* 1996 SC 217, at 220E–F.
9 Indeed, in *O'Brien's CB*, Lord Hope made rough and ready decisions in relation to residential care costs, though he attributed them to deduction from the evidence rather than a jury approach.
10 Jury Trials (Scotland) Act 1815.
11 [1966] 1 QB 273, [1965] 2 WLR 455, [1965] 1 All ER 563.

English Court of Appeal, sitting with five judges, decided that no personal injury case should go before a jury, save in exceptional cases, as jury awards lacked accessibility, uniformity and predictability. The (English) Law Commission[1] considered the matter and recommended abolition of jury assessment of damages on those grounds, save in defamation cases, essentially because juries cannot apply tariffs[2]. Defamation formed an exception only because it was appropriate to continue jury assessment of liability in such cases, and that could not in practice be split from assessment of damages.

The jury approach is, however, again possible in the case of patrimonial losses, 'equivalent' being hardly an exact term. Indeed, it is difficult to avoid if choice between alternative calculations is required. However, like the tariff approach, it is also more obviously suited to the 'substitute or solace' compensation of personal losses[3]. 'Reasonableness' (or a 'felt-fair factor'), however vague a term, is another obvious criterion of justifiability. The approach may also be unavoidable where, by reason of unclear evidence or otherwise, heroic decisions are required of judges to determine appropriate sums as, for instance, Lord Stewart found in *Hosie v Arbroath Football Club*[4] in relation to future care costs. Allotment to past and future is readily done, again, presumably ultimately seeking to reflect how long future pain and suffering etc are likely to last. However, in the *Girvan* cases, (discussed below), the first (reasonable) jury attributed 60 per cent to the past, 40 per cent to the future, and the second (reasonable) jury reversed the proportions.

The jury approach and other approaches

The jury approach does not necessarily produce a different result from other approaches. The jury's role may be to apply common sense in choosing between alternative calculations to produce the 'reasonable sum', and it would no doubt be influenced by any tariff in choosing a 'reasonable sum'. However, the essence of the approach is that the jury is not bound by any method of quantification, and is effectively obliged not to explain its verdict[5].

Indeed, juries have no expertise other than assessing an arbitrary 'reasonable sum'. It is difficult not to see a calculational approach as superior for most patrimonial loss (subject to questions of choice between rival calculations), and although a jury may apply commonsense to calculations put before it, it is ill-equipped to form conclusions on technical questions such as future rates of return on investment. Also, while a tariff is not self-evidently better for *solatium*, as a matter of practice, it is difficult for juries to take tariffs into

1 *Damages for Personal Injury: non-pecuniary loss*, (Consultation Paper no 140 (1995)) paras 4.82–4.104, and Law Com no 257 (HC Paper 344 (1997–98)) paras 4.1–4.30.
2 A 'reasonable sum' is not the same thing as a tariff. Eschewing explicit tariffs makes it difficult to argue that awards are too high or (as the Law Commission argued) too low.
3 In *O'Brien's CB* 1991 SLT 477, at 481H Lord Hope observed that the approach had 'obvious advantages in regard to those parts of an award for damages, notably *solatium*, which are not susceptible to calculation or measurement in terms of arithmetic'.
4 1978 SLT 122.
5 The (English) Law Commission *Damages for Personal Injury: non-pecuniary loss* (Consultation Paper no 140 (1995)) para 2.22 considered that 'consistency and predictability [of non-pecuniary awards] has been facilitated by the disappearance, for all practical purposes, of the jury (which could not be referred to previous awards) in personal injury actions'.

account as they do not receive specific assistance as to current levels of *solatium* (even though judges sitting alone do, despite needing it less). In any case, juries may even be unclear as to the very purpose of delictual damages, and be swayed by irrelevancies.

Thus, this approach is simple, and to a degree unavoidable, but risks evasion of responsibility towards the pursuer, and Lord Hope, in *O'Brien's CB* and *Girvan (No 2)*[1], wished to discourage its use where actual calculation was possible. It also risks evasion of responsibility towards the defender, especially in relation to *solatium*, in that even where jury awards are within the limits accepted (discussed below), their unpredictability means that the defender must doubt the 'reasonableness'. Further, lack of uniformity is likely to discourage settlement[2].

The jury approach, appeal and 'excess of damages'

Also, if a jury has given a decision which is deemed reasonable *ex hypothesi*, on what grounds could it be appealed? In fact, appeal has long been allowed on the ground of excess or inadequacy of damages[3]. It is by means of a motion for a new trial, however, which does not allow the appeal court to substitute its own award[4], thus risks discovering two juries awarding markedly different sums for precisely the same *damnum*, something the courts are happy to accept (as in the *Girvan* cases)[5].

Further appeal to the House of Lords was permitted by the Administration of Justice Act 1982, s 2. The first such appeal, *Girvan (No 2)*, usefully raises the question of the role and use of the jury. A jury awarded £120,000 *solatium* (divided 60/40 between past and future). At retrial on the ground of 'excess damages', a second jury awarded £95,000 for *solatium* (divided 40/60)[6]. A third trial was refused by a majority only in the Inner House[7], and on further appeal the House of Lords also refused it[8].

Girvan (No 2) is thus the principal authority on 'excess of damages'. Lord Hope, giving the leading opinion in the House of Lords[9], concluded that the 'proper approach' had been laid down in *Landell v Landell*[10]. 'Excess' did not mean a sum considerably greater than judges would have awarded, but one so large as to constitute gross injustice and to be higher than any reasonable jury could have awarded fairly and without gross mistake[11]. He observed that

1 1991 SLT 477, at 481H and 1998 SC (HL) 1, at 17C respectively.
2 As Lord Hope conceded in *Girvan (No 2)* 1998 SC (HL) 1, at 20G–H, although finding the argument overwhelmed by other considerations.
3 See now the Court of Session Act 1988, ss 29 and 30.
4 As is possible in England and Wales by virtue of the Courts and Legal Services Act 1990, s 8.
5 In *Girvan (No 2)* 1998 SC (HL) 1, at 17E, Lord Hope said 'Reasonably fair minded jurors may quite properly arrive at widely different figures in making their assessment of the amount to be awarded for pain and suffering and general inconvenience'.
6 See *Girvan v Inverness Farmers Dairy* 1995 SLT 735.
7 1996 SC 134, 1996 SLT 631.
8 1998 SC (HL) 1, 1998 SLT 21, 1998 SCLR 72.
9 1998 SC (HL) 1 at 10E–F.
10 (1841) 3 D 819. A wrongful imprisonment case, in which, at 827, Lord Cockburn remarked, perhaps ironically, that the pursuer's reputation 'could hardly suffer by so common a calamity, with respectable people, as a short imprisonment for supposed debt'.
11 This test, like the traditional one for remoteness of damages in *Allan v Barclay* (1864) 2 M 873 (see ch 3), has several terms of uncertain relationship. Presumably, the test of 'gross injustice' is 'that which no reasonable jury could have awarded'.

this opinion respected the distinction of functions as between judge and jury; recognised that 'excess of damages' was incapable of exact definition; and indicated that judges should be slow to interfere with jury awards. As he noted 'if a series of new trials is to be avoided, a fairly broad approach [to jury verdicts] must still be taken'[1].

The actual jury award is to be compared with a hypothetical jury award, not with a hypothetical judicial award[2]. Lord Hope concluded that the proper procedure was to make an assessment of what judges and juries had awarded in similar past cases[3] and then compare it with the award actually given.

Where the award is for patrimonial loss, a small departure of the actual award from the hypothetical one would be sufficient to justify a new trial. Thus a 'market' approach (discussed below) provides a criterion for 'excess of damages'. However, in *Tate v Fischer*[4], the Second Division decided that the award as a whole should be looked at, so that if the challenged patrimonial loss formed only a small part of the whole, the challenge could be rejected.

For *solatium*, the position is different. In *Girvan (No 2)* Lord Hope concluded[5] that the 'working rule' of *Young v Glasgow Tramway and Omnibus Co (Ltd)*[6], that 'excess of damages' meant those more than twice what a jury might have been expected to give, remained useful in relation to *solatium* for personal injuries, provided that account was taken of the fall in the value of money, as judges commonly do[7]. However, Lord Hope added two points[8]. Firstly, comparison should be with the upper end of the assessment of past cases. Secondly, the sums appealed against should not be excluded from the assessment of past cases, and a third trial where similar figures are produced as in the first two should not be regarded as improper. Thus, the general thrust of Lord Hope's opinion was that the jury's discretion should be so far as possible untrammelled in respect of *solatium*, and a tariff approach was not a closely binding criterion of 'excess of damages'. While applauding the increased publicity which might be given to jury awards in the published tariffs[9], he reiterated his opinion as Lord President in *Currie v Kilmarnock and Loudon District Council*[10] that 'by adhering to the relatively narrow band within which judges operate, judges would become increasingly out of touch with awards made by juries'[11]. In other words, it was not for juries to be guided by judges, but the reverse.

Indeed, on the basis of experience with the Court of Session Rules Council, he explicitly doubted whether juries could sensibly be given more guidance on awards because of the complex nature of the procedures involved, and explicitly doubted whether it was sensible to consider giving judges the

1 1998 SC (HL) 1 at 7E–G and 16G.
2 Disapproving in part *MacGregor v Webster's Exors* 1976 SLT 29.
3 1998 SC (HL) 1, at 11G–12C. Thus admitting elements of tariff.
4 1998 SLT 1419.
5 1998 SC (HL) 1, at 10C and 17G.
6 (1882) 10R 242.
7 He considered that Lord President Cooper's doubts in *McGinley v Pacitti* 1950 SC 364, 1950 SLT 276, related only to awards other than *solatium*, and to taking inflation into account.
8 1998 SC (HL) 1, at 17G and 18C.
9 See above.
10 1996 SC 55, 1996 SLT 481.
11 See also his remarks at 1998 SC (HL) 1, at 17F on the 'justification for preserving the present system'.

power to substitute their own awards on appeal without the whole area being considered by the Scottish Law Commission[1].

In *Tate v Fischer*[2] the Second Division seems to have reinforced the un-challengability of jury decisions by noting that s 29(1) of the Court of Session Act 1988 requires such a motion for a new trial to be 'essential to the justice of the cause'.

The 'calculational' or market approach

The third approach assumes there is a lump sum which will accurately provide *restitutio in integrum*. The task of quantification is to calculate it, essentially by discovering a relevant market price. This clearly fulfils the injunction upon judges to have reasons for their awards[3].

It is unclear if this approach has any application to personal losses for, in so far as they are 'substitute or solace' compensation, there is no means of calculation, and no market[4]. However, it readily reflects the idea of 'equivalent' compensation, and is clearly a possible approach to any patrimonial loss. Thus, for example, consequential expenses can be seen as the price of those goods or services on the market, and loss of income as the price the pursuer would have obtained on the market for his or her services. Quantification is by calculation on relevant market information, which is relatively simple in principle. Examples, such as *McMillan v McDowall*[5], are numerous.

There is always discretion in the decision, however, and calculation is not necessarily straightforward. In relation to lost assets, there are several alternative bases of calculation available. The difficulties are well illustrated in *Clyde Navigation Trustees v Bowring Steamship Co*[6]. The facts and arguments are too complicated to be fully recounted. In essence, however, the dispute was about how to value a dredger which had been negligently sunk and subsequently replaced by a converted vessel. Did *restitutio in integrum* require damages to be quantified as the cost of the old vessel (subject to depreciation, but also to expenditure on it); as the cost of a second-hand vessel suitably converted; as the insurance value; or as the price of a similar vessel sold not long before? And did it require separate compensation for loss of use? In the event, the Inner House upheld the Lord Ordinary, who had decided that *restitutio in integrum* required '(i) the cost of a reasonably efficient second hand barge, (2) the cost of its adaption to [the pursuer's] special purpose, and (3) a sum for the loss of the service of [the dredger] for a period of two years'[7]. He estimated

---

1 1998 SC (HL) 1, at 21H–22B and 22C–F.

2 1998 SLT 1419.

3 *Robertson's CB v Anderson* 1996 SC 217, at 220E–F.

4 Although a 'functional approach', assessing damages according to what may be purchased as 'substitute or solace', seeks to apply such an approach. See Ogus 'Damages for Lost Amenities: for foot, a feeling or a function?' (1972) 35 MLR 1. The (English) Law Commission *Damages for Personal Injury: non-pecuniary loss* Consultation Paper no 140 (1995) in paras 4.9–4.10 considered this approach, which is used in Canada (paras 3.38–3.51), but its Report (Law Com no 257) (HC Paper 344 (1997–98)), in paras 2.4–2.7, rejected it, in part because the Canadian experience is not wholly happy.

5 1993 SLT 311.

6 1929 SC 715, 1929 SLT 603.

7 Though it is not clear if this meant a sum for the hire of a substitute during conversion; the loss of revenue otherwise obtained; or both. The Inner House seems to have thought it meant loss of revenue.

this at £5,700. However, he did so by 'applying [his] mind as a juryman . . .' without disaggregating the sum, and eschewed explicit calculation.

The use of market principles, and some of the attendant difficulties, were evident in the better-known English case in the House of Lords *Owners of the Dredger Liesbosch v Owners of the Steamship Edison*[1] which had remarkably similar facts. They were further complicated by questions of causation and remoteness of damages. However, in relation to the loss of assets Lord Wright declared[2] the principle to be 'the value of the ship to her owner as a going concern', that is, 'the capitalized value of the vessel as a profit-making machine'. This meant that the profit or otherwise that might be earned in the future had to be taken into account and might be reflected in the price. This meant in turn that different types of ship might have to be treated differently. In *Liesbosch*, the court decided that the plaintiffs were entitled to the market price of a comparable substitute, and to associated expenditure, that is the costs of adaption, transport, insurance etc. They were also entitled to a sum for disturbance and loss in carrying out their contract during the period between the loss of the *Liesbosch* and the time when a substitute could have been provided, including overhead charges, expenses of staff and equipment which was 'thrown away' in that period.

It is worth noting that in modern current cost accounting, accountants distinguish between several types of cost or value based on market prices. 'Historic cost' ('HC') refers to the amount originally paid for the item, which could be discounted to reflect its age. 'Replacement cost' ('RC') is the amount payable to replace the item, which might be for a new replacement, a second hand one, or a new one discounted to reflect the age of the lost item. 'Net realisable value' ('NRV') is the amount the item could be sold for in its existing condition, subtracting transactional costs. 'Net present value' ('PV') or 'Economic value' ('EV') is the amount of benefit expected to be derived from the item over its future life, discounted to present value. Which of these is the most appropriate depends on circumstances. However, what an asset is worth to a company is sometimes referred to by a further term, the 'Deprival value' ('DV') or 'value to the business'. This is defined as either the RC or the 'Recoverable amount', whichever is lower, where 'Recoverable amount' is the NRV or the EV, whichever is higher[3]. The reasoning is not complicated. Essentially, the company will replace an item when the cost of doing so is less than the company would get by selling it, or the profit it would get by using it: and vice versa. However, while such ideas may well be fed into the construction of claims for losses of assets, there is little evidence that they are used by judges to quantify damages.

In any event, it is clear that a calculational approach must overlap with a jury or 'reasonable sum' approach. It is also an approach of particular significance in relation to future damages, where the courts have gone a good deal further in taking on board technical actuarial information, as discussed below.

---

1 [1933] AC 449.
2 Above, at 464.
3 See eg Alexander *Financial Reporting: the theoretical and regulatory framework* (2nd edn, 1990) pp 18–20 and 39–43; and Parker, Harcourt & Whittington *Readings in the Concept and Measurement of Income* (2nd edn, 1986) pp 27–32 (and references therein).

QUANTIFICATION OF FUTURE LOSSES

As noted, future losses raise particular difficulties. The precedential or 'tariff', and jury or 'reasonable sum' approaches cope easily with the difficulties by, in effect, being arbitrary. The calculational or 'market' approach, however, must confront the difficulties, and does so as one or another form of an 'annuity' approach.

CALCULATIONS AND MARKETS IN THE FUTURE: THE ANNUITY APPROACH—TRADITIONAL VERSION

Origins and nature

A form of annuity approach has been employed at least since *McKechnie v Henderson*[1], where the Inner House upheld an ambiguous use of it, although it has usually been only a rough 'multiplier/multiplicand' sum until recent times[2]. It takes on board that future losses occur over a continuing future period, and asks what capital sum would produce an annual return of the appropriate level to pay for the relevant continuing heads of damages (for example, loss of income, or continuing consequential expenditure such as nursing services[3]) for the appropriate number of years (for example, until predicted date of recovery, date of retirement or date of death[4]). It is fundamental that both capital and interest are to be exhausted at the end of that period[5]. The simplicity of the concept conceals difficulties, for instance what rates of interest, inflation and taxation can be expected. Also, an actuarial approach necessarily averages out individual cases.

The traditional rough 'multiplier/multiplicand' version has been commonly used by courts, and received explanation and reiteration in *O'Brien's CB*, where it was described as 'simple, economic and easy to use'[6].

Multiplicands

The multiplicand is the amount to be generated annually, that is, the annual sum designed to compensate for the annual loss suffered, such as the cost of

---

1 (1858) 20D 551.
2 Thus, for example, on the face of it, it does not seem to have been used in *Riddell v Reid* 1941 SC 277, 1941 SLT 179 or *Paterson v London, Midland and Scottish Railway Co* 1942 SC 156, 1942 SLT 117, but see comment on those cases in *Smith v Boyd* 1944 SC 499, at 500–501, 1945 SLT 108. *Smith v Boyd* itself exemplifies the rough multiplier/multiplicand approach.
3 See eg Lord Hope in *O'Brien's CB* 1991, SLT 477, at 483A.
4 In personal injury actions the Damages (Scotland) Act 1976, s 9 requires a court, in respect of a pursuer whose expectation of life is reduced, to consider a 'notional date of death', that is, the date until which he or she would otherwise be expected to survive. For patrimonial losses, it may calculate as if he or she would survive until then, but may reduce living expenses which will not be expended because of the reduction in expectation.
5 In *Wells v Wells* [1998] 3 WLR 329 [1998] 3 All ER 481 (an English case in the House of Lords), at 356–360, Lord Hope of Craighead gave a clear exposition of the issues. Other classic expositions are *Cookson v Knowles* [1979] AC 556, at 568, per Lord Diplock, and *Hodgson v Trapp* 1989 AC 807, at 826, per Lord Oliver of Aylmerton, [1988] 3 WLR 1281, [1988] 3 All ER 870.
6 Per Lord President Hope 1991 SLT 477, at 486L: see also at 481, and now *Wells v Wells*, discussed below.

nursing care, or lost earnings. This is worked out broadly speaking by the usual means of quantifying such past losses (discussed in ch 5), and grossing up to an annual figure.

It is possible, though unusual, to have different multiplicands for different future periods. Thus in *Stevenson v Sweeney*[1], three increasing levels of care were proposed as necessary over the pursuer's lifetime[2].

Multipliers[3]

The multiplier is the number applied to the multiplicand to produce the capital sum. It is not the predicted number of years till recovery, retirement, or death (or notional date of death) as appropriate. Indeed, although commonly referred to as being 'a multiplier of *x* years' or '*x* years' purchase', it is not a number of years at all. Such a 'full multiplier' would overcompensate by preserving the capital intact at the need of the relevant period, rather than exhausting it along with the interest[4]. A discount for payment in advance of most of the expenditure (since the sum can be invested and produce interest) is a necessary part of an annuity approach[5].

Thus the multipliers in fact used are usually markedly less than 'full multipliers'. Traditionally, they are the product of precedent, justified by reference to comparable cases[6], though occasionally, they appear to be a form of jury approach, produced intuitionally[7]. However, assuming that the judges are familiar with basic economics in general and annuities in particular, it can be inferred that there is a two-stage process in producing a multiplier in practice. The first, implicit, stage is to generate a 'notional basic multiplier', that is, one which is presumed to produce an appropriate annuity until the relevant date, making the necessary discount for early payment and assuming exhaustion by the relevant time. This 'notional basic multiplier' might be taken to assume a 4–5 per cent return and certainly ignores not only inflation and taxation, but also any factors particular to the case. These become the precedents used by other judges as their starting points for pursuers of different ages and other characteristics (for instance: 'woman; aged 35; disabled for life'). In the second, commonly explicit, stage the judge takes account of the factors particular to the case in hand, such as redundancy or illness from an unrelated cause which might have led to loss of job in any case. Multiplier-increasing vicissitudes are referred to from time to time as well as

---

1   1995 SLT 29, at 33E ff. But, at 331, not different levels of lost income. Also reported 1995 SCLR 988.
2   In some cases, it seems that the multiplier is varied for such contingencies, rather than the multiplicand, presumably on an analogy with variation in length of time the annual sum will be required. This is a handy device, but logically unsound.
3   Not to be confused with the multiplier produced by the Retail Price Inflation Index, noted in relation to the effect of inflation on tariffs.
4   It may nevertheless be effectively given, as in *Davidson v Upper Clyde Shipbuilders* 1990 SLT 329.
5   A clear explanation is found in *Wells v Wells* [1998] 3 WLR 329, at 333C–F, per Lord Lloyd of Berwick.
6   In *O'Brien's CB* 1991 SLT 477, at 483C, Lord Hope stressed that in relation to multiplier cases generally 'it will be sufficient to rely on the figures used in comparable cases'.
7   Compare the multipliers, and the lack of reasoning, as between *Tuttle v University of Edinburgh* 1984 SLT 172 and *MacIntosh v National Coal Board* 1987 SLT 172.

multiplier-reducing ones[1], though rarely. An example of both stages being undertaken fairly explicitly is *Fullemann v McInnes's Executors*[2].

On such an approach, different heads of damages should often attract different multipliers. Loss of earnings ceases at retirement age. Costs of care for a permanently disabled person continue until expected date of death. Because the multiplier is used to reflect contingencies such as redundancy or promotion and premature death from an unrelated cause[3], and since these contingencies are greater in relation to employment than to other heads of damages, differences of multipliers are increased[4].

Critique of the traditional annuity approach

The traditional 'multiplier/multiplicand' annuity approach is simple, and does allow a very high level of individuation[5]. A judge looks at the facts revealed by the proceedings, and (if they are not agreed between the parties), can fix multiplicand and multiplier based on those facts. Different multiplicands and multipliers can be fixed for different heads of future damages, taking into account different likelihoods of work, etc. It is commonly argued that this possibility of individuation is an important advantage of the delict system. However, there are problems.

Multiplicands

Firstly, there may be difficulties of evidence and arithmetic in quantifying annual losses. See, for example, the review of the evidence on the multiplicand for future care in *Byrnes v Fife Health Board*[6], *O'Brien's CB*[7], *Stevenson v Sweeney*[8], and *Allan v Greater Glasgow Health Board*[9]. Further, where there are several heads of damages, such as nursing care, and personal care under the Administration of Justice Act 1982, s 8, they must clearly not overlap, an issue

---

1 Thus Lord Hope in *O'Brien's CB* 1991 SLT 477, at 481J referred to 'the risks of accident, illness or redundancy', but also 'the prospect of promotion and variations in the amount of wages or salary'. He might also have added 'unusually secure employment' and 'the likelihood of an unusually long life'.
2 1993 SLT 259, per Lord Cullen, at 267. The position is complicated by reference to the Ogden Tables, discussed below. The report notes that 'Both parties have marked reclaiming motions against the Lord Ordinary's interlocutor'. However, no appeal is reported.
3 See *O'Brien's CB* 1991 SLT 477, at 481J, per Lord Hope.
4 See *O'Brien's CB* above, at 481L, per Lord Hope. In *Stevenson v Sweeney* 1995 SLT 29, Lord Morton of Shuna fixed the multiplier for lost earnings at 14, but that for care costs at an unprecedented 20. At 32F, he observed that '[n]either counsel could suggest any circumstance other than premature death that would diminish the quantity of care that the pursuer will require', but this figure may have been influenced by the Ogden Tables (discussed below).
5 Lord Hope not only described it as 'simple, economical and easy to use', but also as 'flexible enough to allow for the special features of individual cases in deciding what is appropriate': *O'Brien's CB* 1991 SLT 477, at 486L–487A.
6 1978 SLT (Notes) 66, at 67. Curiously, a poor work record was treated as reducing the multiplier for income loss, not the multiplicand, risking double prejudice to the pursuer.
7 1991 SLT 477 at 479–480.
8 1995 SLT 29 at 32–33.
9 1998 SLT 580, at 586J–587D. This was a particularly difficult case because, although it is not easy to make sense of all the figures quoted, evidence showed the relevant continuing costs as greater than the entire family income at the time, which was in the form of state benefits: see Lord Cameron of Lochbroom, at 586I–586J. It is now impliedly overturned by *McFarlane v Tayside Health Board* (1999) Times, 26 November, HL.

arising in *O'Brien's CB*, for instance. Most simply, parties may disagree on the likelihood of redundancy or other vicissitudes.

Secondly, the multiplicand may be contingent or changing because the loss which it represents varies over time. For example, the level of care which an accident has rendered necessary may vary though amelioration or deterioration of the condition. This was coped with in *Stevenson v Sweeney* by fixing different multiplicands for different periods (as discussed above).

Thirdly, in a time of significant inflation, multiplicands decline in real value. Atiyah cites[1] an Australian case[2] in which a quadriplegic was awarded damages of about £120,000 (an exceptionally high award) in 1965. Over £50,000 of this was to cover nursing and medical expenditure, at a rate of about £70 per week. By 1973, because of inflation, the entire award was inadequate to pay for even nursing services, costs of which had doubled in a decade. This might suggest that multiplicands should be planned to increase over time. However, judges have treated inflation as something falling within the question of multipliers rather than multiplicands, and in any event, something that can be ignored, arguing that in times of inflation the real rate of return on capital remains much the same, and the nominal rate merely reflects the real rate plus the current rate of inflation[3]. This view was approved by Lord Hope in *O'Brien's CB*, relying on English House of Lords cases. He said[4] that it 'was now well established that the "risk of further inflation on the one hand, and the high interest rates which reflect fear of it on the other" should be left out of account', and quoted Lord Scarman in *Lim Poh Choo v Camden Area Health Authority*[5] to the effect that the problem was best left to investment policy[6]. This attitude was, however, attacked in the English House of Lords case of *Wells v Wells*[7] (discussed below) and may not survive.

Fourthly, irrespective of changes in wages through redundancy etc, or increases in care costs though deterioration, and of the effects of inflation, there is another factor. In a time of increases in wages in real terms, multiplicands for future continuing consequential expenditure and future loss of earnings will automatically be insufficient in the future. Future care costs are likely, for instance, to increase in real terms because medical staff will be paid more, and because new treatments may be developed which are expensive, and which prolong life and thus costs[8]. This factor appears to be completely ignored; subsumed in the question of inflation; or deemed to be taken care of in the choice of multiplier[9].

---

1 Cane (ed) *Atiyah's Accidents, Compensation and the Law* (6th edn, 1999) p 133.

2 *Thurston v Todd* (1966–67) 84 WN (NSW) (Pt 1) 231, discussed in *Compensation and Rehabilitation in Australia: report of the National Committee of Inquiry* (1974).

3 Thus if the real rate remains constant at 4–5%, a nominal rate of, say, 14% merely indicates 9–10% inflation. By the same token, 9–10% inflation automatically produces a nominal rate of about 14%.

4 1991 SLT 477, at 483F.

5 [1980] AC 174 at 193, [1979] 3 WLR 44, [1979] 2 All ER 910.

6 See also *Mallett v McMonagle* [1970] AC 166, per Lord Diplock at 176, and *Cookson v Knowles* [1979] AC 556, per Lord Fraser at 577, [1969] 2 WLR 767, [1969] 2 All ER 178.

7 [1998] 3 WLR 329, [1998] 3 All ER 481.

8 Certainly, other new treatments might prove cheaper and might speed recovery, so reducing costs.

9 See now (English) Law Commission Report *Personal Injury Compensation: How Much is Enough?* (Law Com no 225) (HC Paper 666 (1993–94)), discussed above.

Multipliers

Firstly, the two stage process described above is inference. Courts have tended to eschew explanations of how they are generated, save by reference to precedent[1], treating as sufficient the broad assertion of the aim of *restitutio in integrum*, with occasional reference to the underlying principles of annuities. Even *O'Brien's CB* does not constitute a very clear account. Secondly, generating a 'notional basic multiplier' appears a simple arithmetic process, but depends on various assumptions, such as a rate of return on the investment of the lump sum, and the effects of future inflation. These are discussed below in more detail. Thirdly, individuation is certainly possible, but alteration of the multiplier is necessarily a crude method. This is also discussed below in more detail. Fourthly, traditionally generated multipliers in any case appear low, and have rarely exceeded 15.

Overall, it is important to note that multipliers do more than one job. They seek accurate prediction of exhaustion of capital; reflect assumptions about future rates of return on investment, and related assumptions about the relationship of such returns and inflation; and also seek individuation by reflecting presumed lengths of time before pursuers recover, and contingencies and opportunities in their lives which would have occurred had they not suffered the *damnum*. These factors require further examination.

Multipliers and rates of return on investment

It has long been argued that traditionally generated multipliers are too low in part because the tariff has assumed that a return of 4–5 per cent can be obtained if the lump sum is invested. This often repeated assertion, traced by Lord Hope in *O'Brien's CB* as far as *McKechnie v Henderson*[2] and reinforced by pronouncements of the House of Lords in English cases[3] does not often seem to have been checked against reality[4]. It is intuitively implausible that the real rate of return on investment has remained constant for 150 years, and there is strong contrary evidence[5]. It is also worth noting that 4–5 per cent covers a wide range, for a 5 per cent rate of return is 25 per cent higher than a 4 per

---

1 One of the few exceptions is *Forsyth's CB v Govan Shipbuilders* 1988 SC 421, 1989 SLT 91, 1989 SCLR 78, where Lord Clyde fixed a multiplier for life at 'about one third of the life expectancy' of the pursuer. In other cases, multipliers may give the impression of being half the number of years from proof to recovery, retirement or death, whichever is relevant.
2 (1858) 20D 551. In *Wells v Wells* [1998] 3 WLR 329, at 358F Lord Hope hazarded the guess that then this represented the return given by banks on deposit accounts, rather than on equities.
3 Lord Diplock in *Mallet v McMonagle* 1970 AC 166, at 176, (before the principal rise in inflation) and *Cookson v Knowles* [1979] AC 556, at 571, and Lord Fraser of Tullybelton at 576–577 (during a period of high inflation). Both cases concerned the Fatal Accidents Acts, which do not apply in Scotland, but the issues are the same.
4 In *Cookson v Knowles* [1979] AC 556, at 571G, Lord Diplock observed that 'in times of stable currency the multipliers that were used by judges were appropriate to interest rates of 4 per cent or 5 per cent *whether the judges using them were conscious of this or not*' (emphasis added).
5 See *Structured Settlements and Interim and Provisional Damages* (Consultation Paper no 125) (undated), App A, which purports to show that between 1970 and 1990, the annual real rate of interest ranged from –9.66 (1975) to 6.47 (1986), averaging –0.70% from 1970 to 1979, but 3.55% from 1980 to 1990. These figures are arrived at by deducting the rate of inflation from the nominal rate of return.

cent rate. However, it is now unlikely that the assumption will survive since the English House of Lords decision in *Wells v Wells* (discussed below).

Multipliers and future inflation

Argument on rates of return is confused by the existence of inflation. However, judicial statements have assumed that inflation can be ignored because, as noted above, it is argued that in times of inflation, the real rate of return on capital remains much the same, the nominal rate merely reflecting the real rate plus the rate of inflation. Such statements are sometimes qualified by the declaration 'in times of stable currency'. Yet notoriously, there has been continuous, if variable, inflation over the last 50 or more years, on occasion at high rates[1].

In *Cookson v Knowles*[2] Lord Diplock, after an examination of the issues in a time of high inflation, reiterated the principle[3]. However, he did so observing that equities and growth stocks had not kept pace with inflation, but fixed interest securities had, and in any case calculations concerning future inflation in relation to fatal accidents are 'artificial'[4] (and indeed all future loss calculations are 'conjectural'[5]) so rough and ready methods were justified. As noted above, there is considerable doubt about such conclusions, and they are unlikely to survive *Wells v Wells*.

Multipliers and individuation

It is not clear how far judges can individuate accurately. There are few variables for future care costs, more for future loss of earnings[6]. Individuation by modifying the multiplier by one or two whole numbers (as is usually done) is necessarily rough and ready (for changing a multiplier from 5 to 4 is a reduction of 20 per cent), and may seem very impressionistic[7]. Also, the argument would be more convincing were modification of the 'notional basic multiplier' not usually downwards. More sophisticated attempts to come to

---

1 See p 101, footnote 5 above. Paradoxically, it is deducting inflation from the nominal rate which shows the enormous variation in real rates.
2 [1979] AC 556 at 570–571. See also the arguments of counsel of the plaintiff at 561C.
3 In the context of the Fatal Accidents Acts, which do not apply in Scotland, but the issues appear the same, as noted above.
4 [1979] AC 556, at 571D. Commercial insurance and national insurance benefits, etc and prospects of remarriage were to be ignored (which considerations apply in Scotland) so the purpose 'is no longer to put dependants, particularly widows, in the same economic position as they would have been in had their late husband lived': at 568E. Also, at 568G, the assessment 'calls for consideration of a number of highly speculative factors' such as the widow's possible premature death, the likelihood of the husband continuing in work until the usual retiring age, interruptions to his work by unemployment or ill-health, possible increases in his earnings, possible increases in the proportion of earnings passed on to dependants, and possible work by the widow.
5 [1979] AC 556, at 571F.
6 In *O'Brien's CB* 1991 SLT 477, at 481J, Lord Hope observed that they included 'the risks of accident, illness, redundancy and the prospects of promotion and variations in the amount of wages and salary'.
7 For instance, in *Byrnes v Fife Health Board* 1978 SLT (Notes) 66, at 67, Lord Ross referring to the pursuer's work record, used phrases such as 'it seems not unreasonable', 'I feel that it is likely' and 'I do not feel able to'.

terms with the difficulties may even seem at odds with the rationale of an annuity approach. In *Stevenson v Sweeney*[1], Lord Morton of Shuna decided on a single multiplier of 20 for future care costs, and applied it to two different multiplicands. He considered that the first should be used for five-and-a-half years (so multiplied it by five-and-a-half), and the second, for the balance of 20 years (so multiplied it by fourteen-and-a-half), then added the two sums together. This does not seem a very exact way of ensuring that capital and interest would be exhausted by the relevant date.

Further, modification in the light of the variables is done by means of the 'experience' of judges[2]. Any such decision is always open to criticism on appeal, but more importantly, to a large extent, 'experience' is merely precedent[3]. It is thus a significant misnomer. Although often presented with arithmetic calculations[4], judges have no means of discovering whether their awards actually produce the required annual sum over the relevant number of years, being exhausted in the process, or leave unexpended capital (thus overcompensating), or run out too soon (thus undercompensating). The obvious analogy is a panel of doctors frequently prescribing a treatment without the means to discover how efficacious or otherwise it is[5]. Indeed, as noted above, there is now strong evidence from an (English) Law Commission Report[6] that sums awarded do not in fact constitute *restitutio in integrum*.

CALCULATIONS AND MARKETS IN THE FUTURE: THE ANNUITY APPROACH – ACTUARIAL VERSION

The 'Ogden Tables', Index Linked Government Stock and rates of return

Proper actuarial tables for use in personal injury actions, long called for, have now been produced in the 'Ogden Tables', that is the 'Actuarial Tables with

---

1 1995 SLT 29.
2 Thus in *O'Brien's CB* 1991 SLT 477, at 483J, Lord Hope observed that '. . . since awards [for loss of earnings] are very frequently made by the courts, every judge has a wealth of experience to draw down when it comes to select the multiplier . . .', and regretting the lack of such experience in future cost of care cases. At 486L he added '[i]t is important that whenever possible, the court should follow the traditional approach of basing its award on a conventional figure derived from experience and from awards in comparable cases'. See also *Taylor v O'Connor* [1971] AC 115, at 128, per Lord Reid, [1970] 2 WLR 472, [1970] 1 All ER 365.
3 Thus Lord Weir's reasoning in his selection of a multiplier of 11 for future care costs at first instance in *O'Brien's CB* was criticised on appeal at 1991 SLT 477, at 486A. He had, it was suggested, simply increased the agreed 10 for future loss of earnings because the care costs were to last for a few more years, while discounting for the possibility of epilepsy. He should have relied on precedent (no actuarial evidence having been led): see 487I.
4 Thus in *O'Brien's CB* 1991 SLT 477, counsel for the pursuer offered such calculations, demonstrating that (making the usual assumptions about rates of return and inflation) a multiplier of 11 for future care costs was grossly insufficient, since the fund intended to last a 19-year-old for life would be exhausted after 16 years, and a multiplier of 16 after 29 years, despite which the court awarded one of only 15.
5 'Experience', Oscar Wilde is said to have remarked, 'is the name we give to our mistakes'.
6 *Personal Injury Compensation: How Much Is Enough: a study of the compensation experiences of victims of personal injury* (Law Com no 225) (HC Paper 666 (1994–5)).

Explanatory Notes for use in Personal Injury and Fatal Accident Cases'[1]. These are a set of 22 principal Tables[2].

Use of the Tables is fully explained in the Introduction and Explanatory Notes. In brief, however, each contains actuarially generated multipliers to use instead of traditionally generated ones, with a range of rates of return from 1.5 per cent to 5 per cent. Thus, for instance, to discover the sum likely to be required to pay a woman of 30 a given annual sum (say £10,000) for a certain consequential expenditure such as nursing care for the rest of her life, firstly, the relevant Table for that type of loss and that person's sex is identified (Table 12, 'Multipliers for pecuniary loss for life (females) ... calculated with allowance for projected mortality from the 1996-based population mortality ...'). Secondly, a rate of interest, say 4.5 per cent, is selected. Thirdly, the relevant multiplier for that person's age is read off the Table (in this case 20.17). Fourthly, that multiplier is applied to the given multiplicand, as in the traditional approach (thus 20.17 × £10,000 = £201,700).

Features of the 'Ogden Tables'

Firstly, the Ogden Tables are essentially predictions of length of life. They reflect ordinary population mortality, thus averages only[3]. They are based on data for England and Wales, thus not Scotland[4]. Also, they are based on historical data, thus relating to people living in a period with different risks of disease, accident, etc, although alternative Tables now provided and recommended attempt to take account of the trends of declining mortality[5].

Secondly, the multipliers are designed to produce a figure net of tax, so a lower rate of return than would be used otherwise is required.

Thirdly, the Tables give a range of rates of return on capital wider than the traditional 4–5 per cent. The Introduction and Explanatory Notes have recommended the use of Index-Linked Government Stocks ('ILGS'), usually producing 2.5–4.5 per cent[6], lower than currently obtainable on a basket of equities, even discounting for inflation. However, being index linked and guaranteed by the Government, IGLS provide a more predictable return,

---

1 (3rd edn, 1998), produced by the Government Actuary's Department for a representative joint committee of lawyers and actuaries, chaired by Sir Michael Ogden, and based on the English Life Tables. Note, however, the concerns of the Association of British Insurers in App C. In *Fullemann v McInnes's Exrs* 1993 SLT 259 counsel for the pursuer, a Swiss resident, sought to use 'Barwerttafeln', a Swiss equivalent. The defender's objection that they were not foreshadowed in the record, were incomprehensible, and had not been proved, was sustained at 267B.

2 Ie basic male and female Tables giving multipliers for each of 'pecuniary loss' (ie consequential expenditure) for life; loss of earnings to 65 and 60; loss of pension rights to 65 and 60; together with the same, adjusted for '1996-based population mortality' (discussed below); plus Tables giving discounting factors for specific numbers of years; and multipliers for 'pecuniary loss' for specific numbers of years. There has been increasing sophistication. The first edition had only six Tables. Paragraph 45 refers to software used by the English High Court Family Division for related calculations.

3 See the concerns of the Association of British Insurers in App C, including the observation (para 6) 'People show a marked disinclination to die in strict accordance with their life expectancy': but also para 6 of the Explanatory Notes.

4 But see below in relation to 'geographical variation'.

5 Ie the Tables 11–20, adjusted for '1996-based population mortality'.

6 App A: see also 'Introduction to the Third Edition' and paras 11–13 of the Explanatory Notes.

reducing the pursuer's risk in investing a lump sum. In particular, as a measure of real return, inflation can be ignored. The Damages Act 1996, s 1 gives the Secretary of State the power[1] to prescribe a rate of return which courts, '[i]n determining the return to be expected from the investment of a sum awarded as damages for future pecuniary loss in an action for personal injury ... shall ... take into account' unless a party shows another to be 'more appropriate'.

Fourthly, because a lower real rate of return is indicated by these Stocks, higher multipliers result[2].

Lastly, individuation is rendered more accurate, because the multipliers go to two decimal places, while traditional ones were almost always whole numbers, and because there are subordinate Tables and calculations in the Explanatory Notes giving 'ready reckoner' modifications to the basic Tables[3]. Thus, there are three additional Tables indicating further multipliers to introduce a 'Basic Deduction for Contingencies other than Mortality'[4]. There is also indication of further variation for occupation[5], and for geographical region[6]. However, it is interesting how little difference these modifications make[7]. Given the heroic assumptions and speculative variables employed in generating multiplicands and predicting recovery rates, the traditional treatment of rates of return and inflation, and difficulty in confronting rises in real wage rates, this level of adjustment seems hardly worth making. Also, no attempt is made to take into account contingencies such as ceasing work to care for children or other dependants.

Conclusions on the 'Ogden Tables'

Thus, clearly, the Ogden Tables do not remove all difficulties. However, they do eliminate many problems of the traditional multiplier/multiplicand approach. They provide a firm justification for an annuity approach, and for those multipliers in fact generated. These can be demonstrated to do what they are supposed to do, that is, provide a sum the size of the multiplicand every year for the requisite number of years, taking inflation into account properly, by indicating a reliable measure of the rate of return on investments available. They even provide a more solid base for some individuation.

---

1 Not exercised at the time of writing.
2 In the example given at p 104 above, using a 4.5% rate of return which is in the middle of the traditionally assumed span of rates, a multiplier of 20.17 was produced, much higher than the traditional method would be likely to produce. If a 3% rate were used, as recommended by *Wells v Wells* [1998] 3 WLR 329, the multiplier would be a quarter higher yet, at 25.52.
3 See, however, the concerns of the Association of British Insurers in App C.
4 'Loss of Earnings to Pension Age 65 (Males)' (Table A); 'Loss of Earnings to Pension Age 60 (Males)' (Table B); and 'Loss of Earnings to Pension Age 60 (Females)' (Table C). Each gives a range of representative ages, and has a 'High', 'Medium' and 'Low' column, corresponding to levels of economic activity, and assume a 3% rate of return.
5 Thus, paras 37 and 38 recommend increases or decreases in the Table A–C multipliers to reflect risky occupations.
6 Thus, paras 39 and 40 recommend increases or decreases in those multipliers for certain areas (Scotland being an area for reduction).
7 The Table A 'Medium' column alters multipliers by a factor no greater than 0.9 (ie would reduce the lump sum to 90%); occupational variation alters them by no greater than 0.03: and geographical variation by no greater than 0.05.

Judicial and legislative response to the 'Ogden Tables'

The first edition of the Ogden Tables was considered in *O'Brien's CB*. Lord President Hope's leading judgment[1], indicated that in cases of future costs, multipliers were normally appropriate, and that precedent or 'experience' would be sufficient guidance, even where 'more sophisticated methods of calculation' were available. However, in special or unusual cases (possibly including future care costs) courts should be more willing to consider checks where practicable. He rejected a number of examples of purported sophistication found in English cases as irrelevant and took the opportunity to underline the desirability of the traditional annuity approach and in particular its reliance on a 4–5 per cent rate of return.

On the Ogden Tables specifically[2] Lord Hope considered that the fact that they were published by HMSO and available in the literature meant that there was no reason why the court should not take judicial notice of them 'by way of general background', and, that they could be assumed to be arithmetically correct. In particular, he considered them useful for various purposes such as the provision of an insight into the variations produced by different variables (including the rate of interest)[3].

However, he had two objections to greater reliance upon them, in particular as a starting point for the decision on a multiplier in that case. Firstly, they were based on English Life Tables, which might require adjustment in relation to Scotland. Secondly, they worked on the assumption that IGLS produced a rate of return of 2.5–3.5 per cent, whereas it was admitted that such stock, by the time of the case, was producing 4 per cent. Neither of these reasons appear to rule out the use of adapted actuarial tables in the future. Indeed, the adjustment for geographical variation, and the extending of the presumed range of rates of return on relevant Stocks to 2.5–4.5 per cent[4] in subsequent editions meet both objections. Nevertheless, the whole trend of Lord Hope's (and indeed, the court's) judgment is that the traditional method should be maintained.

Since *O'Brien's CB* there have been Outer House cases in which the question of the use of actuarial tables has been discussed, and which have heeded Lord Hope's opinion to differing degrees. In *Fullemann v McInnes's Executors*[5], for loss of income with a retirement age of 65, the precedents indicated a multiplier of 8, while the Ogden Tables indicated 11. However, there was evidence that the pursuer would have worked beyond that age, indicating a higher multiplier. Lord Cullen selected 11[6], apparently on the ground that the 'notional basic multiplier' (as it has been described here) should therefore be 13, but discounted by 2 for the vicissitudes of the pursuer's life. This conclusion appears heavily influenced by the Ogden Tables.

Shortly thereafter, in *McMillan v McDowall*[7] Temporary Judge Coutts seemed to go even further in relation to consequential expenditure on future care costs, effectively using actuarial evidence, including the Ogden Tables, as

---

1 1991 SLT 477 at 483C.
2 Above, at 484C.
3 Above, at 484G.
4 Albeit at the loss of some exactitude, given the size of this range: 4.5% is nearly twice 2.5%.
5 1993 SLT 259.
6 Above, at 267D.
7 1993 3 SLT 311.

a starting point. In *Stevenson v Sweeney*[1], also in relation to future care costs, Lord Morton of Shuna, while reiterating that they were only to be used as a check on traditional methods, was heavily influenced by such evidence. Having observed that there was no 'wealth of previously decided cases' as there was for lost income, and that for future care costs premature death appeared to be the only contingency, he decided on the unprecedentedly large multiplier of 20[2].

Later cases *Swan v Hope-Dunbar*[3] and *Burns v Harper Collins*[4], have seemed, however, closer to Lord Hope's injunction.

A modified actuarial approach: 'annualised cost'

A special form of the actuarial approach can be used for specific non-continuing items, as in *McMillan v McDowall* in respect of a house built for the pursuer. This may be appropriate for an award of a simple capital sum which might otherwise create a windfall for others, typically heritable property. The multiplicand is fixed at the annual additional expenditure undertaken, rather than the annual cost of acquiring the property, and the multiplier is generated in the usual way.

ENGLISH DEVELOPMENTS

The (English) Law Commission

The (English) Law Commission considered the traditional multiplier/multiplicand system and use of the Ogden Tables, noting that it had in the past supported the traditional method, and seen the actuarial method as only a checking device[5]. However, it accepted criticism of the traditional method on grounds similar to those outlined above, and in particular, drew attention to 'double discounting' of multipliers[6]; the arbitrary nature of such discounting in any case; the lack of realism in assuming real rates of return on investment are constant; and the fact that multiplicands might not reflect a realistic assessment of the plaintiff's expectations. With the availability of ILGS and Scottish experience, legislation to promote the use of actuarial evidence might thus be 'an idea whose time has come'[7]. The Damages Act 1996, s 1 followed, but did not reproduce, its recommendations.

1 1995 SLT 29.
2 The Ogden Tables gave 28.9, and an actuary's evidence, 28.7.
3 1997 SLT 760, 1996 SCLR 1118.
4 1997 SLT 607, 1996 SCLR 1135.
5 *Structured Settlements and Interim and Provisional Damages* (Consultation Paper no 125) (undated) paras 2.9–2.42; (Law Com no 224) (Cm 2646 (1994)) paras 2.1–2.48.
6 A good example was provided by *Wells v Wells* [1998] 3 WLR 329, where, at 345H–346D, where Lord Lloyd criticised the Court of Appeal for reducing a multiplier by 20% 'to cater for the hazards of life' because, it appeared, 'courts had tended to [do so]' when the multiplier already took account of them. He pointed out that one might as well increase it by 20%. At 346H–347D, he made a similar criticism of the House of Lords' own recent similar decision in *Hunt v Severs* [1994] AC 350, [1994] 2 WLR 602, [1994] 2 All ER 385.
7 Interestingly, it was suggested that judicial reluctance to use the Ogden Tables in England and Wales flowed from the senior judges having been barristers taking personal injury actions before juries, without expert evidence, without awards broken down into heads of damages, when a greater stress was placed on uniformity, and at a time when inflation was not a problem.

A radical idea which was not favoured by legislation was to 'decouple' the court's role in identifying loss from its role in capitalising a relevant sum. It could, in short, identify the multiplicand (which could remain steady, increase, or decrease), and simply require evidence of the capital lump sum required to produce this annually for the relevant number of years.

The House of Lords

The House of Lords' decision in *Wells v Wells*[1] concerned English law. However, it must be likely that it will be followed in Scotland, not least because two Scottish judges sat, and one expressly referred to Scotland. *Wells* comprised three linked personal injury cases of markedly different facts. However, they had in common that they included large awards for future damages. The judges at first instance assumed a rate of return of 2.5–3 per cent instead of 4–5 per cent and made correspondingly higher awards, overturned by the Court of Appeal. All the plaintiffs appealed to the House of Lords which upheld the original decision. The House of Lords consciously took its decision in the light of the Law Commission's Report (discussed above), and the opinions are models of clarity on the process of quantifying future damages. Opinions were given by the whole Bench, including Lords Hope and Clyde, but all agreed on all essentials.

The leading judgment is perhaps that of Lord Lloyd of Berwick[2]. For him, the starting point was the need to identify a capital sum which would provide the required annual income for the intended number of years. In principle, this was not difficult to calculate, but inflation is a problem, traditionally assumed to be solved by investment policy, a mixed basket of gilts and equities doing the job. The advent of ILGS now provided an alternative which took account of inflation and was risk free. Arguments might be produced to the effect that a prudent investor would have a mixed portfolio of 70 per cent equities and 30 per cent gilts, producing a good balance of income and safety. However, plaintiffs in tort actions were not in the same position, for they relied on their damages for income, and required more protection against loss, which might be catastrophic for them, even if short-term[3]. Thus, for them ILGS were the most sensible option. That inflation proofing did not protect against real rises in costs was not an argument for the traditional method.

In any case, the existence of the 'Ogden Tables' and other critiques of the traditional method of quantification of future damages, supported the general conclusion, and no authority prevented it. Thus the judges at first instance were right to assume that the plaintiffs would invest in ILGS. It was the most accurate way of calculating damages, was not unfair to other parties, protected the investor, and might be cheaper. That not all plaintiffs used ILGS was irrelevant. Since ILGS rates are published daily, it was simple to discover the current rate, from which a deduction for tax required to be made. A deduction at the standard rate was inappropriate, for it ignored allowances

---

1 [1998] 3 WLR 329, [1998] 3 All ER 481.
2 Although that of Lord Hope of Craighead is probably easier to follow.
3 It was also noted that one witness had given misleading evidence in that the rate of return for equities was calculated assuming reinvestment of the return produced, which would not happen in respect of a plaintiff for whom the return was income.

and the fact that an annuity comprises an increasing proportion of capital, so 14 per cent was 'about right'.

Thus, the House of Lords should set guidelines to replace the traditional 4–5 per cent. A bracket rather than a figure was preferable to allow flexibility in exceptional cases, such as higher tax rate payers, but Lord Lloyd was happy to fall in with the majority which preferred a single figure. Given the existence of short-term fluctuations, an average over a period might be better, and he proposed 3 per cent.

QUANTIFICATION AND INTEREST ON DAMAGES

THE ISSUE

Decree may be long after the *damnum* was suffered, and damages paid long after that. *Restitutio in integrum* therefore raises the question of interest on those damages.

THE COMMON LAW BACKGROUND

Direct authority on interest on delictual damages at common law is surprisingly thin. This is true of nineteenth-century cases. *Lenaghan v Monkland Iron & Steel Co*[1] concerned assythment. *Caledonian Railway Co v Carmichael*[2] concerned compulsory purchase. Also, although it was a House of Lords case, it overturned the First Division with the only Scottish judge dissenting. Further, its frequently cited dictum on interest (mentioned below) was made by an English judge, and was probably obiter. *Flensburg Steam Shipping Co v Seligmann*[3] was an admiralty case decided without reference to *Caledonian Railway v Carmichael* (or any other case), and Lord President Inglis' opinion opens with words which, read in context, do not mean what they seem[4]. *Martin v Robertson, Ferguson & Co*[5] was a contract case and primarily concerned the competence of the appeal. Also, while the Lord President discussed interest, the other judges reserved their positions. *Dunn & Co v Anderston Foundry Co*[6], another contract case, depended heavily upon the facts and imaginatively avoided the principle apparently laid down by the earlier cases.

The twentieth-century cases are equally thin. *AS Kolbin & Sons v William Kinnear & Co*[7] concerned the liability of agents, and the *ratio* in relation to interest was laid down by another English judge (despite the presence of three Scottish judges) in a more complicated repetition of *Caledonian Railway Co v*

---

1 (1858) 20 D 848.
2 (1870) 8 M (HL) 119.
3 (1871) 9 M 1011.
4 Above, at 1014: 'The rule that interest does not run on damages is well fixed' clearly means 'until they are quantified'.
5 (1872) 10 M 949.
6 (1894) 21 R 880.
7 1931 SC (HL) 128, 1931 SLT 464.

Carmichael (and used the term 'chattel'). *FW Green & Co v Brown & Gracie Ltd*[1] was a contract case and is not fully reported, but in any case, the House of Lords dealt with interest in terms of the Court of Session Act 1808. More recent undoubtedly delictual cases, such as *Clancy v Dixon's Ironworks Ltd*[2], tend to rely on the nineteenth-century precedents, or their restatement in *Kolbin*, and legislative regulation for over 40 years means cases from *Macrae v Reed & Mallik Ltd*[3] onwards primarily concern statutory interpretation.

Nevertheless, because the operation that legislation is only explicable in terms of the common law, and because of drafting problems, there is frequent reference back to the common law.

Common law principles—the relevant rate of interest

Curiously, given the centrality of the question, little in the cases indicates or explains the appropriate rate of interest. Clearly, if interest is a substitute for the pursuer's investment of the money, it might reflect what prudent investment would produce.

There is some direct reference. For instance, in *Clancy*, Lord Carmont, giving the opinion of the court, decided upon 5 per cent per annum. There is also indirect reference, as in *Kolbin*[4] where Lord Atkin noted that the Second Division had awarded interest at bank rate, and in *Caledonian Railway v Carmichael*[5], where the rubric discloses that the pursuer concluded for interest at 5 per cent. There may be no reference at all, even where interest was to be paid, as in *Lenaghan*.

Generally, 5 per cent per annum seems to have been assumed appropriate, and reflected a presumed rate of return on investment. In *Dunn v Anderston Foundry*[6], one of the few cases in which the rate was actually discussed, Lord Rutherfurd Clark said that '[t]he old rule was 5 per cent, and I do not think it has been altered. It may, however, be worthy of reconsideration, looking to the fact that investments now earn so much less than they used to do'. The Lord Justice-Clerk rejoined 'I think we must adhere to the old rule, and calculate the interest at the rate of 5 per cent'[7]. However, this was a contract case.

Common law principles—periods for which interest might be paid

At common law, an important distinction was made between damages before decree, on which interest was payable, and damages after, on which it was not.

---

1 1960 SLT (Notes) 43.
2 1955 SC 17, 1955 SLT 36.
3 1961 SC 68, 1961 SLT 96.
4 1931 SC (HL) 128 at 137 and 140.
5 (1870) 8 M (HL) 119, at 121.
6 (1894) 21 R 880, at 882.
7 In *Jefford v Gee* [1970] 1 QB 130, at 148E–H, [1970] 2 WLR 702, [1970] 1 All ER 1202, Lord Denning said that in England and Wales the post-decree rate had been fixed in 1838 at 4% and ought to be changed; that 'a realistic rate' ought to be awarded; that the Bank Rate was then 8% but fluctuated too much; and that money paid into court was placed on a short term investment account, at a rate fixed by the Lord Chancellor, and that this was particularly suitable.

In *Caledonian Railway v Carmichael*[1], Lord Westbury declared interest was only payable for non-contractual damages 'by virtue of the principal sum of money having been wrongfully withheld'[2]. This was restated by Lord Atkin[3] in *Kolbin* as 'a pursuer may recover interest by way of damages where he is deprived of an interest-bearing security or a profit-producing chattel, but otherwise, speaking generally, he will recover interest, apart from contract, by virtue of a principal sum having been wrongfully withheld ...'. The principle is completed by Lord Justice-Clerk Thomson in *Macrae v Reed & Mallik*[4], observing that only at the date of final decree 'the illiquid claim for damages is quantified and made liquid'[5]. Summing up these cases, damages are a debt once they are awarded, so only then is interest payable.

There are limits, complexities and exceptions to this principle. Firstly, the limit on pre-decree interest applies to delictual damages, but not necessarily to contractual damages. This deserves mention because, as noted, several of the authorities concern contract, where other principles may apply.

Secondly, there are complexities. The Lord President noted in *Lenaghan*, that a jury may increase damages where there has been delay to tacitly include a sum for interest for the period before its verdict. Also, there may be uncertainty as to when the award is actually final. With a jury trial, there must be a motion for the verdict to be applied, and a line of Inner House authority from *Lenaghan* and *Flensburg* to *Clancy*, indicates it is this date. If there is an appeal, the final interlocutor may be delayed for a long time, particularly if the appeal is a motion for a new jury trial. However, such a case might fall to be treated as an exception.

Thirdly, then, in exceptional cases, interest might be backdated to a limited extent[6]. For instance, in *Lenaghan*, delays caused by appeals meant that the final interlocutor was delayed by more than four years. Although these delays were not improper, the Second Division allowed interest from the date of the verdict rather than the application of the verdict. *Flensburg* concerned unconscionable delays, but the First Division only backdated interest to the date on which the verdict would have been applied had there been no unjustified proceedings, and not even to the actual verdict, thus hardly constituting an exception. *Clancy* was somewhat similar.

Common law principles—problems and criticisms

The common law principles created problems and thus criticisms, though not in relation to rates of interest awarded so much as the period for which it was awarded.

---

1 (1870) 8 M (HL) 119 at 131.
2 Lord Westbury is quoted in later cases. The Lord Chancellor, giving the leading judgement, decided the question on the facts. The only Scottish judge (Lord Colonsay), dissented on another point, and so had no need to approach this one.
3 Three Scottish judges were sitting (Viscount Dunedin, Lord Thankerton and Lord Macmillan), all of whom simply concurred.
4 1961 SC 68, at 72.
5 See also the Lord President in *Martin & Sons v Robertson, Ferguson & Co* (1872) 10M 949, at 951.
6 The *Third Report of the Law Reform Committee for Scotland ...* (1957) (Cmnd 141) para 2 asserts that the Inner House and House of Lords have this power, implying the Outer House does not, and that it is not clear what is the earliest date from which interest might be awarded, but offered no authority.

On the one hand, the principle reflects the truth that until final decree, the pursuer's claim is no more than that, and may be contested as to liability, *quantum*, or both. On the other hand, even normal delays in litigation may have an unfortunate effect on pursuers. In *Lenaghan*[1], the Lord President pointed out that the pursuers were 'widows [who] had been living with large young families for several years' and continued that '[c]onsidering the nature of the loss sustained by the pursuer, I should have wished to allow interest from the date of the accident'. Ultimately successful pursuers bear all their losses until decree, indeed might have to borrow equivalent sums and pay interest on them[2]. Further, as a mirror image, even such normal delays 'may tend to give defenders an undue advantage at the expense of pursuers' because for that period they have the money, as Lord Justice-Clerk Thomson observed in *Macrae v Reed & Mallik*[3]. Indeed, he noted that it might be possible for a defender to finance an appeal out of the interest gained.

Incidentally, this casts doubt on the distinction in Lord Atkin's commonly used expression of the common law in *Kolbin* between, on the one hand 'interest-bearing security' or 'profit-producing chattel', and on the other an ordinary delictual award. On the former, a pursuer might recover interest from the date of deprivation, but on the latter only from the date of final decree. Yet money is 'interest-bearing' or 'profit-producing', and future damages are actually calculated on the assumption that the lump sum will be invested. Indeed, in effect, interest is being earned on the potential sum, whoever holds it. The question is simply who keeps it[4].

In any case, as discussed in *Macrae v Reed & Mallik*[5] and other cases, the problem is more complicated than simply backdating interest to the date of the cause of action, for losses may manifest themselves at different times. Property losses occur at that date, but might be considered to actually manifest themselves only when a replacement is acquired or repair paid for, giving two possible dates from which interest might run. Consequential expenditure, such as nursing care, however, may manifest itself over a lengthy period after that date, in occasional or periodic instalments, producing an accumulating sum. Interest on that sum from that date, or even from first expenditure, would overcompensate, while interest on that sum from the last payment would undercompensate. Conceivably, interest on each payment could be made individually[6], but it could be calculated on half that sum (or interest at half the rate on the whole sum)[7]. Loss of income, as another regularly accumulating sum, can be dealt with in essentially the same way, as

---

1 (1858) 20 D 848 at 849.

2 The (English) Law Commission Report no 225 *Personal Injury Compensation: How Much Is Enough?* (1994) (Cm 666) paras 8.7–8.9 notes that after an accident, costs increase while income declines, and records that of the respondents, most experienced financial difficulties after an accident: a third borrowed or accumulated debt; a quarter stopped saving; and half had to use savings.

3 1961 SC 68, at 73.

4 This may have been the reasoning behind *Dunn v Anderston Foundry* (1894) 21R 880.

5 See, for example, Lord Justice-Clerk Thomson at 1961 SC 68, at 74, and Lord Patrick at 76–78.

6 As, *mutatis mutandis*, in *Dunn v Anderston Foundry* above.

7 This was suggested by Lord Denning in *Jefford v Gee* [1970] 2 QB 130 at 146G, [1970] 2 WLR 702, [1970] 1 All ER 1202 for loss of wages because the *Dunn* method 'would mean too much detail'. For medical expenses (there only £6), in principle it 'should run from the date on which they are paid' but 'are not usually so large as to warrant separate calculation' (an implausible assertion now).

occasionally specifically suggested, for instance by Lord Ross in *Byrnes v Fife Health Board*[1]. *Solatium*, however, is more complicated[2]. The pain and suffering etc continue over a period from the cause of action onwards. It can hardly be assumed to be suffered in regular instalments, like nursing bills, but it could be assumed that it accumulated over time, but at a decreasing rate. Thus, while it may be rough justice, with possible exceptions, the same principle seems appropriate.

STATUTE

The provision

The Interest on Damages (Scotland) Act 1958, applying to all damages actions, first gave a power to award pre-decree interest[3]. This was amended by the Interest on Damages (Scotland) Act 1971.

The substituted s 1(1) provides that a court pronouncing an interlocutor decerning for a sum of money as damages may include decree for interest:

- for the whole or any part of the period from the date of the cause of action;
- on the whole or part of the damages;
- at different specified rates on different parts or periods.

In a personal injury or fatal accident action, s 1(1A) requires a court to give decree for interest on all or part of any 'damages or *solatium*' [sic][4] as it 'considers appropriate', unless there are 'reasons special to the case'[5]. The issue is required to be raised before final interlocutor[6].

Original and amended provisions

The 1971 Act effected four amendments. Firstly, the original provision permitted the decree only 'if the circumstances warrant such a course'. The removal of these words was discussed in *Smith v Middleton*[7]. The Lord Ordinary (Emslie) concluded, somewhat surprisingly, that it made no difference[8]. Despite dubiety expressed by Lord Maxwell in *James Buchanan & Co v*

---

1 1978 SLT (Notes) 66 at 68.
2 In *Macrae v Reed & Mallik Ltd* 1961 SC 68, at 77–78, Lord Patrick argued that *solatium* 'is not a *surrogatum* for monetary loss', so should never bear interest, which seems to run counter to common law principles, and be illogical. See also Lord Denning in *Jefford v Gee* [1970] 2 QB 130, at 147E–G.
3 The *Third Report of the Law Reform Committee for Scotland* .... (Cmnd 141) (1957) observed that the power had existed in England and Wales since the Law Reform (Miscellaneous Provisions) Act 1934, but recommended no change.
4 An odd form of drafting, discussed below.
5 Drafting is again slightly odd in that the court is required to include the interest 'in' the damages.
6 *Handren v Scottish Construction Co Ltd* 1967 SLT(Notes) 21, although where the pursuer forgot to ask for it per *incuriam*, the Inner House awarded it in *Forsyth's CB v Govan Shipbuilders Ltd*.
7 1972 SC 30.
8 Above, at 34.

Stewart Cameron (Drymen) Ltd[1], this view has prevailed. Secondly, originally, the date from which pre-decree interest might run was the date of citation[2]; thirdly, originally, it appeared that only one rate might be specified; and fourthly, s 1(1A) was inserted.

The general effect of the changes effected by the 1971 Act is clear. Courts are to be more generous to pursuers and are enabled to be more subtle. Nevertheless, no clue is given as to the exercise of the discretions on period, proportion, or rate, nor on jury awards of an undifferentiated sum[3], though the discretion is reviewable if based on wrong principles or wholly unreasonable[4].

Judicial interpretation—general

The principal case on the original provision was *Macrae v Reed & Mallik*[5]. It offers no clear *ratio*, and has been heavily re-interpreted, but its authority is regarded as surviving the amendment of the original legislation.

Where the Lord Ordinary (Wheatley) had allowed 5 per cent on the whole of a jury award, the Inner House was unanimous that this was wrong; that there should be no interest on future damages; and that a 'selective' approach was required, that is, individual heads should be looked at individually[6]. Beyond that, it is not clear how far there was any agreement. In particular, while Lord Justice-Clerk Thomson would allow interest for normal delays on past *solatium*, even where quantification was speculative, Lord Patrick would not allow it on *solatium* at all; Lord Strachan would only allow any interest at all where delays were caused by the defender's obstruction[7]; and Lord Mackintosh (who gave what is possibly the leading judgment) would include any delictual losses only with difficulty, and probably only those where *quantum* was not disputed[8].

Not surprisingly, the *ratio* required to be explained, but was applied, in a number of subsequent Outer House cases, including ones for loss of support

---

1 1973 SC 285.

2 See the Interest on Damages (Scotland) Act 1971, s 1(1), read with s 3(2) both as originally enacted.

3 In *Orr v Metcalfe* 1973 SC 57, at 59, Lord President Emslie said the Act 'has already been the subject of much judicial criticism, all, in my opinion, fully deserved' and at 61, Lord Cameron that it 'would be difficult to find a section of any recent Act of Parliament of recent years which presents, from the obscurity of its language, so many problems of construction or operation' and hazarded that the draftsman had overlooked the fact that it would have to be operated in jury awards.

4 *Macrae v Reed & Mallik* 1961 SC 68, reiterated by Lord Justice-Clerk Ross in *Boots the Chemist Ltd v GA Estates* 1993 SLT 136 at 142F.

5 1961 SC 68. Other cases include *R&J Dempster Ltd v Motherwell Bridge and Engineering Co Ltd* 1964 SC 308, 1964 SLT 353, a contract case. There, without reference to *Macrae*, the Lord President simply declared the Act to allow departure from the common law in unusual cases only. There was no undue delay or other special circumstance (and no indication as to what 'special circumstance' might mean). The case has been largely ignored since, and regarded as overtaken by legislative amendment (see eg *James Buchanan & Co v Stewart Cameron (Drymen) Ltd* 1973 SC 285, at 288).

6 This is sometimes referred to as a 'selective and discriminating' approach, although that phrase does not appear in this case.

7 Lord Hunter in *Fraser v J Morton Wilson Ltd* 1966 SLT 22, at 23, considered Lord Strachan to have dissented, although this 'was not made clear by the rubric'.

8 In a fit of cynicism, at 1961 SC 68, 82, he declared that in delict actions 'the sum sued for is usually a random round figure which becomes the ceiling of the amount which the pursuer can get in the action, but which in most cases is very considerably above what he expects to get if successful . . .'.

for widow and children following a fatal accident in *Killah v Aberdeen & District Milk Marketing Board*[1], and *Webster v Simpson's Motors*[2] and for loss of moveable and heritable property following a negligently started fire in *Fraser v J Morton Wilson Ltd (No 2)*[3] and *Bell's Sports Centre (Perth) Ltd v William Briggs & Sons Ltd*[4]. The view of the *ratio* of *Macrae v Reed & Mallik* which emerged was effectively Lord Justice-Clerk Thomson's, that is, that provided the claim was properly broken down into heads of damages, any reasonably ascertainable past loss could be claimed for[5], even where damages were not clearly ascertainable.

The essence of this explains most of the amendments to the original provision, but none of the Outer House cases dealt with the central problem in *Macrae v Reed & Mallik*, that is, what to do where a jury awards an overall figure for damages, without any way of itemising the different heads of damages.

Judicial interpretation – rate of interest

The Act does not give any guidance on appropriate rates of interest. However, 'judicial rates of interest'[6] were 'the only feasible yardstick' for Lord Emslie, as Lord Ordinary, in *Smith v Middleton*. They were used explicitly by the Inner House in a number of cases, such as *Ross v British Railways Board*[7] and *Prentice v Chalmers*[8]. In *Boots the Chemist Ltd v GA Estates Ltd*[9], the Lord Ordinary (upheld by the Second Division) described it as 'the usual practice' although the defenders had argued that the contemporary rate of 15 per cent was excessive because the pursuers could not have obtained that if they had had the money and invested it, and because such a high rate was an incentive for pursuers to delay proceedings. This does not mean the full rate for the full period is necessarily used. For instance, as noted above, where the sum is an accumulating one, a half rate on the accumulated sum may be used, and where a period has more than one rate applying these rates should be used or averaged[10].

Judicial interpretation – interest for the whole or part of the period from date of the cause of action

There is no presumption that interest should be allowed from the date of the cause of action. This was confirmed in *Boots the Chemist Ltd*. Lord Justice-Clerk

---

1 1961 SLT 232.
2 1967 SLT (Notes) 36.
3 1966 SLT 22.
4 1971 SLT (Notes) 48.
5 Save, possibly, *solatium*: see Lord Wheatley in *Killah* 1961 SLT 262, at 233.
6 *Alias* 'legal rate' or 'court rate': at the time of writing it was laid down as 8% by SI 1993/769 (sheriff court) and SI 1993/770 (Court of Session). Immediately previously it was 15%. For the current rate, see *Parliament House Book* Div D (sheriff court) and Div C (Court of Session).
7 1972 SLT 174.
8 1985 SLT 168.
9 1993 SLT 136, particularly at 141H, 1992 SCLR 859.
10 See also *Purryag v Greater Glasgow Health Board* 1996 SLT 794, where there had been a lapse of 18 years between cause of action and proof, and half the 'court rate' was generally agreed following 'longstanding Scottish practice'. The defender argued for 2% on the *solatium* because the pursuer would have got it at current levels, not those of 18 years earlier.

Ross, giving the opinion of the Inner House, affirmed Lord Mackintosh's view in *Macrae v Reed & Mallik* that the legislation did not sweep away the common law. He thus relied on the principle laid down in *Caledonian Railway Co v Carmichael* and *Kolbin* (affirmed in *Green v Brown & Gracie*), that limited pre-decree interest to where the money claimed is quantified, because only then can it be said to be wrongfully withheld and the pursuer to be 'standing out of his money'[1]. This begs the question of when a loss can, in Lord Ross's words, 'reasonably be regarded as quantifiable or capable of ascertainment'[2].

The answer can be sought by noting that Lord Ross approved *Fraser v Morton* and *Bells' Sports Centre*. Both were cases of property damage by fire. Both relied on an interpretation of *Macrae v Reed & Mallik* generous to the pursuer. Both thus allowed interest from the date of citation (the earliest date them possible) insofar as the losses of assets represented by the heritable and moveable property were suffered at the time of the fire, even though precise sums were not fixed till later. This seems to suggest that 'capable of ascertainment' means 'capable of ascertainment, in principle, albeit at some later date'. *Buchanan v Cameron* concerned goods lost in transit. Lord Maxwell distinguished *Fraser* and *Bell*, taking a more restrictive line, and in *Boots the Chemist*, Lord Ross seemed to approve the opinion only in so far as it maintained that there must be some 'ascertainment'.

Boots the Chemist itself, a case of property damage by flood, increases the problem, however. Lord Ross distinguished between 'loss of stock', items 'analogous to what might be termed "out-of-pocket expenses"', and 'loss of sales'. In respect of 'loss of sales', agreed as at a date which was apparently the approximate date of loss, there is no problem as such (but see below). In respect of some items 'analogous to ... "out-of-pocket expenses"', however, there is. They included repair costs apparently dated as at the time of repair. Lord Ross said (under reference to *Caledonian Railway v Carmichael*) that 'once the injured party has incurred the expenditure to repair the loss, it appears to me entirely reasonable to regard the wrongdoer as wrongfully withholding the money ...'[3]. But this is difficult to reconcile with *Fraser* and *Bell*. The *damnum* which was repaired occurred at the date of the flooding. Repair goes to the question of the size of loss, not the date of ascertainment. Is there no loss if there is no repair?

In respect of 'loss of stock', there are also problems. Lord Ross observed that 'the stock was lost on 3 November, but there was no material before the Lord Ordinary to enable him to conclude whether that stock, if not destroyed, would have earned profit for the pursuers from any particular date'[4], and approved the conclusion that interest might be awarded from the date of citation since 3 November had no particular significance. This raises several issues. Firstly, this again seems to confuse loss and its ascertainment. Possible profit is merely a means of determining the size of loss, and even goods sold

---

1 1993 SLT 136, at 143F. Unfortunately, in *Bell*, Lord Emslie had distinguished the date on which damages were agreed (so clearly ascertained) from the date on which the pursuer was 'standing out of his money', apparently when repairs were paid for.
2 Above, at 143H.
3 Above, at 143.
4 Above, at 143J. In *James Buchanan & Co v Stewart Cameron (Drymen) Ltd* 1973 SC 285, at 290, Lord Maxwell used the same argument, relying on *Carmichael*, distinguishing cases like *Bell* on the ground that money spent on repairs could be seen as examples of 'deprivation of an interest-bearing chattel' because 'money not otherwise expended can always earn interest'.

at a loss have a value[1]. Secondly, the date of citation had no more relevance than had 3 November, so this hardly indicates a 'selective and discriminating' approach. Thirdly, if the measure of 'loss of stock' is loss of profit, what was 'loss of sales'[2]?

Thus, it is far from clear what constitutes 'ascertainment' in relation to losses of assets. It may be that if claims are presented as capital losses, they will be treated as ascertainable at the date of loss, whereas if they are presented as repairs, they will be treated as ascertainable at the date of repair.

In relation to loss of income and loss of support, the same difficulties seem not to have arisen. A clear example is *Prentice v Chalmers*[3], where the Inner House, without comment, specifically awarded interest on loss of support from the date of the accident. Thus, in general, Lord Maxwell's explanation of the word 'ascertainment' in *Buchanan* as 'being known to or readily discoverable by the defenders' is useful, but its application by him, and by later judges, seems unnecessarily restrictive and sometimes unpredictable.

This leaves open the question of the effect of delays by the pursuer. In *Boots the Chemist*, the pursuer had made no judicial demand for some five years after the cause of action and (despite reminders and requests) a further two years had elapsed before adequate information had been sent. However Lord Ross rejected the argument that the period of interest might be restricted on this account, disapproving Outer House decisions[4] in so far as they suggested that. He concluded that the pursuer merely delays receipt of sums owed to him and this should not be a reason for benefitting the defender who, *ex hypothesi*, owes the money. This seems a little hard upon a defender who admits liability and cannot properly settle his affairs because the pursuer is dilatory on *quantum*.

Judicial interpretation—interest on the whole or part of the damages

The drafting is effectively the same as in the original provision, and despite the wide wording, *Macrae* interpreted it to exclude future damages, a restriction which clearly remains.

It has also been regarded as excluding *solatium*. Since the Interest on Damages (Scotland) Act 1958, s 1(1A) explicitly requires interest in personal injury actions on 'damages and *solatium*', this restriction does not remain for personal injury actions (although it could be argued that as this distinguishes *solatium* from damages, for the purposes of s 1(1) it is excluded thus preventing interest on *solatium* in, for example, defamation).

'Part' includes any broad head of damages, such a *solatium*, and any separate category within one. In *Boots the Chemist Ltd*, interest was allowed on seven items in an agreed list from one date, and on one on the list from another.

---

1 Boots the Chemist's stock control in the 1980s was no doubt capable of determining stock and its book value at the press of a button.
2 The defender raised this at first instance. Lord Cameron of Lochbroom appeared to accept the point in part saying, at 1992 SLT 136, 141B, '[i]t may reasonably be said that the head of loss of sales may encompass a return on stock which was in fact destroyed', but seems to have regarded the difficulty as identical with the problem of when to allow interest for loss of stock.
3 1985 SLT 168.
4 1993 SLT 136, at 144C–G. The decisions disapproved included *Nacap Ltd v Moffat Plant* 1986 SLT 326, *Buchan v J Marr (Aberdeen) Ltd* 1987 SLT 521, 1987 SCLR 96, and *M&I Instrument Engineers Ltd v Varsada* 1991 SLT 106.

Judicial interpretation – different rates on different parts or periods

The original provision referred only to 'rate'. In *Boots the Chemist*, 'full judicial rate' was awarded explicitly by the Lord Ordinary, but taking into account a change of rate during the time between cause of action and settlement.

Different rates are commonly awarded upon single payments and cumulating sums. Thus, in *Porter v Dickie*[1], Lord Ross awarded the 'full judicial rate' upon funeral and headstone expenses, and half that rate on loss of support.

Judicial interpretation—interest on 'damages and *solatium*' in personal injury actions unless there are 'special reasons'[2]

Ross v British Railways Board[3], provides an interesting parallel with *Macrae v Reed & Mallik*. The Lord Ordinary (Stott) was faced with an undifferentiated award and awarded interest on the whole sum, including *solatium* and future damages, for the whole possible period. The Second Division concluded that a jury award was not a 'special reason'. There being no practicable way of disaggregating the award, interest had to be allowed on the whole sum, but for less than the whole period, and/or at a lower rate than otherwise, and the Second Division itself decided upon interest from the date of citation. Lord Justice-Clerk Grant acknowledged that this was 'very rough justice'[4].

Judicial interpretation—the effect of the award of interim damages

The Inner House has not yet delivered an opinion and Outer House decisions have varied in approach. In *Redman v MacRae*[5], in respect of a claim for *solatium*, the Lord Ordinary (Weir) simply noted that while there should 'normally' be an award of interest, the receipt of interim damages 'effectively discounted[ed] the requirement'. Lord Morton of Shuna was subtler in *Jarvie v Sharp*[6], though unfortunately, the report is not entirely clear. Seemingly, interim payments approximated the size of the final award, and because it was made after three of the four years between cause of action and proof, interest was given at the full rate on two thirds of the sums due. For careful treatment see the somewhat brief discussion of Lord Cullen in *Bhatia v Tribax Ltd*[7], where it was decided that interim payments could only be applied to past losses, to reduce principal and any interest to date.

Judicial interpretation—the relationship with social security payments

The relationship of damages to social security payments generally is deal with in ch 6. However, it should be noted that the Social Security (Recovery of Benefits) Act 1997, s 17[8] was held by the Inner House in *Wisely v John Fulton*

---

1 1983 SLT 234.
2 For an unintended result of the drafting, see *Orr v Metcalfe* 1973 SLT 133.
3 1972 SC 154, 1972 SLT 174.
4 1972 SC 154 at 158.
5 1991 SLT 785, at 786F–G.
6 1992 SLT 350.
7 1994 SLT 1201.
8 'In assessing damages in respect of any accident, injury or disease, the amount of any listed benefits paid or likely to be paid is to be disregarded'.

(Plumbers) Ltd[1] to require courts assessing interest on damages to disregard the fact that certain social security benefits may be clawed back from those damages[2]. This does appear a curious result[3]. However, Lord President Roger observed the Act to be a compromise, no worse than others which have obtained in this area[4]. Equally, as a matter of construction, the interest on damages must count as part of the 'Compensation for earnings lost during the relevant period' for the purposes of Sch 2 to the Act, thus from which the listed social security benefits are deducted.

1 1998 SLT 1026, 1998 SCLR 954.
2 Approving *Spence v Wilson* 1998 SC 433, 1998 SLT 689 and over-ruling *George v George C Peebles & Son* 1998 SLT 685.
3 And may differ from that under the Social Security Act 1992, which previously governed the situation. Therefore cases such as *Morrison v Laidlaw* 1994 SLT 359 and *Cavanagh v BP Chemicals* 1995 SLT 1287 are irrelevant.
4 1998 SLT 1026, at 1030I.

5. Quantification in practice

Atiyah's analysis of the concept of compensation, and a four-fold typology of damages based on it, were outlined in ch 1 and developed in ch 2. The four types are:

patrimonial losses—I : losses of assets;
patrimonial losses—II : actual and notional consequential expenditure;
patrimonial losses—III: loss of profit, loss of income, and loss of support; and
personal losses: *solatium* and loss of society.

Chapters 3 and 4 considered *restitutio in integrum* as the basic principle of damages, its implications, limitations upon it, and three approaches to its general application to past and future losses. This chapter considers the specific application of those principles to this four-fold typology.

PATRIMONIAL LOSSES—I: LOSSES OF ASSETS

GENERAL

Chapter 2 pointed out that losses of assets were of a wide variety of types, according to the nature of the delict which caused it, the nature of the loss and the nature of the property. It concluded that, in practice, classification had to be in terms of the traditional categories of corporeal and incorporeal. However, it observed that the distinctions between heritable and moveable and between destruction and lesser damage; the fact that incorporeals could not suffer physical damage; and that, in general, loss to incorporeals was treated as loss of income, rather than loss of assets, all had to be borne in mind[1].

Chapter 4 pointed out that Atiyah's 'equivalent' compensation is likely to be appropriate for losses of assets, and therefore a calculational approach since, in principle, assets are on the market. However, various markets might be involved, and as cases like *Clyde Navigation Trustees v Bowring Steamship Co*[2] and *Owners of the Dredger Liesbosch v Owners of the Steamship Edison*[3] showed, there are considerable possible difficulties, and any calculational approach is in practice likely to require an element of 'reasonableness' in choice of form and its application. Nevertheless, the question remains as to what form or forms of calculational approach principles the courts have applied.

---

1 Damages for loss caused by breach of a Convention right under the Human Rights Act 1998 are subject to limits described in ch 3.
2 1929 SC 715, 1929 SLT 603.
3 [1933] AC 449.

There are broad statements of principle, for instance, in *Admiralty Commissioners v SS Susquehanna*[1]. This was an English House of Lords case but the leading opinion was given by Lord Dunedin, a former Lord President, and it was explicitly approved by the Inner House in *Clyde Navigation Trustees*. Unfortunately, however, it seems to amount to little more than saying that where calculation is possible it should be used, but that otherwise quantification is a jury matter. Indeed the cases generally, and comment on them, even when seeming to consider a calculational approach, sometimes muddy the waters. They may do so by subsuming the whole question into that of remoteness of damages by referring to 'all natural and probable consequences' or the like. They may also do so by referring to 'the value' of the item, or its 'actual', 'fair, 'real', 'reasonable' or 'true' estimates, losses or values, all of which are question-begging adjectives. Some may go further and refer to costs of repair, of reinstatement, and of substitution, and to depreciation and diminution of value, but also to the problems of enhancement of value and increase in value. There may also be reference to 'constructive total loss' and other complications.

Nevertheless, in fact, almost all examples can be reduced to just two forms of calculation: either the cost on the market of restoration of the asset, or the reduction in the market price of the asset[2]. These two forms do require unpacking. Firstly, in this context, 'restoration' includes both repair of damaged but reparable assets, and replacement or reinstatement of assets destroyed or damaged beyond repair. Secondly, substitution could be seen as a third form, but is best seen as either restoration by means of replacement (if final), or as actual consequential expenditure (if pending restoration by repair or replacement). Thirdly, both are net calculations, so restoration of moveable property is likely to mean, for instance, the cost of replacement minus the 'scrap value' of the replaced item. Fourthly, reduction in market price can be expected to assume willing buyer and willing seller. Fifthly, references to recovery of profits are best regarded as income loss. Sixthly, quantification almost invariably assumes the item in question is to be regarded as an economic asset, although there is no reason a claim for loss of assets should not also include *solatium*, as Lord President Emslie observed in *GUS Property Management Ltd v Littlewoods Mail Order Stores Ltd*[3] (discussed below).

TOTAL LOSS OF CORPOREAL PROPERTY

'Total loss' encompasses both physical destruction and permanent loss of control to another[4]. Difference of market values is the standard measure of

---

1 [1926] AC 655, [1926] All ER Rep 124.
2 See eg *GUS Property Management Ltd v Littlewoods Mail Order Ltd* 1982 SC (HL) 157 at 178, 1982 SLT 533, per Lord Keith of Kinkell. Cases and comment may further confuse by treating these two forms as identical. They may produce the same answer on occasion but manifestly do not always do so. In *GUS Property Management* itself, the pursuer averred that value of the property was reduced by £350,000, but it would only cost £100,000 to repair it. But this can operate both ways. A dent in a new car may cost £500 to repair, but would reduce its market value by £5,000. An identical dent in an old car might also cost £500 to repair, but have no effect on its market value.
3 1982 SC (HL) 157, 1982 SLT 533.
4 As by unrecovered theft or other permanent loss of title.

damages for total loss of both heritable and moveable property. Other measures may be used, but require special justification.

The principal authorities are *Hutchison v Davidson*[1] and *Pomphrey v James A Cuthbertson*[2]. In *Hutchison* an estate cottage burned to the ground through the defender's negligence. The sheriff-substitute awarded damages measured by the reinstatement cost, as the pursuer sought. On appeal, the sheriff substituted the difference between market values before and after the fire, and was upheld by the Inner House. Lord Russell, giving the leading judgment, observed that broad statements of principle were in fact of little help, though he considered *The Susquehanna*[3] accurately stated the position in Scots law, and cited *Liesbosch*. The principle he laid down was that:

'[i]n the case of total destruction of an article for which there is an available market in which a reasonably similar type as regards age, quantity and utility can be purchased (eg a motor vehicle or household furniture), the rule [that the measure is the difference between market value before and after the damage] would, in the ordinary case, provide the measure of ascertaining the sum required reasonably to make reparation to the injured party ... But not every case of damage will necessarily be met by that rule'[4].

The case concerned heritable property, but Lord Russell exemplified his opinion with moveable property. Also, the Inner House came to the same conclusion in *Pomphrey*, concerning a car which was a total loss (relying in part on *Hutchison*, and also *The Susquehanna* and *Liesbosch*). The pursuer sought the cost of replacement, including costs of modification required for business purposes, but minus scrap value. He asserted this replacement was cheaper than repair. The Inner House concluded the proper measure was neither replacement nor repair, but the market value of the car immediately before loss including the effect of modifications[5] minus scrap value. (It also included the cost of hiring a substitute, which is consequential expenditure.) That replacement was cheaper than repair was irrelevant. The principle of minimisation of loss did not mean the pursuer could choose his method of quantification and justify it by citing a more expensive one. Lord Justice-Clerk Thomson explicitly stated that '[m]arket value is recognised as the measure of damages in all cases of total loss."The worth of a thing is the price it will fetch".'[6]

The market value approach also seems sound doctrinally. It measures the *damnum* which exists whether or not the pursuer replaces. If he or she does not replace, does he or she suffer no loss? On the other hand, if assets are replaced, the claim is for replacement to the same condition, and not 'new for old'.

Both *Hutchison* and *Pomphrey* conceded that in certain circumstances, the market value approach might not apply. In *Hutchison*, Lord Russell mentioned cases where market values were not readily obtainable or otherwise not

---

1 1945 SC 395, 1946 SLT 11.
2 1951 SC 147, 1951 SLT 191.
3 [1926] AC 655.
4 1945 SC 395, at 407.
5 It was assumed the effect was to increase its value: see Lord Thompson at 1951 SC 147, at 153. However, in principle, it could reduce it.
6 1951 SC 147, at 153.

appropriate. There, citing Lord President Clyde in *Duke of Portland v Wood's Trustees*[1], he considered that a jury should be presented with several estimates based on different measures for comparison. On the facts of the case he considered that to make his case for reinstatement the pursuer required to aver and prove that the premises were 'a necessary and indispensable pertinent of [his] estate, viewed as a composite unit and conducted as a going concern'[2].

A clear example of a case where market value might be inappropriate arose with *Co-operative Wholesale Society Ltd v Motherwell District Council*[3]. Again, premises had been damaged by fire, but in this case the defender had immediately ordered demolition contractors to raze the entire premises, which the pursuer considered wholly unnecessary and without statutory authority. The Lord Ordinary (Davidson), following *Hutchison v Davidson*, held that it was open to the pursuers to argue for reinstatement cost, or some other unusual method of quantification in special circumstances. In the instant case, it was not clear that they were. If they were, he considered that the fact that there was no opportunity to discover the market value of the fire damaged premises before demolition might 'persuade the court that the general rule ... is not applicable' and further, the averments in relation to loss (save perhaps those relating to lost rents) could 'provide an adequate basis for reaching a reasonable estimate'[4].

Both market value and repair might also be inappropriate where the item in question is of essentially sentimental value[5].

Where one method of calculation is significantly cheaper than the other, it is a matter of speculation whether a court would prefer it on that ground, applying the principle of minimisation of loss, as may have been suggested in *GUS Property Management Ltd*, discussed below.

There are a number of cases concerning specialised examples of total loss to which statutory provisions may apply, such as subsidence through mining, now governed by the Coal Mining Subsidence Act 1991. Also, claims for total loss of corporeal property may involve claims for consequential expenditure, which may be difficult to distinguish from claims for destruction of the asset, as such[6].

LESSER DAMAGE TO CORPOREAL PROPERTY

'Lesser damage' encompasses both damage less than destruction and temporary or partial loss of control to another[7]. Both *Hutchison* and *Pomphrey*

1 1926 SC 640, 1926 SLT 417.
2 1945 SC 395, at 408–9.
3 1985 SLT 89.
4 Above, at 91.
5 In *GUS Property Management Ltd*, 1982 SC (HL) 157, at 172, Lord President Emslie quoted counsel as giving the example of a father wishing to give to a child a watch which is then damaged. Regardless of how the economic value of the watch is arrived at, sentimental 'heirloom' value might be claimed for as *solatium*.
6 Claims for loss of profit would seem incompetent provided total loss were measured by difference of market values, for those values would include any element of future profitability. However, they would seem competent if total loss were measured by replacement cost (if the asset were replaced) for the period from loss to replacement: cf *Clyde Navigation Trustees* and *Liesbosch*.
7 As by trespass or encroachment without damage.

concerned total loss, and in *Hutchison*, Lord Russell explicitly stipulated '[i]n the case of total destruction', and in *Pomphrey* Lord Justice-Clerk Thomson made a similar proviso[1]. Further, in *Pomphrey*, the opinions all turned on the assumption that the car was a 'constructive total loss', that is, that repair would cost more than replacement, and Lord Jamieson specifically stated that '[i]f the article can economically be repaired the measure of damages is the cost of the repairs'[2].

Nevertheless, the argument that the difference of market values is doctrinally more sound remains. If assets are merely damaged, does the pursuer suffer no *damnum* if he or she chooses not to repair? Also, the repair might improve the asset to a better condition than it was.

The point is interestingly raised in a more complicated way by *GUS Property Management Ltd*[3]. There, negligent building works damaged neighbouring heritable property. The damaged property was then, by coincidence, sold in an administrative arrangement to another subsidiary of the same holding company, at 'book value'[4], that is, without reference to market value. The seller then assigned its rights to the buyer. On the strength of this, the buyer sued in respect of the damage. At first instance, it was argued, inter alia, that the seller and assignor could not sue because it could not show it had lost anything as it had not sold at a reduced price, and the buyer and assignee could not sue either, as it could not sue for anything the seller could not. The Lord Ordinary's interlocutor on proof before answer was appealed to the Inner House, and again to the House of Lords.

Giving the opinion of the House Lord Keith of Kinkell said

'Where the property is disposed of in an arm's length transaction for the price it is fairly worth in its damaged condition, the difference between that price and the price it would have fetched in an undamaged condition is likely to be the best measure of the loss and damage suffered'[5].

This is clearly a special example of the difference of market values approach. He continued

'[b]ut it may happen that the owner of the property disposes of it otherwise than by such a transaction. He may, for instance, alienate it gratuitously ... It is absurd to suggest that in such circumstances the claim to damages would disappear, as the Lord Ordinary put it, into some legal black hole ... There would be no agreed market price available ... so some other means of measuring it would have to be applied, such as the estimate of depreciation in value or of the cost of repair'.

The 'book value' price was irrelevant.

1 1951 AC 147, at 153.
2 Above, at 161.
3 1982 (SC) HL 157. Another interesting case is *Bristol & West of England Building Society v Rollo Steven & Bond* 1998 SLT 9, where solicitors advised a building society to lend on premises which they negligently did not inform had a sitting tenant. Allowing proof before answer, Lord MacLean held the loss, when the premises were sold following the buyer's default, was the difference between the sum advanced and the net sum received (ie sale price minus both rent received from the tenant and transactional costs). It was not the difference between the sum lent and the value of the premises at the time of lending. However, he also held that the pursuers could claim the loss of profit which they would otherwise have made on the money lent.
4 Possibly 'Historic cost': see ch 4.
5 1982 SC (HL) 157, at 177.

Lord Keith also said that '[i]t may well be that at the end of the day, the proper measure of [the seller and assignor's] loss will turn out to be the estimated cost of making good the damage to the building, rather than the diminution in its market value. It may also be that there will not be found to be any substantial difference between the two measures'[1]. This reflects the fact that the pursuer averred that the damage had reduced the value of the property by £350,000, but that it would only cost £100,000 to repair. There is thus at least a suggestion that where there is a substantial difference, the cheaper will be preferred, on the principle of minimisation of loss, even if it is not the difference of market values.

As with total loss, it is possible that a claim based on sentimental value might be made. As also noted in relation to total loss, some examples may be covered by statute, such as the Coal Mining Subsidence Act 1991. Also, a claim for lesser damage may be accompanied by claims for consequential property loss (as where an asset, temporarily wrongfully possessed, is damaged[2]) and for consequential expenditure, which may be difficult to distinguish[3].

INCORPOREAL PROPERTY

Incorporeal property is physically indestructible and undamageable, so cannot literally be destroyed or damaged. It can be rendered worthless, or worth less, by infringement. Thus, a claim for diminution of market value appears perfectly competent[4].

However, in practice, claims in respect of incorporeal property have concerned infringement as such, that is, in effect loss of income (as discussed below). Also, as noted elsewhere, while '[i]nfringement of a moral right [in copyright] is to be treated as a breach of duty[5] . . .[i]t is not wholly clear what this means . . .'[6]. Such cases are perhaps claims for *solatium*[7].

PATRIMONIAL LOSSES—II: CONSEQUENTIAL EXPENDITURE

ACTUAL CONSEQUENTIAL EXPENDITURE AND APPROACHES TO QUANTIFICATION

The compensation which consequential expenditure attracts is clearly of Atiyah's 'equivalent' type. In principle, any approach to quantification could apply, but (as noted in ch 3) a tariff would be difficult to operate, given the

---

1 1982 SC (HL) 157, at 178–9.
2 Permanent dispossession would render a claim for damage otiose.
3 A claim for loss of profit would seem competent where the asset was repaired and could not produce profit during repair, but not otherwise.
4 See *Gerber Garment Technology Inc v Lectra Systems Ltd* [1977] RPC 443, at 456–457, 478 and 481. In *Sutherland Publishing Co Ltd v Caxton Publishing Co Ltd* [1936] 1 Ch 323, at 336, Lord Wright MR said that in such cases 'the measure of damages is the depreciation caused by the infringement to the value of the copyright as a chose in action' (ie as incorporeal moveable property). Damages did not fall to be awarded in that case, however.
5 Copyright, Designs and Patents Act 1988, s 103(1).
6 18 *Stair Memorial Encyclopaedia* para 1144.
7 Note also 'additional damages' under CDPA 1988, ss 97(2) and 229(3), discussed below in relation to loss of profit.

manifold varieties of claim, and a calculational approach is more obviously appropriate[1]. Deductions for compensation from other sources may fall to be made from a calculation, by virtue of the Administration of Justice Act 1982, ss 10 and 11, or recovered through the Social Security (Recovery of Benefits) Act 1997 (dealt with in ch 6).

Past consequential expenditure

A straightforward calculational approach appears in principle simple. Where goods or services have been purchased, their price on the market will be known or capable of estimation. In *Gordon v Wilson*[2], Lord Penrose (albeit obiter) required claims for such expenditure to be founded on actual costs[3]. Such claims have become more common, and have often been argued with great specificity. For instance, in *Tuttle v Edinburgh University*[4] Lord McDonald explicitly adopted the lengthy and detailed list of 'appliances, aids and equipment' acquired, including the prices indicated, in an expert report[5].

There may be minor questions of rounding sums up or down. Beyond that, however, choices may have to be made between the different calculations offered by the parties. Thus, unless such consequential expenditure is agreed, this approach inevitably merges into the jury approach, and at the other end of the spectrum from mere rounding up or down, a judge may (as a jury may), simply decide on a reasonable (albeit informed) figure. Thus Lord Grieve in *Gardner v Howard Doris*[6] (after seeing a report on the pursuer's needs[7]), simply 'consider[ed] a capital sum of £6,000 should be awarded' for costs incurred in buying and running a vehicle.

'Reasonableness' is explicitly invoked by the Damages (Scotland) Act 1976, s 1(3), which limits funeral costs to 'any reasonable expense'. The few reported cases chiefly concern whether a headstone is a funeral expense at all, but in the Inner House in *Prentice v Chalmers*[8], Lord Hunter observed that it was not argued that the cost of the headstone 'was unreasonable in amount having regard to the station in life of the deceased and his family'. 'Reasonableness' is a variable quality.

1 Damages for loss caused by breach of a Convention right under the Human Rights Act 1998 are subject to limits described in ch 3.
2 1992 SLT 849, at 855K-856H.
3 1992 SLT 849, at 856A, in relation to extra travel costs, having demonstrated considerable weakness in the evidence of an expert witness, he observed that '[i]t is far from clear that expert evidence is either necessary or appropriate on a topic which might readily have been dealt with on precognition of the pursuer. But if it is tendered, it is important that it reflects the result of research into actual costs . . .'. There were similar criticisms of telephone, heating equipment and holiday costs.
4 1984 SLT 172, at 174.
5 See 7 below note.
6 1983 SLT 672, at 674.
7 As noted in ch 2, this report was, it seems, the first produced by the Spinal Injuries Association which was admitted in evidence (see 1983 SLT 672 at 673). It was spoken to by a named individual, who was mildly criticised for including 'items [which] ought to be regarded as luxuries, for example the electric buggy'. He was also criticised in *Tuttle v Edinburgh University* 1984 SLT 172, at 173–174, as to his costings, but was seriously criticised in *McMillan v McDowall*, 1993 SLT 311 at 314IH–315A for inaccuracy and exaggeration. It is interesting to note, however, that such an electric buggy was not necessarily regarded as a luxury by the time of *McMillan v McDowall*. See also the use of the National Foster Care Association report on the costs of bringing up a child in *McLelland v Greater Glasgow Health Board* 1999 SLT 543, at 553C–D.
8 1984 SLT 168 at 171.

Future consequential expenditure

Difficulties chiefly arise in relation to future losses in serious personal injury cases. Lord President Hope observed in *O'Brien's CB*[1], that it is only comparatively recently that future care, now a major item in many such cases, has emerged as a distinct claim and 'there has been little opportunity for analysis of how [such claims] should be approached'[2].

In respect of the specific circumstances of the future maintenance costs of a child, in *McLelland v Greater Glasgow Health Board*[3], Lord MacFadyen rejected the argument that they were not payable because the parents would have had another child had the handicapped one been aborted, and accepted the argument that the costs would be for life, not merely for the duration of the obligation to aliment, or until majority. However, he deducted sums on the ground that there would be state provision, distinguishing the operation of the Administration of Justice Act 1982, s 10(c) on the ground that future additional care costs consequent upon the handicap were not 'damages payable to the injured person in respect of personal injuries' (the child's handicap being congenital and the pursuers being his parents)[4].

Calculations and the jury approach

In the case of purchase of items of property (especially moveable), and services, straightforward estimates can be used. In *Geddes v Lothian Health Board*[5] and *McMillan v McDowall*[6], specific items were individually listed and costed (though in the latter, evidence of the costs was 'somewhat vague').

However, as with past consequential expenditure, the judge (or jury) has a discretion, necessarily introducing 'reasonableness'. This is especially obvious in older cases concerning estimates for costs such as future care over lengthy periods. Thus in *Hosie v Arbroath Football Club*[7] Lord Stewart, in some difficulty in relation to costs of future physiotherapy and nursing, explicitly rejected the annuity method on the ground that '[a]warding damages is far from being an exact science and logic certainly cannot be pushed too far'. He plumped for the informed, but round, figure of £8,000. This reasoning was followed in *Gardner v Howard Doris* and *Tuttle*.

'Reasonableness' may be appropriate in relatively small claims; may allow rounding sums up or down; may involve choosing between alternative calculations; and may disallow unproved claims. However, such broad uses of the 'reasonable sum' approach for lengthy future costs are now disapproved. Lord President Hope in *O'Brien's CB*[8] laid down the principle that,

1 1991 SLT 477, at 482J.
2 At 480D, he observed, particularly in relation to multipliers, but also more generally, that 'I have the clear impression from the Scottish cases to which we have been referred, that the principles which should be applied have not always been appreciated'.
3 1999 SLT 543, particularly 550D–F, 554L–555J and 557B.
4 It is not clear why there was no discussion of the Social Security (Recovery of Benefits) Act 1997 (for which, see Ch 6, which also discusses s 10(c) of the Administration of Justice Act 1982).
5 1992 SLT 986, at 987I–J, 1992 SCLR 216.
6 1993 SLT 311, at 315B–D.
7 1978 SLT 122, particularly at 128.
8 1991 SLT 477, particularly 480D, 480F, 482J and 480H.

in general, future patrimonial losses should be quantified by means of an annuity approach. In relation to future expenditure generally, he declared 'I have the clear impression from the Scottish cases to which we were referred that the principles which should be applied have not always been appreciated', and that '[t]he purpose of an award of damages for future expenditure is to place the pursuer as near as may be in the same financial position as he would have been in if the accident had not occurred'. He went on to explain and approve the annuity approach, and to note a 'trend towards greater accuracy in the assessment of the annual cost and towards the use of a multiplier', conceding only that '[t]here may be cases where, because the period is so short or the circumstances so uncertain, this method is inappropriate and it is better to make a broad estimate of the damages in the form of a lump sum'. The annuity calculation Lord Hope preferred was the traditional form, the actuarial (in the form of the 'Ogden Tables') being used as a check. As noted in ch 4, since *O'Brien's CB*, there has tended to be greater reliance on the actuarial form.

Interesting examples of the interaction of calculation and reasonableness arose with some 'wrongful conception' and 'wrongful birth' cases, straddling the date of *O'Brien's CB*. In *Allan v Greater Glasgow Health Board*[1], Lord Cameron of Lochbroom expressly referred to 'reasonableness' and suggested obiter that he would allow capital costs associated with birth, such as a pram, but not private school fees or provision for a wedding[2], nor for the time and trouble in bringing up a healthy child. (He left open whether public policy would admit a claim for the cost of an abortion.) In *McFarlane v Tayside Health Board*[3] Lord Gill would operate a more exiguous reasonableness test, but was overturned on the issue of relevancy. The Inner House (which did not refer to *Allan*) would accept child-rearing costs generally. It did not look specifically at what costs would be involved, simply invoking *restitutio in integrum*, but expressly excluded arguments that the benefits of having a child outweighed the detriments whether wholly or in part only, and that public policy disallowed such claims[4]. However, the House of Lords decided that the costs of rearing a healthy child could not be admitted. The majority did so on the ground that it was 'pure economic loss': the minority on the ground that it was either unreasonable, or that the benefits of a healthy child outweighed the detriments[5]. In *McLelland v Greater Glasgow Health Board* Lord Macfadyen accepted the capital costs of birth and expenses of extra maintenance applying, a three-fold test of (i) whether the expenditure has been incurred or is likely to be incurred, (ii) whether incurring it was foreseeable, and (iii) whether it is reasonable[6].

Calculations and annuities

Having deprecated loosely reasoned 'reasonable sum' approaches, in *O'Brien's CB*, Lord President Hope noted that 'it will normally be appropriate

1 1998 SLT 580, at 583C–D and 585B.
2 References to the English cases *Benarr v Kettering Health Authority* (1988) NLJ 179 and *Allen v Bloomsbury Health Authority* [1993] 1 All ER 651, respectively.
3 1997 SLT 211.
4 See Lord Justice-Clerk Cullen, at 311K–L, Lord McCluskey at 317F, and Lord Allanbridge at 318G–H.
5 (1999), Times, 26 November, HL; see also *Anderson v Forth Valley Health Board* 1998 SLT 588, 1998 SCLR 632.
6 1999 SLT 543 at 550F–G.

to resort to the use of a multiplier in all cases where . . . costs [will be] incurred over a future period of years'[1].

Calculation by the annuity method, both traditional and actuarial, is again straightforward in principle, and is described at length in ch 4. Annual consequential expenditure is multiplied by the multiplier deemed appropriate to cover the relevant number of years[2] to recovery, retirement, or to death or 'notional date of death', where it is likely to be premature. (Section 9(2)(c) of the Damages (Scotland) Act 1976, read with s 9(1), requires a court to reduce damages by a sum representing the living expenses not expended where death is likely to be premature[3].) Chapter 4 also noted the practical difficulties and limitations of the traditional and actuarial versions of the annuity approach.

Several reported cases, which should be read in the light of the criticisms, well exemplify the annuity approach applied to actual consequential expenditure. These include *McMillan v McDowall*[4]. As noted elsewhere Temporary Judge Coutts criticised the method of assessing future costs in the expert report which used a projection of future costs on an annual basis[5], disapproved in *Tuttle v Edinburgh University* and elsewhere. So far as specific items were concerned, a multiplicand of £1,560.80 was claimed for continuing outlays in relation to the specific items, with a suitable multiplier. The defender argued simply that the sum of £5,000 would be adequate to cover all future needs for out-of-pocket expenses (a jury approach). The judge decided that an annual outlay of £750 was adequate as a multiplicand for continuing costs. For the multiplier, he chose the figure of 18, as suggested by the pursuer (giving a total of £13,500)[6]. It is not clear why these multipliers were appropriate. Expert evidence, based on the Ogden Tables, was led in respect of other future losses (as discussed below), and it is likely that this influenced the figure as well as the precedents (or tariff) for multipliers in cases with pursuers with similar characteristics. The judge noted that he was departing somewhat from the approach of Lord Macdonald in *Tuttle*.

In addition to these specific items and maintenance costs, there was a claim for future expenses of holidays, which would require an accompanying relative, for which an annual sum of £400 was sought[7], and this was in principle accepted. However, the judge noted that the pursuer's ability to go on holiday would become restricted by being in residential care[8]. Rather than reducing the £400 per annum he considered this a matter of reducing the

---

1 1991 SLT 477, at 483C.
2 For some examples, see Bennett *Personal Injury Damages in Scotland* (1999) App V(C)3.
3 This would be a difficult feat for a jury. Strictly speaking, s 9(2)(b) of the Damages (Scotland) Act 1976 allows a court to use the 'notional date of death' rather than the expected date of death to calculate damages for consequential expenditure, including nursing care. However, this would be manifestly absurd.
4 1993 SLT 311, which also included claims for notional consequential expenditure.
5 Above, at 314L.
6 Above, 315D–F.
7 Above, at 318B.
8 The position that he would still need holidays, but that they would become more expensive, was not taken.

multiplier[1]. The figure of 18 was suggested by the pursuer, but in the light of the reducing possibilities of holidays, one of 13 (explicitly, and perhaps surprisingly, observed to be the same as for wage loss) was allowed.

Also noteworthy is *Stevenson v Sweeney*[2], where different levels of care for different future periods were assessed as requiring different multiplicands.

In brief, multiplicands for future consequential expenditure are produced in essentially the same way as for such past expenditure. However, while the difficulties of evidence and arithmetic, and other contingent and changing losses, noted in ch 4, are considered in the cases, those of inflation and the effects of real rises in wages are not.

By the same token, multipliers have been produced by precedent (in effect, a tariff), but are increasingly relying on the Ogden Tables, to which extent, they are necessarily taking account of real rates of return on investment and inflation, previously ignored, while continuing to provide individuation (although this still relies heavily on judges' 'experience'[3]).

Calculations and the tariff approach

Thus, the use of the annuity approach relies traditionally on tariffs to supply multipliers, as argued in ch 4.

Calculations and modified annuities: 'annualised cost'

This has been used in respect of specific non-continuing items where award of a simple capital sum would have the effect of creating a windfall for others, such as family and inheriting descendants. By agreement, it was applied in *McMillan v McDowall*[4], following the English Court of Appeal decision in *Roberts v Johnson*[5]. Both cases show the unavoidable overlap with a jury approach.

In *Roberts*, the item was a house requiring conversion. At first instance, the judge awarded a sum representing consequential expenditure on accommodation, which could be regarded as the cost of interest foregone on capital spent on the new house, or as extra mortgage payments. It was arrived at by subtracting from the total cost of house (net £68,800) and conversion (£32,284) some £10,000 representing its increased value; a further 10 per cent because the house was in a more desirable area; and then arbitrarily taking one-third of the resultant amount as representing 'the increased charges element'.

However, the Court of Appeal considered this was the wrong approach, and authority required another. It concluded[6] that the answer lay in the observation of Lord Diplock in *Wright v British Railways Board*[7], that low-risk non-inflation-proofed investments produced a real rate of return of 2 per cent. Admittedly, this concerned non-economic loss, but could apply equally to economic loss, like the notional cost of mortgage interest, as well at least

---

1 1993 SLT 311, at 318C.
2 1995 SLT 29.
3 A concept criticised in ch 4.
4 1993 SLT 311, at 317G–318A.
5 [1989] QB 878, [1988] 3 WLR 1247.
6 Above, at 892B–893H.
7 [1983] AC 773 at 783–784, [1983] 3 WLR 211, [1982] 2 All ER 698.

where it concerned residential property in a desirable area where property values could be assumed to be rising[1]. Thus the extra accommodation cost was 2 per cent of the £68,000 net price, that is, £1,370, and this should be the multiplicand. The same multiplier as was fixed by the trial judge should be applied to it[2]. The sum thus arrived at was £21,920. To this, however, should be added the net conversion cost of £28,284 (that is the conversion cost of £38,284 less £10,000 consequential added value of the house), giving a final total of £50,204. The Court of Appeal admitted this to be a complicated calculation, though no worse than in *George v Pinnock*[3], on which the trial judge had purported to rely.

In *McMillan* itself, the item was a bungalow built for the paraplegic pursuer. There was dispute about the cost of the bungalow, which the judge decided should not, in any case, be reduced to reflect the features necessary for a paraplegic which another ultimate purchaser would not want. However, it was agreed, following *Roberts*, that the multiplicand should be 2% of the cost. Pursuer and defender argued for multipliers of 18 and 11 respectively, but the judge fixed it at 15, taking into account that the money had not yet been expended and had the pursuer continued in employment, he would have had to quit his tied cottage at the age of 65.

'NOTIONAL' CONSEQUENTIAL EXPENDITURE IN GENERAL

'Notional' consequential expenditure includes those sums payable under ss 8 and 9 of the Administration of Justice Act 1982 for 'necessary' and 'personal' services. Their nature was described in ch 2. Section 10 of this Act may require deductions in respect of compensation received from other sources, and the Social Security (Recovery of Benefits) Act 1997 may require recovery of some social security benefits. This is dealt with in ch 6.

Section 8: 'necessary services'

The claim is for 'reasonable remuneration for those services' and 'reasonable expenses incurred in connection therewith'.

'Reasonable remuneration and . . . reasonable expenses'

There has been criticism of failure to specify the services adequately, for example, in terms of the nature, duration per day, and length of period.

---

1 Their Lordships were further reinforced by the *ad hoc* observation that the house was purchased out of interim payments. Thus (at [1989] QB 878, 893H), the return on the sum representing net price of the house which would have been obtained had it not been spent on the house should be compared with the 'tax-free yield of 2% in risk-free investment' in fact obtained.
2 The Court of Appeal also observed, at [1989] QB 878, 893B–E, that no reduction should have been made to the net house price for its greater attractiveness, and more attractive surroundings, if it had already been decided that the choice of house was reasonable. However, despite his reference to 'what was called during the hearing the Rolls Royce element', the trial judge's 10% reduction was in fact for the enhancement of the value of the house by reason of the conversion, and his reference to 'betterment' should be understood in that sense. This was acceptable.
3 [1973] 1 WLR 118.

Examples include Lord Osborne in *Galbraith's Curator ad Litem v Stewart*[1], and Lord Clyde in *Forsyth's CB v Govan Shipbuilders*[2].

'Reasonable remuneration' raises difficulties of interpretation in any case. The Scottish Law Commission, though using the word 'remuneration' in its recommendation, referred to 'compensation' in the text, directly examining its nature only briefly[3] (though rejecting allowing the service provider to sue for lost income as inappropriate). Moreover, many of the services are difficult to quantify, traditionally undervalued on the market and arguably cannot be provided for by the market as they depend on love and affection. Thus there is little clue in the legislation as to the basis for quantifying 'reasonable remuneration', and there has been no guidance from the Inner House.

In contrast, 'reasonable expenses in connection therewith' has seemed to cause little difficulty in practice.

Quantification of past remuneration

The tariff approach

It would be possible, given the lack of clarity, for such claims to be regarded as attracting a conventional sum, in effect, creating a tariff, but this has not occurred[4].

The jury approach

The jury approach was suggested (usually obiter) in a number of cases, from *Denheen v British Railways Board (No 2)*[5] onwards[6]. Thus there is a line of Outer House authority for such a rough and ready approach, albeit justified by reference to the nature of the claim, as by Lord Cameron of Lochbroom in *Mitchell v Inverclyde District Council*[7]. He observed that '[i]n the assessment of services rendered by relatives, it is, I consider, to be borne in mind that there are natural ties which should not convert the assessment of any award into a purely commercial transaction'. However, in the light of criticisms of unspecific claims, it would be inadvisable to rely on this, and fail to provide in the pleadings detailed information on the type, frequency, duration and possible cost of such services, even if they are ignored at the end of the day.

---

1 1997 SLT 418 at 424G–I.
2 1988 SC 421 at 427, 1988 SLT 321, 1989 SCLR 78.
3 *Damages for Personal Injuries: Report on (1) Admissibility of Claims for Services, (2) Admissible Deductions* (HC Paper 557 (1977–78)) paras 8–33, especially 26 and 33.
4 See, however, Bennett *Personal Injury Damages in Scotland* (1999) App V(E).
5 1988 SLT 320. Lord Coulsfield would have awarded £3,000 for several years housekeeping. The pursuer's preferred calculational approach would have produced perhaps ten times that sum.
6 Eg *Fowler v Greater Glasgow Health Board* 1990 SLT 303: £5,000 for complete nursing care for ten months for a comatose baby 'at great personal sacrifice'; *Johnstone v Hardie* 1990 SLT 744: £3,000 for housework, in part falling under the Administration of Justice Act 1982, s 9, for some years; and *Kennedy v Lees of Scotland* 1997 SLT 510, 1996 SCLR 978: approximately £2,000 including interest (ie one third of £5,898) for help in dressing and bathing, and housework for five years.
7 1998 SLT 1157 at 1160F–I, 1998 SCLR 191.

The market approach in general

Consequential expenditure thus lends itself to a calculational approach, modified, as always, by an admixture of 'reasonableness'.

Despite particular difficulties in quantification, s 8 can be seen as an extension of the existing common law right to sue for the cost of nursing services. This might indicate the market for such services as the source of the appropriate calculation, but as shown below, other markets for the carer's services offer an alternative. *Gordon v Wilson*[1] provides an extensive discussion of the issues, albeit obiter.

The calculational or market approach II: 'professional rates'

If s 8 is seen as an extension of claims for nursing services and the like, the 'professional rate' for the job is an obvious means of calculation, though there must be a choice as to the appropriate rate, and that rate may require modifying.

In *Gordon v Wilson*[2], so far as s 8 was concerned, discussion centred upon five matters. Firstly, a claim for s 8 damages had been made for a period when the pursuer was in hospital, and Lord Penrose decided it should not be paid for this period[3]. Secondly, although some of the s 8 services would normally be given by a nurse, the carer had no relevant qualifications, so comparison should be made with professional home help rates. Thirdly, in any case, professional rates were to be discounted as including an agency fee and tax and national insurance. Fourthly, the fact that the services were being provided in the carer's own home reduced the figure by a further 25 per cent[4]. (This is important as it will commonly be the case.) Fifthly, however, the additional stress of caring for a loved one wiped out this deduction. (This is also important as it will almost inevitably be the case). However, the defender was assoilized, so all such discussion was obiter.

Similar issues arose in *McMillan v McDowall*[5], but Temporary Judge Coutts was not wholly at one with Lord Penrose, and said, 'I do not consider that the use of the word remuneration means that the provider has to be paid as if she were an independent employee; indeed there is something repugnant about the idea of a caring relative being awarded an hourly rate'[6]. Thus, such rates were only 'material against which the court can check its impression', and in any case, precise recording of time spent was not possible. Despite this inclination towards a 'reasonable sum'[7], his actual award relies heavily upon

1 1992 SLT 849.

2 Above, particularly at 855D, 855E–G, 855H and 855I.

3 It is not clear whether this was because, on the facts, he concluded no such services were in fact rendered, or whether he considered that hospitalisation precluded any s 8 claim (past medical and nursing services having, seemingly, been claimed separately). The former would seem better in accordance with the Act, but he refused a modified claim for £100 for additional visiting by relatives, saying, in 1992 SLT 849, at 855D, 'I consider it to be clear that the claim must be reduced to exclude the eight weeks of services [while the pursuer was in hospital], but that there is no basis for substitution'.

4 In *McMillan v McDowall* 1993 SLT 311, discussed below, Temporary Judge Coutts said at 315K that Lord Penrose 'declined to make any further deduction to reflect the fact that services were provided in the home'.

5 1993 SLT 311.

6 Above, at 315L.

7 Above, at 316F–H.

such calculations, albeit subject to different modifications from those Lord Penrose used.

The difficulty in recording time was also referred to in *Stevenson v Sweeney*[1], and *Kennedy v Lees of Scotland*[2], where Lord Morton of Shuna and Lord Gill drew attention to the difference between 24-hour care and occasional care that might be required at any time in the 24, and the difficulty of assessing short periods of time of different and unpredictable length and frequency. Again, despite toying with a jury approach, both finally awarded calculation-based sums.

The market approach III: 'opportunity cost'

If s 8 is seen as compensating the carer for giving up time, however, another market on which calculations can be based is what the carer could command in the market for the skills he or she is not deploying while acting as carer, to do what is traditionally low paid work, and which may require love and affection not available on the market. The relevance of this is obvious if the carer is highly skilled in another area, and is giving up a well-paid and satisfying career to look after a relative.

This 'opportunity cost' view was approved in the English High Court in *Mehmet v Perry*[3] in a case under the Fatal Accidents Acts[4], but disapproved by the English Court of Appeal in *Roberts v Johnstone*[5].

Occasionally, Lords Ordinary have referred to it. In *Forsyth's CB*, the wife of the incapax was compelled to give up her part-time job, worth £40 per week, to look after him. The Lord Ordinary (Clyde) noted the language of the Scottish Law Commission report, and remarked[6] that '[i]f one was [sic] to envisage a negotiation between the injured person and the relative to agree reasonable remuneration for the services required to be performed by the latter for the former it seems reasonable to suppose that in such a discussion notice would be taken of the level of wages which the relative would require to surrender in order to perform the services in question'. *Howie v Upper Clyde Shipbuilders Ltd*[7] presented similar facts and a concordant opinion from Lord Cameron of Lochbroom.

On the other hand, there are inherent difficulties. It may be unfair to a defender who ends up paying the salary of, say, a professor of biochemistry who has chosen to give up that career to provide services available professionally at a fraction of that rate, and hardly constitutes the pursuer minimising his or her loss. (Moreover such a carer would commonly provide

---

1 1995 SLT 29.
2 1997 SLT 510.
3 [1977] 2 All ER 529.
4 The couple had five children. The youngest two suffered a blood disorder requiring considerable medical and nursing attention, and considerable emotional security and support, which the wife and mother, who was devoted to them, provided. She was killed in a car crash. The husband gave up work to care for the family, and sued, inter alia, for the loss of his wife's housekeeping services, at the rate of wages he had to forgo. It was found by Deputy Judge Brian Neill QC, at [1977] 2 All ER 529, 535f–j, to be reasonable on his part to give up his job and, at 536f–g, (relying on dicta in the Court of Appeal in *George v Pinnock* [1973] 1 All ER 926, and *Donnelly v Joyce* [1973] 3 WLR 514, [1973] 3 All ER 475), that the means of calculating the relevant expenses should be the 'opportunity cost' method.
5 [1989] QB 878 at 888C–E.
6 1998 SLT 321, at 326L–327A.
7 1991 SLT 2, 1990 SCLR 381.

a lower standard than the cheaper professional.) It may also be unfair to the unemployed carer who would presumably get nothing. Thus, combined with English Court of Appeal disapproval, these difficulties seem to make the 'opportunity cost' approach unattractive.

Quantification of future remuneration[1]

In principle, any of the methods of quantifying remuneration for past services might be used, *mutatis mutandis*, for future services. Precedents are few.

Tariff and jury approaches

These approaches, as such, clearly have even less application than in relation to past remuneration but are sometimes used[2], and still operate to provide a basis for multipliers, and to modify or choose between competing multiplicands and multipliers.

The market approach

How the multiplicand is to be calculated has been little touched on, although the problems are essentially the same as for calculation of past notional consequential expenditure. *McMillan v McDowall* is one of the few examples. Temporary Judge Coutts used an explicitly calculational approach (as he did with actual consequential expenditure). He relied on professional rates and included considerable detail, for example, determining the multiplicand included the housekeeper's costs of £50 per week plus the carer's living expenses plus some weekend relief, totalling £7,883, but also allowing for increasing professional help as the pursuer's mother would be less able to assist etc. Some of the calculation is unclear, and the conclusion relies on a mixture of pursuer's and defender's figures thus evidencing elements of a 'jury approach'[3]. He had some difficulty in relation to deductions for state benefits[4], and regarded it as a matter for the multiplier.

Stevenson v Sweeney[5] is another, and turned largely upon the factual issue of the number of hours of care provided. No explicit attempt was made in Lord Morton of Shuna's calculation to distinguish between care to be provided by the pursuer's mother in the short term, and that to be provided professionally in the long term, but a modified professional rate was implicitly accepted for the former[6], and another for the latter[7]. The sum arrived at may be a

1 Until amendment by the Law Reform (Miscellaneous Provisions) (Scotland) Act 1990, s 69, the Administration of Justice Act 1982 appeared to limit s 8 damages to past losses. In *McMillan v McDowall* 1993 SLT 311 at 316L, the pursuer surmounted this difficulty by entering into a contract with his mother for the relevant services, putting them in the realm of actual consequential expenditure.
2 As in *Mitchell v Inverclyde District Council*, 1998 SLT 1157, at 1160I.
3 See 1993 SLT 311, at 316L–317F.
4 See ch 6.
5 1995 SLT 29.
6 The precise figure awarded is difficult to explain. Lord Morton seems to have accepted £4.10 per hour for six hours a day, less four weeks at £210 per week, which produces £8,625, but at 33C, he actually awarded £9,195. Also, the respite care thus appears to be costed at about £3.75 an hour.
7 1995 SLT 29, at 33F, he awarded £18,500, reflecting a higher, but unspecified cost of a carer and an unspecified number of hours per day.

compromise between pursuer's and defender's estimates, and thus also evidences elements of a jury approach. He did declare that it was inappropriate to make such awards net of tax (distinguishing *Gordon v Wilson* where they were so provided at the pursuer's request), and assumed that not only would income tax be payable by the pursuer as employer on the periodic payments to third parties but also on those to his mother[1].

There has been somewhat more discussion on multipliers. Indeed, it was in *O'Brien's CB*[2] that Lord President Hope laid down the principle that in future patrimonial claims generally a calculational approach was normally to be preferred over a jury approach (as described in ch 4). On *O'Brien's CB* itself, Lord President Hope criticised the Lord Ordinary's choice of 11[3]. No reasoning had produced the figure, though it seemed to take into account both whether the pursuer would remain likely to benefit from the services and whether the carer would remain able to provide them. The multiplier was raised to 15 on the ground that it should be the same as for a claim for future care not provided by relatives (that is, actual consequential expenditure), although the point was not rigorously argued[4].

Subsequent cases, as noted in ch 4, have tended to rely more heavily upon the Ogden Tables, although the calculations have not always been simple and straightforward. Thus in *McMillan v McDowall* Temporary Judge Coutts performed a number of arithmetic procedures on figures taken from the Ogden Tables and elsewhere to produce an historically high multiplier. In brief, for a paraplegic aged 18, two periods were to be catered for, that is, to the age of 45 (when he would become more dependent), and thereafter. A multiplier of up to 20 for whole life seems to have been arrived at on the basis of actuarial evidence, including the Ogden Tables, with a reduction of 10 per cent for the vicissitudes of life in the later period. A multiplier of 14.5 for the first period, similarly arrived at, was adopted, and subtracted from the multiplier for whole life to give a multiplier 'in the order of 3' for the second period, which was said to give an overall multiplier of 17.5[5].

Rather similar difficulties arose in *Stevenson v Sweeney*, and there was also argument as to the appropriate rate of interest, and on risks other than mortality, including marriage. Lord Morton of Shuna seems to have used the Ogden Tables as his sole source of information in producing the very high multiplier of 20.

Thus, it may be that the difficulties of multiplicands and multipliers outlined in ch 4 are more closely examined in such cases.

Quantification of reasonable expenses

There are few cases on 'reasonable expenses' under s 8. *McMillan v McDowall*[6] is one, but even there, the matter arose in part indirectly. What had appeared

---

1 1995 SLT 29 at 33B.
2 1991 SLT 477.
3 Above, at 487L–488C.
4 For some multipliers for future necessary services, see Bennett *Personal Injury Damages in Scotland* (1999) App V(C)4.
5 1993 SLT 311 at 316J–K, 317B–C and 317D–F. In fact, the sum of the multiplicands was not multiplied by 17.5, but that for the first period by 14.5 and that for the second by 3, the two products being then added together.
6 1993 SLT 311.

in the pleadings as past consequential expenditure by the pursuer emerged as services performed on his behalf by his parents. The Administration of Justice Act 1982 was mentioned only in passing, and the character of certain items as 'reasonable expenses' (costs of visits by relatives, of alterations to a house, and of two buggies) was not expressly mentioned at all. They were, however, clearly implicitly treated as 'reasonable expenses' for the 'necessary services' of visiting etc.

Temporary Judge Coutts allowed the sum conceded by the defender for costs of visits, despite the reduction from the pursuer's claim (which was 'not fully established') being 'somewhat arbitrary'. It is not clear what evidence was produced, but there was a question as to whether some of it might relate to family members who were not 'relatives' within the meaning of the Act. The costs of the house alterations were agreed. The costs of the two buggies were accepted at the pursuer's figure, that for the first having taken into account a discount, and that for the second having taken into account a trade in[1].

Future consequential expenditure also arose in that case, and was dealt with by 'annualised cost', as discussed above. It is likely that future s 8 reasonable expenditure would have been dealt with similarly, but the matter has not been decided.

Accounting to the service provider

The pursuer recovers the remuneration and expenses for the person who actually provides the service so must, by virtue of s 8(2), 'account to the relative [providing the service] for any damages recovered from the [defender] under this section'. Lord Hamilton in *Blackhall v MacInnes*[2], and Lord Gill in *Kennedy v Lees of Scotland*[3], both considered this meant the court must apportion such damages between relatives where more than one had rendered them. However, this does not seem generally to have been done, and in *Kennedy* the parties were agreed that no such apportionment was required.

Section 9 'personal services'

Section 9 entitles the injured person to claim a 'reasonable sum' for the defined 'personal services'.

'Reasonable sum'

Neither the Scottish Law Commission Report[4], nor the legislation, gives any real indication as to how the courts should interpret the phrase. There are comparisons to be made with claims for actual consequential expenditure, and s 8 notional consequential expenditure, but there are significant differences. In particular, the word 'remuneration' is not used. Again, there has been a paucity of Inner House cases.

---

1 See 1993 SLT 311, at 314A, B, F and G.
2 1997 SLT 649, at 653L–654A.
3 1997 SLT 505, at 514I–K.
4 *Damages for Personal Injuries: Report on (1) admissibility of Claims for Services (2) Admissible Deductions* (Scot Law Com no 51) (HC Paper No 557 (1977–78)) paras 34–44.

Quantification of past reasonable sums

Tariff and jury approaches

In principle, both these broad approaches are available. A tariffs could be used were a conventional sum considered appropriate[1], and the idea of 'reasonableness' is inescapable, whether in the form of simple rounding up or down of sums, in choosing between different calculations, or more generally. Indeed, given the use of 'reasonable sum' rather than 'reasonable remuneration', the legislation might invite that view. However, that temptation has been resisted.

A market approach

In practice, it seems courts have preferred a market approach. However, the 'opportunity cost' version, considered in some s 8 claims, does not seem to have any application. The services are, by definition, those otherwise provided gratuitously.

The 'professional rates' version was clearly used in *Brown v Ferguson*[2]. Lord Sutherland suggested that, in the absence of guidance as to how a 'reasonable sum' might be assessed, if a person had actually been employed to provide the services, using that cost 'was not unreasonable'. The pursuer had in fact paid out to another person (in fact the deceased's mother), some £100 per month for childcare services, about £500 per annum for various other purposes, and had bought her a car and paid the running costs. There was evidence that professional rates for a housekeeper were at the time of the accident £35 per week if living out, and if living in £60, and that these figures were appropriate. He therefore decided the average living out figure would have been about £60 per week 'making a total of £15,000 for the period to date'[3].

Lord Sutherland specifically rejected any suggestion that the loss of earnings which the deceased's mother suffered in giving up her job to provide the childcare should be taken into account. He did not explain his reasoning, but it might be that the loss was regarded as too remote. Also, as noted above, the 'loss of opportunity' approach is inappropriate where the 'personal services' are ones otherwise provided gratuitously.

However, in *Ingham v John G Russell (Transport) Ltd*[4], this was not unequivocally approved. On appeal as to the relevancy, where the principle issue was the nature of 'personal services', Lord Ross concluded that because the pleadings asserted that the deceased could have obtained work for at least £5 per hour doing the services in question, and because s 9 allowed a 'reasonable sum', there was sufficient specificity. Lord McCluskey went further observing that the words of the statute are 'an instruction to the court to approach the matter very broadly', and do not require detailed enquiry averring rates of pay of relevant tradesmen and apportionment of hours, which would involve extremely complicated pleadings and proof. Strictly speaking, the 'professional

---

1 See, for example, Bennett *Personal Injury Damages in Scotland* (1999) App V(E).
2 1990 SLT 274, particularly at 276F–H, 1990 SCLR 577.
3 Ie, presumably £60 × 52 = £3,120 per year, for the five years from accident to proof (ie July 1983 to June 1988).
4 1991 SLT 739, particularly at 744D–E, 747F–H, 1991 SCLR 596.

rate' given by Lord Ross is an irrelevant one (and could be mistaken for adopting a 'opportunity cost' approach). What is required is the price of the 'personal service' now provided on the market, rather than the price an injured or deceased person might have got on the market for doing it.

Quantification of future reasonable sums

Mutatis mutandis, quantification of future s 9 services seems to proceed upon the same principles as for s 8. The principal *mutanda* is the non-applicability of the 'loss of opportunity approach'.

Tariff and jury approaches

As elsewhere, a tariff may be relevant in indicating a multiplier in the absence of an actuarial approach, and an element of 'reasonableness' is inevitable.

A market approach

A market approach (subject to such applications of tariffs and 'reasonableness') seems preferred[1]. In *Worf v Western SMT Co Ltd*[2] Lord Mayfield heard evidence that the relative had spent about 200 hours per year performing some of the s 9 services which the deceased had previously done. This was estimated on a professional rate at some $6,000 (the pursuer being American), and that, with the other s 9 services 'would be in the region of $10,000 per year'. The defender suggested half that figure, and Lord Mayfield felt that 'the sum of $8,000 was an appropriate figure'. To that he applied a multiplier of 10 (producing £80,000), giving no explanation, although that figure is midway between the pursuer's 12 and the defender's 7 or 8.

Lord Sutherland, in *Brown v Ferguson*[3], followed his quantification of past losses based on a professional rate for a living out housekeeper by taking the current rate of £70 per week for the future 'and allowing a further seven years this would amount to £25,000'. This seems to have been a very rough multiplier/multiplicand approach. What is not clear is why a multiplier of 7 was chosen. The child was born in 1980, so was 10 years old at the time of proof, so Lord Sutherland was, by explicitly mentioning seven years, presumably concluding that by adulthood the child would be independent.

Nevertheless, given the close link of ss 8 and 9, it is possible that the problems of the annuity approach are more closely looked at than elsewhere.

PATRIMONIAL LOSSES—III: LOSS OF PROFIT, LOSS OF INCOME, LOSS OF SUPPORT

Chapter 2 noted that loss of profit, loss of income and loss of support raise the same questions. It also distinguished loss of income from 'loss of employ-

---

1 For some multipliers for personal services, see Bennett *Personal Injury and Damages in Scotland* (1999) App V(C)5 and 7.
2 1987 SLT 317, particularly at 318I–L.
3 1990 SLT 274, at 276J.

ability' and loss of pension rights and 'loss of congeniality of employment' which is regarded as an aspect of *solatium.*

LOSS OF PROFIT

Quantification of loss of profit in general

As always, in principle, any approach to quantification is possible, but in relation to loss of profits, the calculational approach seems most apt, albeit modified by 'reasonableness'[1]. However, few cases have examined the questions raised.

An exceptional example is that of 'violent profits', that is profit which a wrongful possessor has acquired by means of the wrongful possession. These are distinguished from compensatory damages, and have been referred to as 'penal'[2]. Methods of calculating them have been suggested[3], but the better view may be that they are a form of restitution rather than damages[4].

Cases which considered loss of profit have generally done so in relation to intellectual property. As noted above, such losses are usually treated as loss of income rather than loss of assets. Although there is little authority, it seems appropriate that awards of damages for loss of profit be quantified net of tax, as are those for loss of income (discussed below)[5].

Quantification of past loss of profit in patent cases

Complications exist. Such claims depend upon statutory provision, the Patents Act 1977. Also, the principal remedy may be interdict and an account for profits (on which there is little authority), rather than damages. Further, most cases are English ones (for the 1977 Act is a United Kingdom statute). There is also little authority on related actions such as breach of confidence and passing off. On the other hand, subject to exceptions, the same principles govern the quantification of damages for infringements of other forms of intellectual property.

The Patents Act 1977, s 61(1)(c) merely provides that a court may make an award 'for damages in respect of [an] infringement', and gives little help on quantification. However, the basic measure of damages in all cases is probably the difference between profits which have been received, and those which would otherwise have been received[6]. This may not be appropriate in all

---

1 Damages for loss caused by breach of a Convention right under the Human Rights Act 1998 are subject to limits described in ch 3.
2 Walker *The Law of Civil Remedies in Scotland* (1974) p 770.
3 *Walker* pp 772–773.
4 Stewart *Delict* (3rd edn, 1998) pp 24–25, 250–252.
5 See eg the English Court of Appeal case *Gerber Garment Technology Inc v Lectra Systems Ltd* [1997] RPC 443 (in relation to the circumstances of a multi-national company) at 458, per Staughton LJ; 465–466, per Hobhouse LJ; and 483, per Hutchison LJ.
6 In principle, there could be an element of *solatium,* for instance to recognise lack of public recognition. The reported cases do not show examples. Possibly damages of the same nature are available under statute in relation to breach of copyright or of unregistered design, as discussed below.

cases[1], and in any case, requires explication. Various criteria have been suggested as general guidelines (and the cases often stress that rules are too confining[2]), and the chief authority is Lord Wilberforce's leading judgement in an English case, *General Tire and Rubber Co v Firestone Tyre and Rubber Co Ltd*[3], decided under the Patents Act 1949, s 13, similar to the later provision[4].

Loss of sales

Firstly, if the pursuer exploits the intellectual property him- or herself, the *damnum* of the infringement is taken to be the diversion of sales to the defender. Thus, damages are normally the profit the pursuer would otherwise have obtained. Lord Wilberforce outlined this principle in *General Tire Co*[5] but it can be traced to *United Horse Shoe & Nail Co Ltd v John Stewart & Co*[6]. There, the defender admitted infringement, but claimed he could have manufactured the nails in question without it, so the pursuer had in fact lost nothing. Lord Watson observed that '[h]owever large [the defender's] gains, he is only liable in nominal damages so long as his illegal sales do not injure the trade of the patentee; and however great his loss he cannot escape from liability to make full compensation for the injury which his competition may have occasioned'. He admitted that loss of sales 'must always be more or less a matter of estimate'. The pursuer had reduced his prices to counter the infringement and Lord Watson noted that he could not claim all profits in the relevant market, for he would be subject to legitimate competition as well (and found it probable that the pursuer derived benefit from the defendant's marketing efforts). Lord Macnaghten more explicitly distinguished between loss of profit from the reduction in price and that from the infringement. The former was too remote because the reduction was not reasonable. The Lord Ordinary's award was upheld after somewhat brief consideration of the relative numbers of items sold by pursuer and infringer[7].

The principle was widely applied, and somewhat elaborated, on much more complicated facts by the English Court of Appeal in *Gerber Garment Technology Inc v Lectra Systems Ltd*[8]. The plaintiff had patents on a computer-assisted manufacturing (CAM) process, and sold examples, usually with a matching computer-assisted design (CAD) process. The defendants infringed the patent by selling the CAM process machines, and sold the CAD process

---

1 In *Goswami v Hammond* [1985] Sol J 653, research work by the plaintiff was published by others, reducing 'the professional value he might have been able to obtain by referring to [it under his own name]'. This 'might not have been great, [but] could not be described as nominal', per Lawton LJ at 653.

2 'Reported authorities . . . may be useful as illustrations of judicial reasoning, but are capable of misleading if decisions on a particular set of facts and observations in judgments leading up to such decisions are later relied on as establishing a rule of law', per Lord Wilberforce in *General Tire & Rubber Co v Firestone Tyre & Rubber Co Ltd* [1975] 1 WLR 819 at 824F.

3 [1975] 1 WLR 819, [1975] 2 All ER 173.

4 See also Cornish *Intellectual Property: patents, copyright, trade marks and allied rights* (3rd edn, 1996) p 60 ff. See further, 18 *Stair Memorial Encyclopaedia of the Laws of Scotland* vol 18, esp Pt I paras 803, 1452, 1489–90, and Pt II paras 868–871, 915, 1088, 1089–90, 1144, 1209, 1234, 1400, 1438.

5 [1975] WLR 819 at 824F–H.

6 (1888) 15 R (HL) 45, 13 App Cas 401, 25 SLR 447.

7 (1888) 15 R (HL) 45 at 48–50.

8 [1997] RPC 443.

with them without infringement. Damages were awarded at first instance under several heads. These were: lost profit on sales of CAM machines which the pursuers would have achieved during the currency of the patent but for the defendant's sales (and royalties on other infringing machines which would not have been sold but for the defendant), and 'springboard damages' for loss of profit on CAM machine sales which they would have made after the expiry of the patents but for the defendant's illegally early entry into the market; lost profit on sales of CAD machines which they would have sold with the CAM machines; spare parts and servicing on the machines; and 'price depression', that is, reduced profit on sales they had actually made. The defendants appealed against the award of damages in terms of four points of principle, which were, effectively: what sorts of damages could be awarded; whether the plaintiff could sue for losses to their subsidiaries; what degree of detail of calculation of lost profit could be required of the judge; and another point in relation to royalties.

In the leading judgment[1], Staughton LJ held that, as matter of interpretation, the Patents Act 1977 did not distinguish between loss of profit on the patented items and loss of profit on those sold with them, so both could be claimed, as could 'springboard damages' and loss of profit on spares and servicing. Further, as loss of profit was essentially the same as loss of income, he considered expenses saved should be deducted from such loss. This would appear to mean that not only the marginal cost of production and sale[2] but also an element of overheads should be deducted. However, there was no authority on the question, and he declined to offer any. Also, he was content with the rough and ready calculation of lost profit at first instance, whereby the judge estimated the number of lost sales (15), took the proportion of the infringer's total sales which that represented (60 per cent), and awarded that proportion of the defendant's profits as the plaintiff's lost profit.

The case was further complicated as the plaintiff had suffered the harm by way of loss of value of its wholly-owned subsidiaries. The Court of Appeal agreed that as it was the plaintiff which had suffered the harm, this was no barrier to recovery, at least so long as the subsidiaries had no right of action themselves. The plaintiff as owner had suffered the loss, so no difficulty arose in relation to the separate legal personalities. Loss of value of the shareholding was thus simply the measure of the harm. However, a majority (Staughton LJ dissenting) required each legal person to prove its loss, rejecting the argument that loss of a certain value to a subsidiary could be treated as loss of the same value to the owner, since tax regimes may vary, and accounting practices within groups of companies[3].

Loss of royalties

Secondly, if the pursuer licenses others to use the intellectual property (whether or not exploiting it himself or herself), the *damnum* of the infringement is taken to be the unauthorised use of the property. Thus, damages are normally the loss of royalties, though this may be difficult to establish. The

---

1 [1997] RPC 443 at, 453–456, 458–460.
2 Ie the extra cost to the company of producing an extra item.
3 [1997] RPC 443, at 478–480, 481–483.

principle was outlined in *General Tire Co* by Lord Wilberforce[1] and *General Tire Co* itself fell into this class[2]. The plaintiffs patented a method of making tyres and licensed other companies to use it, subject to payment of royalties at a particular rate. The defendants infringed the patent. The House of Lords, following *Penn v Jack*[3] and *AG fur Autogene Aluminium Schweissung v London Aluminium Co Ltd (No 2)*[4] held that if a particular rate had been in fact negotiated, that represented the rate it was willing to accept. The evidence relied upon by Lord Wilberforce included that the tyre rubber market was international and highly competitive, that the patentees had offered a particular royalty rate generally, and this rate (despite an ambiguity) had been used generally. Where some licensees had paid lump sums instead, this effectively reflected out-of-court settlements of disputes about use. The Court of Appeal had erred in considering that either a 'reasonable sum' should be paid, or that a hypothetical bargain between parties on equal terms should be imagined. Neither was warranted by authority or principle, the former risked being punitive and the latter ignored the facts.

Indeed, in principle, a 'going rate' for licences was an appropriate measure. In a slightly different context Lord Wilberforce approvingly quoted[5] Fletcher Moulton LJ in *Meters Ltd v Metropolitan Gas Meters*[6], to the effect that where a patentee grants licences at a certain fee, then the court simply multiplies that fee by the number of infringing articles. This approach had 'almost become a rule of law'. It must be shown, however, that the circumstances in which that rate was applied were comparable to those between plaintiff and defendant. Thus in *Boyd v The Tootal Broadhurst Lee Co*[7], one rate agreed between the pursuer and several others was irrelevant because it had been agreed when the patent was in doubt. The facts of *General Tire Co* were implicitly distinguished by Lord Wilberforce[8].

Reasonable royalty

Thirdly, if the pursuer holds the intellectual property and loss of sales cannot be calculated nor going rate for licences be determined, the *damnum* is difficult to pin down, and damages are likely to be quantified as a 'reasonable royalty' which might have been obtained from a licensee, following *Meters Ltd*[9]. There, the defendants infringed the plaintiff's patent in pre-paid gas meters. Some 19,500 infringing meters were sold. The plaintiffs argued that they would have sold 14,000 of them but for the infringement. The defendants argued for nominal damages as the plaintiffs had only a small part of the market. In preliminary proceedings, a Master held they would only have sold 5,000, and lost profit at 13/4d per meter, and were entitled to further damages for lost of profit on reduced sales by reason of reduced prices. The court, however, heard evidence persuading it that the plaintiffs would have sold only 3,500,

---

1 [1975] WLR 819, at 824H–826A.
2 Lord Salmon [1975] WLR 819 at 837H–838B, considering otherwise.
3 (1867) LR 5 Eq 81.
4 (1923) 40 RPC 107.
5 [1975] WLR 819 at 826D–H.
6 (1911) 28 RPC 157 at 164–165.
7 (1894) 11 RPC 175.
8 [1975] WLR 819, at 833H–835H.
9 Lord Salmon seems to have regarded *General Tire* as falling into this third class.

reducing damages accordingly. An appeal was dismissed. Fletcher Moulton LJ said that 'where there did not exist a quoted figure for a licence, [the court might] estimate the damages in a way closely analogous to [the loss of royalties approach] ... [and] consider what would have been the price which—although no price was actually quoted—could reasonably be charged for that permission [to use] and estimate the damage that way'[1].

The approach was rehearsed in *General Tire Co* by Lord Wilberforce[2], approvingly quoting Fletcher Moulton LJ. It applies where there have been licences but no 'going rate', or no licences at all (and, no doubt, whether or not the pursuer has exploited it himself or herself). It requires evidence of any licenses in fact granted, and their rates of royalty, and their comparability, but also perhaps practice in the relevant trade, expert opinion, the possibility of profitability, and other factors. The court must hypothesise a bargain between pursuer and defender in the light of such evidence, and in the light of his criticism of the Court of Appeal in *General Tire Co*, this must clearly be a realistic hypothesis based on the evidence.

Quantification of past losses in other intellectual property cases

In general

The same principles broadly apply in other intellectual property cases, subject to differences of statutory drafting. The legislation is United Kingdom statute, and most cases English.

Copyright

The Copyright, Designs and Patents Act 1988, s 96(2) allows 'such relief by way of damages ... as is available in respect of the infringement of any other property right'. This provision is essentially similar to s 17 of the Copyright Act 1956, under which most of the reported cases fall. *Columbia Picture Industries & Others v Robinson & Others*[3] seems close to Lord Wilberforce's first approach in *General Tire Co*. The defendants made and sold pirate videos. Scott J observed that it was 'a loss of profits' which must be proved and, while it was impossible to prove loss of sales, if there were pirated sales, loss of legitimate sales could be assumed. Quantification required an estimate, and the maximum must be the difference between what was sold and what needed to be sold to justify commercial expectations, while the minimum was the number of pirated copies sold. The action concerned many plaintiffs and many defendants, and six films. In some instances, despite infringement, no damages were payable because profit would only be derived if sales reached a certain level which Scott J concluded they would not have reached even without the pirating.

Lord Wilberforce's second approach seems manifested in *Stolvin-Bradford v Volpoint Properties Ltd*[4]. The plaintiff produced drawings for owners of a site for the purpose of obtaining planning permission. He was paid an 'agreed

1 (1911) 28 RPC 157, at 164–165.
2 [1975] WLR 819 at 827C–828C.
3 [1988] FSR 531, particularly at 535, 536.
4 [1971] Ch 1007 particularly at 1016H, [1971] 3 WLR 256, [1971] 3 All ER 570.

nominal sum', and retained the copyright. A particular feature of these drawing was, however, incorporated into a subsequent plan by the defender. It was held that no licence to use them had been given, and the defendants, in the words of Lord Denning MR 'ought to pay as damages an amount equivalent to the fee which they would have had to pay for a licence'.

Lord Wilberforce's third approach is illustrated by *Nichols Advanced Vehicle Systems & Others v Rees & Others (No 3)*[1]. This involved a Formula 1 racing car with no sale or realistic hire market, kept going by sponsorship, transferred to a new owner at an artificial price, and including a proportion of infringing parts which had a manufacturing cost but were now depreciated[2].

One of the few Scottish cases is *Oliver Homes (Manufacturing) v Hamilton*[3]. Temporary Judge Robertson purported to follow *Stolvin-Bradford* (but arguably took Lord Wilberforce's third approach), distinguishing *Columbia Pictures* because that case concerned multiple sales of infringing material by a competitor. The defender had copied house designs of the pursuer, which was a company designing and manufacturing house kits. The pursuer sought damages which were, under the Act, 'at large', and parties agreed that they could cover not only the pursuers' losses, but also benefits or advantages accruing to the defender. The pursuer claimed for the saving the defender had made by not having their plans prepared (which was accepted by the defender); loss of sale of a house kit, including 'contribution to annual overheads' (effectively, the sum they would have received had the defender employed them to prepare plans and had bought a kit from them); and loss of profit on the materials for a house kit (which was not pursued ultimately). They averred that they never licensed use of their designs without sale of a kit. Temporary Judge Robertson held, that the proper measure was nevertheless a 'reasonable charge for the use of their plans based on what would have been a fair remuneration if a licence had been granted'.

Design rights, trade marks, plant variety rights and rights in performance

Section 229(2) of the 1988 Act is drafted similarly to s 96(2) in respect of unregistered designs, as is s 14(2) of the Trade Marks Act 1994, and s 13 of the Plant Varieties Act 1997 is almost identical to the copyright provision, so no doubt both fall to be interpreted like it. So, probably, does s 194 of the 1988 Act, in respect of rights in performance, although it is ambiguously drafted, giving no reference to available remedies[4]. The Registered Designs Act 1949 does not specify what remedies are available, but it can be assumed that damages are[5].

In addition to these oddities, there are some exceptional cases. These depend chiefly upon statutory provision, but also on the common law on passing off and breach of confidence.

---

1 [1988] RPC 71.
2 See opinion of Sir Frederick Lawson [1988] RPC 71, at 93, lines 34–39.
3 1992 SLT 892, particularly at 894G–H.
4 'An infringement of any of the rights conferred by this Part is actionable by the person entitled to the right as a breach of statutory duty'.
5 Registered Designs Act 1949, s 7 ('Right given by registration') says 'The registration of a design under this Act shall give to the registered proprietor the copyright in the registered design ...'. For an example of the application of Lord Wilberforce's third approach in *General Tire Co*, see *PB Cow Ltd v The Cannon Rubber Manufacturers Ltd* [1961] RPC 236.

'Additional damages' for copyright and design right infringements

In relation to both copyright and unregistered designs, by virtue of the Copyright, Designs and Patents Act 1988, ss 97(2) and 229(3), the pursuer may obtain 'additional damages' at the court's discretion 'having regard to all the circumstances, and in particular to (a) the flagrancy of the infringement, and (b) any benefit accruing to the defendant by reason of the infringement'. This repeats wording in the Copyright Act 1956, s 17(3), save that a requirement that the court be satisfied that 'effective relief would not otherwise be available' was removed. The original power was intended to allow 'something equivalent to exemplary damages'[1], although at a time when '[t]he distinction between exemplary or punitive damages on the one hand and aggravated but nevertheless compensatory damages on the other had become somewhat blurred'[2]. It was continued under the 1988 Act because, it seems, '[n]o one has submitted [it] should be abolished'[3]. Also, the lack of 'effective relief' provision had been interpreted as referring to remedies outside copyright law[4].

The provision as a whole is apt to cover damage beyond loss of profit. Under the 1956 Act, 'benefit' was defined by Brightman J in *Ravenscroft v Herbert and Another*[5], as implying 'that the defendant has reaped a pecuniary advantage in excess of the damages he would otherwise have to pay', so possibly means damages can reflect profits to the infringer on sales which the pursuer would not have achieved, avoiding the principle of *restitutio in integrum* as applied in *United Horse Shoe & Nail Co Ltd* and *General Tire Co* in patent cases. However, authority lacks, and it is possible that this remedy should be regarded as an example of 'violent profits', suggested in ch 3 to be a form of restitution rather than delictual damages.

'Flagrancy' is a matter of *solatium*, so is dealt with below. In *Redrow Homes Ltd v Bett Brothers plc*[6], the House of Lords did decide that, as a matter of construction, because they are 'additional' such damages can only be awarded where damages have already been awarded (and thus not, for instance, where an account of profit is sought).

Innocence and copyright

Section 97(1) of the 1988 Act disentitles the pursuer from any damages for infringement of copyright if the defender 'did not know, and had no reason to believe, that copyright subsisted in the work'. However, this is 'without prejudice to any other remedy', which means an account of profits is still available.

Groundless threats and design rights

Section 253 of the 1988 Act gives a right, when threatened by certain proceedings for infringement of design right which are not justified, to 'damages in

---

1 Gregory Committee Report (Cmnd 8662) (1952) para 294, quoted by Lord Jauncey in *Redrow Homes Ltd v Bett Brothers plc* 1998 SC (HL) 64 at 66C–D, 1998 SLT 648, 1998 SCLR 325.
2 Per Lord Jauncey in *Redrow Homes Ltd*, above, 1998 SC (HL) 64 at 66H.
3 *Report on the Reform of Copyright Law* (the 'Whitford Report') (Cmnd 6732) (1977) para 704, quoted by Lord Jauncey in *Redrow Homes Ltd* at 650E.
4 The Whitford Report, quoted by Lord Jauncey in *Redrow Homes Ltd* at 650E. However, see *Goswami v Hammond & Others* [1985] Sol J 685.
5 [1980] RPC 193, at 208.
6 1998 SC (HL) 64, 1988 SLT 648, 1998 SCLR 325.

respect of any loss ... sustained by the threats'. This clearly relates chiefly to loss of profit.

Passing off at common law

Although there are a number of passing off actions reported, it is not clear on what principles damages are to be quantified. The *General Tire Co* principles would seem appropriate in most cases, since custom will have been diverted. Where the situation parallels that for 'additional damages' for 'flagrant' infringement in copyright, *solatium* might be relevant, as it might where despite lack of economic right, a 'moral right' such as now exists in copyright was infringed.

Breach of confidence at common law

Confidential information can perhaps now be regarded as a form of intellectual property at common law under some circumstances[1], although authority is thin[2]. Damages are likely to be assessed on similar principles to those outlined for patents in *General Tire Co*, and might also contain an element of *solatium*[3]. English experience is much greater[4].

Moral rights in copyright

'Moral rights' (in addition to the existing 'economic rights') were introduced by ss 77–89 of the Copyright, Designs and Patents Act 1988 for certain copyright work. However, these are effectively matters of *solatium*, so are dealt with below.

Conversion damages in copyright

Until the Copyright, Designs and Patents Act 1988, 'conversion damages' were allowed in copyright cases. 'Conversion' refers to the English law tort of that name, and the essence of the damages was compensation for the property value of copyright articles, in addition to the damages for infringement (or the diminution of the value of the copyright). These are not a matter of loss of profit, and in any case, are no longer available.

Quantification of future loss of profit

In principle, there can be future loss of profit. However, since a primary remedy in loss of profit cases is interdict, in practice the issue does not seem to arise. Were it to do so, presumably, application of traditional multipliers and multiplicands would be employed.

---

1 See *Breach of Confidence* (Scot Law Com no 90) (Cmnd 9385) (1984).
2 See *AB v CD* (1851) 14 D 177, *Brown's Trustees v Hay* (1898) 25 R 1112, *Liverpool Victoria Legal Friendly Society v Houston* (1900) 3 F 42, 8 SLT 320, *Neuman & Co Ltd v A&W Kennedy* (1905) 12 SLT 763.
3 See *Levin v Caledonian Produce (Holdings) Ltd* 1975 SLT (Notes) 69.
4 See eg *A–G v Guardian Newspapers Ltd (No 2)* [1990] 1 AC 109, [1988] 3 WLR 776, [1988] 3 All ER 545 but also *Lord Advocate v Scotsman Publications Ltd* 1988 SLT 490 (IH), 1989 SLT 705 (HL).

LOSS OF INCOME

Quantification of loss of income in general

As usual, any approach to quantification is possible. However, it is clear that a calculational approach is the most apt, save in special cases[1]. As noted in ch 4, it is important to observe that the normal calculation is of the difference between what was actually received during the period of lost income, and what would hypothetically have been received during that period otherwise. With future losses, this becomes the difference between what is predicted will be received over the period of lost income and what is expected would be received during that period otherwise.

What was actually received in the past (and is predicted will be in the future)

If no income is actually received while not working, all income is lost. However, if the pursuer receives 'sick pay' from an employer, he or she has to that extent not lost income, and any claim is for the difference between 'sick pay' and normal pay. Otherwise double compensation results. This basic application of *restitutio in integrum* is enshrined in statute for personal injury actions[2], but this principle must apply to loss of income from any other type of action. Also, the pursuer may receive social security or other benefits. The same principle may require these to be taken into account. Such 'setting off' is discussed with the related question of recovery of benefits in ch 6.

On the other hand, when a pursuer returns to work, he or she may expect to resume normal pay, but may in fact receive a reduced income. An extreme case of such difficulties is *Byrnes v Fife Health Board*[3], discussed below.

What would have been received in the past otherwise (and would be received in the future)

The pursuer might not have continued at the normal pay, but have suffered job loss from redundancy or illness from an unrelated cause. On the other hand, he or she might have expected to receive cost-of-living increases, and/or promotions. Also, not working may reduce travel and other expenses, and *restitutio in integrum* may require this to be taken into account[4].

An approach

Quantification of loss of income is thus best seen as a multi-stage process, ie quantification of basic income in relation to the past; taking account of

---

1 In *Kent v Gourlay* 1990 SLT 516, 1990 SCLR 172, a lump sum was used as a check on a multiplier/multiplicand calculation. Damages for loss caused by breach of a Convention right under the Human Rights Act 1998 are subject to limits described in ch 3.
2 Administration of Justice Act 1982, s 10(i). Section 10(e) also takes into account where the employer pays contingent upon repayment if damages are obtained.
3 1978 SLT 66.
4 As noted in ch 3. There is also the more subtle argument, never in practice deployed, that the pursuer has not had to suffer the detriment of having to work, so replacement of wages automatically overcompensates. It will be recalled that when the unemployed flocked to Paris after the French Revolution, they were given a form of unemployment benefit, but in order that they should not receive something for nothing, were required to engage in the useless task of digging up the Champ de Mars and then filling it in again.

variables, additions and deductions to that basic income; and then considering the future. This is described in relation to employees, directors, partners, and sole traders.

Loss of income of employees

Employees 'basic income'

Employees contract with their employer to work for them in return for a wage or salary. There is a lack of authority, but in the case of an employed wage- or salary-earner, the basis of the calculation is straightforward. A standard 'basic income' would have been received by the pursuer. This can be determined by extrapolating from income received over the preceding three or six months, or by comparing the income actually received by a similar employee.

Over lengthy periods, there may be questions of pay rises and promotions, and it may also be appropriate to take account of possible pay rises reflecting inflation[1]. An example of the extrapolation method and such complications is *Gardner v Howard Doris*[2]. Lord Grieve referred to evidence that '[a] yearly wage of £4,150 in June 1978 would by June 1982 have been a yearly wage of £6,200. Counsel for the pursuer suggested that I took the midpoint of these figures to calculate the loss of earnings over the (now) four years and seven months since the end of June 1978, a period of say 230 weeks. The mid point is £5,175 per annum or for convenience £100 per week. On these figures the pursuer's loss works out at £23,000 from June 1978 to date'[3].

Variables in 'basic income'

Overtime normally worked should be consolidated as 'basic income'. If regularly but not invariably worked, it could be included as an average or estimated from the overtime of an employee in a similar job, as in *McCrum v Ballantyne*[4]. However, there seems no explicit authority for how to treat variables such as irregular overtime, commission or bonuses, although general principle would probably treat them in terms of percentage chances[5]. A share option is in principle simply another bonus, albeit with greater difficulties in valuation, and must be distinguished from share income as earnings.

Variability may also occur through possible redundancy, ill-health or otherwise. Thus in *Hodge v British Coal Corporation (No 2)*[6], Lord Morison observed that '[c]alculation of loss of wages is complicated by the fact that the pursuer

---

1 For instance, by means of the Retail Price Inflation Index, since it is its buying power which is important.

2 1983 SLT 672, particularly at 673. See also *Forsyth's CB v Govan Shipbuilders* 1986 SLT 321.

3 There is an oddity in this example, in that Lord Grieve preceded these remarks by observing that a relevant employee's 'weekly wage in June 1978 was £60.20 per week and four years later by June 1982 was £92.43 per week'. These weekly rates do not aggregate to £4,150 and £6,200 respectively.

4 1993 SLT 788, at 790D–K, 1993 SCLR 182.

5 In *Grant v National Coal Board* 1974 SLT (Notes) 71, a lump sum was suggested, but refused on other grounds.

6 1992 SLT 913 at 914.

would in any event have become redundant on 9 September 1989', and awarded damages for loss of earnings until that date, (but thereafter for 'diminution of prospects of obtaining employment'[1]). In *Byrnes v Fife Health Board*[2] Lord Ross noted that the pursuer had changed jobs frequently before the accident, and had been effectively unemployed for the two years immediately preceding it, by reason of illness and other problems. Lord Ross declared that 'it is doubtful whether he would have resumed gainful employment in the near future if the injury had not occurred, and it is not clear what he could have earned in any employment which he did obtain. On such information as is available, I conclude that if the accident had not occurred, it is unlikely that the pursuer would have worked for more than half the time each year ...'. He fixed damages for past lost wages accordingly[3]. In *Robertson's CB v Anderson*[4], the work record of the *incapax* was very poor, but he appeared to be turning a corner and might have obtained a steady job, though the an Extra Division thought it likely after five years rather than the two claimed. Such cases show that quantification of 'basic income' can be rough and ready, and resemble a jury approach.

Additions to 'basic income'

Fringe benefits include company cars, private health insurance paid for by the employer, etc. They generally require to be included although any item has clearly to be identified as part of earnings to avoid overlapping claims, and may be difficult to quantify, as in *McMillan v McDowall*[5]. A clear example is *Lamont v Cameron's Exrx*[6], where a veterinary surgeon received a car and accommodation in addition to her salary, which were assessed as constituting loses of £11,150 and £13,900 respectively.

It also appears that family income supplement, that is, a benefit paid to 'top up' low wages, and therefore lost if wages are lost, can be included, on the basis of *Webb v MacAuley*[7]. Presumably the principle does not apply to benefits which are not dependent upon being in employment[8].

As noted in ch 2, share income from an employing company is usually irrelevant, as too remote a loss, but in certain cases might not be.

Deductions: income tax, national insurance contributions

Deductions from the 'basic income' must be made for income tax, although this was finally decided surprisingly recently, in *British Transport Commission*

---

1 Ie 'loss of employability', discussed below. See also *Farrelly v Yarrow Shipbuilders Ltd* 1994 SLT 1349, at 1340J–1351C. 1994 SCLR 407.
2 1978 SLT 66, particularly 67.
3 In fact Lord Ross' arithmetic seems at fault. There had been about nine years from accident to proof. If the pursuer had worked for half of that, he would have worked for 4.5 years. He actually worked for some 40 months (treated as 3.25 years), and did not work for the remaining 5.25 years. Thus his loss would appear to be the difference between 4.5 and 3.25, ie 1.25 years. Lord Ross, however, concluded that he lost 2.875 years, ie seemingly half of the 5.25 years he did not work.
4 1996 SC 217.
5 1993 SLT 311.
6 1997 SLT 1147, 1996 SCLR 1139.
7 1988 SC 10, 1988 SLT 138.
8 The relationship of damages and other compensation systems is discussed in ch 6.

v Gourley[1]. This was a majority decision of an English House of Lords case, concerning a fee-earning plaintiff. However, there is no doubt that its principle applies in Scotland, and to wage and salary earners (although not necessarily to the self-employed[2]).

The case is worth examining. The plaintiff had had a very large fee income, and was awarded £37,720 for past and future earnings without reference to tax liability (calculated as £6,695 net of tax).

Substantial opinions were offered by three of the majority of six judges, and Lord Keith of Avonholm dissented[3]. Lord Jowitt[4] founded on the principle of *restitutio in integrum*. He did not consider taxation too remote, and concluded that whether tax was PAYE or not was irrelevant, and that difficulties of calculation were simply an example of the general difficulty of quantifying damages. He regarded the argument that to deduct tax benefitted the defendant as 'fallacious', observing that two people with the same gross income might be taxed differently, so would not be equally compensated by the same sum of damages. Lord Goddard[5] broadly agreed and also found the argument that taxation was *res inter alios acta*[6] misleading, though he doubted the application of the maxim *restitutio in integrum*, embedding his opinion in the English law distinction between 'special damages' and 'general damages'. Lord Reid[7] also broadly agreed, and rejected the *res inter alios acta* argument, while doubting the usefulness of *restitutio in integrum* as a maxim[8], and seeing the matter as one of remoteness. Lord Keith's dissent depended upon taxation distorting compensation by haphazardly benefiting defendants and even plaintiffs.

The principle upon which deduction of income tax rests clearly applies equally to national insurance contributions which are another form of taxation.

Deductions and pension or superannuation contributions

Contributions to a superannuation scheme are different from income tax and national insurance. Though possibly contractually compulsory, they are not a tax but wages deferred and stored by the employer until retirement.

They were deducted on the particular facts of *Mitchell v Glenrothes Development Corporation*[9]. However, that concerned a claim for 'loss of pension rights' (discussed below), and the pursuer's past contributions were returned, so 'no question of duplication of recovery [arose]' with his claim for lost

---

1 [1956] AC 185, [1956] 2 WLR 41 [1956] 3 All ER 796. See *McDaid v Clyde Navigation Trustees* 1946 SC 462, 1946 SLT 127 (Lord Sorn), but *Blackwood v Andre* 1947 SC 333, 1947 SLT 53 (Lord Keith: and see his dissent in *Gourley*).
2 See *MacLennan v Scottish Gas Board* 1985 SLT 2, discussed below, in which *Gourley* was not mentioned.
3 Lord Tucker also noted that he had changed his mind since the Court of Appeal.
4 [1956] AC 185 at 197–198 and 202.
5 Above, at 206–209.
6 Ie 'something done between other persons [than the two parties in question]'. The full maxim is '*res inter alios acta, aliis neque nocet, neque prodest*' ie approximately, 'something done between other persons can neither injure, nor advantage, one'.
7 Above, at 211–212.
8 He nevertheless founded on the substance of it.
9 1991 SLT 284, in particular at 290L.

income, as Lord Clyde observed. In general, therefore, they should be treated as part of income, and not deducted[1].

Deductions and compensation from other compensation systems

Deductions may also have to be made in respect of compensation received from other sources, by virtue of the Administration of Justice Act 1982, or recovered under the Social Security (Recovery of Benefits) Act 1997. These are dealt with in ch 6.

Future loss of income as such

With future loss of income the variables take on a new dimension of difficulty. In *Tuttle v Edinburgh University*[2], the pursuer claimed he would lose £2,000 per annum by being unable to work full time. However, Lord McDonald accepted the defender's assertion that there was evidence that he would be able to work full-time in due course, and that there was no evidence that his employers were going to reduce his salary. In *Campbell v City of Glasgow District Council*[3], Lord Caplan expressed restrained annoyance at the lack of information, observing '[t]he earning potential of an incapacitated man who has to seek fresh employment is essentially conjectural but my task in this case is in no way helped by a total absence of evidence as to the kind of work the pursuer might hope to secure for himself, the training which might be required for such work, the prospect of securing such work in the pursuer's home city, and the earnings such work could yield'.

Approaches to future loss of income

As *Campbell* indicates, estimates may involve an element of the jury approach. Indeed, lump sums for future losses of income are not uncommon[4], as in *Steen v MacNicol*[5] where a nine-year-old boy suffered catastrophic injuries, so would never work and Lord Stott awarded him 'the figure of £12,000 [which] is reasonable ... and takes full account of imponderables'. However, as also in *Campbell*, the usual approach is a market one, whether traditional multiplier/multiplicand, or actuarial, even where there is a high degree of uncertainty.

Future loss through a market approach: the multiplicand

The multiplicand is estimated in accordance with the general principles outlined in ch 4. Some of the difficulties discussed there are taken into account, such as those of evidence and arithmetic, and contingent or changing multiplicands. However, those of inflation and the rise of real wages over time are not.

---

1 Which conforms to the English House of Lords case *Smoker v London Fire and Civil Defence Authority* [1991] 2 AC 502, [1991] 2 WLR 1052, [1991] 2 All ER 449, which concerned a pension actually paid. However, see *Anderson v Gerrard* 1994 SLT 1326, at 1328F–G.
2 1984 SLT 172, in particular at 173.
3 1991 SLT 616 at 623J–K. 1991 SCLR 179.
4 For a list of such awards, see Bennett *Personal Injury Damages in Scotland* (1999) App V(D).
5 1968 SLT (Notes) 77, in particular at 78.

The difficulties of evidence and arithmetic are those of discovering the right multiplicand. Whether it is a case of totally lost, or only reduced, earnings, the multiplicand is the difference between what is predicted will be earned and what is hypothesised would be earned otherwise. However, as noted above in relation to past losses, there may be problems of determining 'basic income' from which to infer the latter. In fact, taking account of variables such as possible redundancy, wage rises etc tends to be dealt with by modification of the multiplier rather than the multiplicand. An example is *Will v Charles Will Ltd*[1] where Lord Ross said '[t]he estimate of future loss can never be precise, and the fact that there is an increased loss for the first eight months can be accommodated in the choice of multiplier'.

There may be changing multiplicands for different periods. For example, in *Campbell v City of Glasgow District Council*[2], Lord Caplan noted that the need to find suitable work, possible retraining, etc meant that two or three years might reasonably elapse between the time that the pursuer was recovered sufficiently to work and his finding any work. For this period, the multiplicand was his net wage loss. Thereafter, the pursuer would be likely to get work, but the light work he would get would not be as well paid as the work he had done, and his experience and abilities made well-paid, responsible non-manual work likely to be unobtainable, so 'he is likely to suffer a continuing permanent wage loss' and a multiplicand of £1,500 was fixed upon[3].

The effect of inflation and of real rises in earnings are obvious by their absence in most cases, most clearly in those concerning children. In *Geddes v Lothian Health Board*[4] a child of eight had suffered catastrophic injures. Obiter, Lord Milligan very usefully gave an extended opinion on the damages he would have awarded. Damages for loss of earnings were sought for the period from the pursuer's age of 18 (in 2002) until his retirement, that is from ten years after the date of proof to some 50 years after it (say, 2041). The multiplicand was £11,019.71. While this might be a reasonable starting salary in 2002 it would not be likely to be worth much in 2041 by reason of inflation, and the calculation wholly failed to include any element for likely increases in real wages. It may be that the multiplier was thought to take these into account, but no such argument was deployed, and as it was fixed at 11.5, this seems unlikely.

Future loss through a market approach: the multiplier

The multiplier is also determined according to the same general principles as described in ch 4. The difficulties of the real rate of return on investment and of inflation have been generally ignored, as noted above in relation to *Geddes*. Multipliers have been used to individuate, but subject to the criticism of the relevance of judges' 'experience' noted in ch 4.

---

1 1979 SLT 37, in particular at 38.
2 1991 SLT 616, particularly at 624A.
3 Lord Caplan concluded that '[i]n the absence of any guidance in the evidence I do not think I can pitch this at more than £1,500 per annum ...' compared with a figure of £7,956 which he would otherwise be earning, (ie less than 20%).
4 1992 SLT 986, 1992 SCLR 214.

Thus, in traditional practice, a form of precedent exists, whereby judges adopt a multiplier from a reported case which they find sufficiently analogous, modified as they think fit. The date at which the multiplier aims is return to work, or if no return is anticipated, to presumed retirement age rather than (as with future care costs) to recovery or, if no recovery is anticipated, to death. The factors tending to reduce the multiplier are also more than, and different from, those for future care costs, so multipliers have tended to be lower[1].

O'Brien's CB was not concerned with future loss of earnings as such, and Lord President Hope regarded the use of the traditional multiplier/multiplicand in this area as generally acceptable, for judges had experience on which they could rely, saying 'it will be sufficient to rely on the figures used in comparable cases without resort to more sophisticated methods of calculation, even as a check'[2]. References to the 'actuarial approach' recommended as a check by the Inner House in *O'Brien's CB* have nevertheless been made in relation to loss of earnings, for example in *McMillan v McDowall*[3], where Temporary Judge Coutts recounted the pursuer's argument based on it (linked to *O'Brien's CB*), and did not criticise him for so doing. However the traditional approach, including examples from before *O'Brien's CB* such as *Tuttle*, clearly remain valid as effective precedents.

Quantification of loss of income of directors

Directors' income as 'quasi-salary'

Directors contract with their company, agreeing to work for it, but are not employees, and receive a fee which can be regarded as a 'quasi-salary'. In principle, this can be treated as if it were an employee's salary. In practice, calculation may be more difficult because the sum paid may be irregular, and/or vary considerably from time to time, particularly with directors of small companies, or those on performance related pay.

An interesting example is *Fullemann v McInnes's Executors*[4]. The pursuer was sole director, and effectively sole owner, of a company. He fixed his remuneration annually, varying it with profit. This sum would be paid into a loan account with the company on which he drew from time to time. The remaining profit was invested in the company and taxed as net profit. This remuneration, described as 'the loss of benefits[5] sustained by the pursuer', was distinguished from loss of profits to the company and loss of goodwill of the company largely on the basis of *Vaughan v Greater Glasgow Passenger Transport Executive*[6].

Lord Cullen considered its quantification[7]. He noted its size in the three

---

1 In *O'Brien's CB* 1991 SLT 477, at 481J, Lord President Hope listed 'variables which must be taken in to account relating to such matters as the risks of an accident, illness or redundancy and the prospects of promotion and variation in the amount of wages or salary'.
2 1991 SLT 477, at 483C.
3 1993 SLT 311.
4 1993 SLT 259, particularly at 265K.
5 This is slightly confusing terminology since (i) 'benefits' does not usually refer to remuneration, and (ii) 'benefits' is used elsewhere in the judgment, apparently to refer to undefined 'fringe benefits'.
6 1984 SLT 44.
7 1993 SLT 259, at 265L–266C.

years before the accident, and was persuaded that this would have increased 'on a broad basis which takes into account the quality of the evidence with which I have to deal and the uncertainties which were inherent in it'. He therefore fixed increasing sums for each of the years between accident and proof, and added this to the agreed annual sum for fringe benefits[1]. From this were subtracted certain sums received and the value of certain other, undefined, benefits[2] (possibly in terms of the Administration of Justice Act 1982, s 10).

Directors' income, dividend upon shares, and capital value of the company

Directors are normally shareholders, and may be remunerated wholly or in part through dividends on shares in the company. As noted in ch 4, *Anthony v Brabbs*[3] now seems clearly to show that where a considerable proportion of a director's income is derived from his or her shareholding in the company, this loss will not be seen as too remote. *Young v Ormiston*[4] must be regarded as doubted or distinguished to the point of extinction on this issue.

As also noted in ch 4, capital value is not income, even if increased, although such increase may make a share holding director better off (and vice versa). However, as also noted, *Fox v Caulfield & Co*[5], applying *Young v Ormiston*, concluded that such increase or decrease is too remote to be treated as *damnum* caused by *injuria* to the director. The principle of *Anthony v Brabbs* does not seem to apply here to alter that.

Directors' future loss of income

Directors' future loss of income can be quantified, *mutatis mutandis*, in the same way as employees'.

Quantification of partners' loss of income

Partners' income as 'quasi-salary'

Partners contract with each other, and with the firm to work for the firm but, like directors, are not employees and receive remuneration. This can be regarded as a 'quasi-salary', in so far as they are 'salaried partners', so receive their income from the firm expressed in monetary terms. To this extent, their remuneration parallels that of an employee. However, there are no cases reported, and doctrinally, it seems preferable to treat all partners as, in effect, shareholders.

Partners' income as a proportion of profits, and capital value of the company

Classically, partners agree between themselves the proportion of profits which they will take, which is thus really share dividend, but may be no more difficult to calculate than a director's 'quasi-salary', as in *Fulleman*.

---

1 See p 155, footnote 5 above.
2 See footnote 1 above.
3 1998 SLT 1137, 1998 SCLR 982.
4 1938 SLT 79.
5 1975 SLT (Notes) 71.

However, a partner prevented form working is likely to reduce the firm's profitability, reducing the worth of his or her share in profits. Thus the problem arises, as noted above, in relation to remoteness. (There is also a problem for the uninjured partners, whose income is also reduced). Whatever application *Young v Ormiston*[1] might have had, *Vaughan v Greater Glasgow Passenger Transport Executive*[2] now makes it clear, as noted in ch 4, that a partner's income derived from the partnership is treated as an exception, and is not too remote. (However, the uninjured partners' problem remains.)

Much of partners' assets are normally to be found in the partnership itself, and reduction in the value of such assets are a loss to the partners. However, as with employees and directors, the distinction between income and capital noted in ch 4, and relied on in *Fulleman*, remains.

Partners' future loss of income

Partners' loss of income can be quantified, *mutatis mutandis*, in the same way as directors'.

Quantification of loss of income of sole traders

Sole traders' income

Sole traders have no employment or service contract with a business organisation, for no such separate organisation exists. They are the real 'one-person companies'. Thus, distinctions between 'quasi-salaries' and share dividends or proportions of profits are meaningless, and the loss is one of profit.

Thus, in *Owenson v Rennie's Lion and Comfort Coaches*[3] the pursuer owned a shop in her own right, and had run it herself. As a result of an accident she could no longer do so, and sold it. The shop had given a profit of £2,500 after tax in the year before the accident. She sold it for £8,000, giving her, after expenses and capital gains tax, the sum of £7,300, which was agreed would produce an income of £500 a year. Net loss of profit from accident to proof was agreed at approximately £5,000, which appears to be the difference between the £500 a year she did receive and the £2,500 she would have received, for the relevant period[4].

Sole traders and the capital value of the business

No distinction can be made between the capital of the business and that of the individual, so questions of remoteness do not arise. However, the distinction between income and capital remains. Thus, on the facts of *Owenson*, had the pursuer continued to trade, rather than selling the shop, and had the value of the shop thereby declined, she would appear not to be able to claim for the difference between the pre-accident and post-accident capital values.

---

1 1936 SLT 79.
2 1984 SC 32.
3 1976 SLT (Notes) 58.
4 Ie, since proof was some 2.75 years after the accident, $(£2,500 - £500) \times 2.75 = £4,500$.

Sole traders' future loss of income

Sole traders' future loss of income can presumably be quantified in the same way as loss of profit, but there is a lack of authority.

Loss of employability

The nature of loss of employability claims is discussed in ch 2.

Quantification of past loss of employability

Given that the touchstone of 'loss of employability' is the contingency of the claim, quantification is clearly a problem, and likely to involve a jury approach.

There is a dearth of authority. *Smith v Manchester Corporation*[1], the case regarded as authority for such claims, did not make such an award for past loss of employability though in the leading judgement Scarman LJ took as his starting point that calculational methods were inappropriate, and the Court of Appeal's figure for future loss was clearly arrived at intuitionally, albeit with a comparison with losses of earnings. *Robertson's CB v Anderson*[2] likewise did not, but suggested a 'lump sum' more appropriate than one arrived at by calculation.

The only reported case specifically upon past loss of employability is *Hill v Wilson*[3]. Again the Inner House did not make an award. It did say that with

'an appropriately broad approach to damages, it may not even be necessary to make a clean choice between a so-called "lump sum"[4] payment and a computed loss of wages, where both have been averred. How, and to what extent, different "heads" of damages will require to be set out in an issue [for a jury] is not a reflection of separate "claims", but merely a suitable way of discovering the makeup, or breakdown, of the jury's total award in such a way as to make it possible, where part of the award is attributable to past loss and damage, to give the pursuer appropriate interest on that part of the principal sum'[5].

This leaves it open to the pursuer to decide how to claim as well as how much, and incidentally runs contrary to the arguable starting point of *Smith v Manchester Corporation*.

Quantification of future loss of employability

As noted, *Smith v Manchester Corporation* itself concerned future loss of employability, and the English Court of Appeal found it difficult to quantify the claim. Scarman LJ suggested that the multiplier/multiplicand approach

1 [1974] KIR 1, particularly at 8.
2 1996 SC 217, at 224G. 'Lump sum', although the phrase employed, is misleading, for damages are always in lump sum form. What is intended is clearly to distinguish between a computational approach, and a non-computational, ie a jury approach.
3 1998 SC 81, 1998 SLT 69.
4 See note 2 above.
5 1998 SC 81, at 85G–I.

was 'clearly inappropriate', and that the court should look at the matter 'in the round', noting the contingencies. Having listed a number of such contingencies, that is, reasons why the employer might not in fact keep the plaintiff in work in the future, he concluded a 'real risk' to exist, and adopted Edmund Davies LJ's comparison with earnings. He thus concluded £300 to be 'a derisory figure'[1]. Nevertheless, the £1,000 the court awarded was clearly largely intuitively arrived at.

A review of cases, such as *Whyte v University of Dundee*[2], *Hoey v British Steel Corporation*[3], *Hodge v British Coal Corporationi*[4], and *McMenemy v Argyll Stores Ltd*[5] suggests that this is the common approach. Indeed, it would be possible for a tariff to grow up.

In *Kennedy v Lees of Scotland*[6], Lord Gill attempted an essentially multi-plicand/multiplier approach (in addition to a sum for loss of earnings, similarly arrived at), concluding that 'a sum representing net wages at the current rate of wage loss for a period between one year and two years would be a reasonable award for [the] disadvantage'. As noted above, however, in *Hill v Wilson* the court somewhat muddied the waters by suggesting it was not necessary cleanly to distinguish loss of employability from loss of earnings.

Loss of pension rights

The nature of lost pension rights

The nature of lost pension rights was dealt with in ch 2. The claim is for a present capital sum (thus discounted for early payment, and assuming a certain rate of return) to represent a pension to be paid some years in the future (but possibly not at all if the pursuer dies before retirement), at a level which may be presently unknown (but which may depend upon what the employee's final wage or salary would have been) and for an unknown length of time (although this is a constant for pensions). The level may be affected by inflation, but the pension may include a lump sum on retirement and be index-linked.

Approaches to the loss of pension rights

Thus quantification of such a sum must be speculative to a degree, but invites an annuity approach, and lends itself to actuarial treatment.

In *Mitchell v Glenrothes Development Corporation*[7] the pursuer, a member of the index-linked local authority superannuation scheme, was disabled and retired on ground of incapacity. His contributions were returned when he left employment, and discussion concerned only the employer's. Pursuer and defender offered essentially similar actuarial calculations of the claim (albeit with different figures) supported by expert evidence, and there was reference

1 [1974] KIR 1 at 8.
2 1990 SLT 545 (at 546L–547C).
3 1991 SLT 196 (at 197I–J).
4 1992 SLT 914 (at 914K–L).
5 1992 SLT 971 (at 972K–L).
6 1997 SLT 510 at 513C, 1992 SCLR 576.
7 1991 SLT 284.

to an English case, *Auty v National Coal Board*[1], which used actuarial evidence extensively on rather similar facts. The principal point of difference was that the defender took the traditional line that inflation could be ignored as real rates of return are constant, though they also differed on what rate of return might be obtained. (There were further complexities concerning the contingent claim of the pursuer's wife.)

Lord Clyde decided the matter on a traditional multiplier/multiplicand basis. Fortified by the clear similarity to a loss of income claim, he said 'no exceptional feature has been suggested in the present case. There seems thus no good reason in principle to depart from the conventional approach'[2], and applied the conventions that inflation is taken care of in the rate of return, and that 4 per cent was reasonably attainable. He decided upon multiplicand and multiplier in a somewhat rough and ready way. The multiplicand was the current annual amount of the pension net of tax, not the annual contribution[3]. The multiplier was arrived at by considering the multiplier for lost wages (which was 8), then applying a net discount (of 2). The net discount was to take account of the fact that, on the one hand, the loss was deferred until the age of retirement, but on the other, the pursuer would have received a lump sum of three times his annual wage on retirement, as well as the pension.

A similar view was taken by Lord Cullen in *Grainger v Fife Regional Council*[4] but, in the light of *O'Brien's CB*, it is likely that a more rigorous attitude will be taken in the future[5].

LOSS OF SUPPORT

Quantification of loss of support in general

A loss of support claim is one made by defined relatives dependent upon a deceased's income, by virtue of s 1(1) of the Damages (Scotland) Act 1976, read with s 1(3). Damages are 'such as will compensate the relative for any loss of support suffered by him since the date of the deceased's death . . .'. This gives no indication of what approach might be taken[6]. The loss of support is typically from the deceased's employment, but could be from a pension.

While claims for consequential expenditure, loss of profit and loss of earnings are commonly only for past losses, claims for loss of support are almost necessarily for future loss as well.

Past lost of support from deceased's employment income

The general view has been that: firstly, the deceased's income should be quantified; secondly, a proportion attributable to the dependents should be

---

1 [1985] 1 WLR 784, [1985] 1 All ER 930.
2 1991 SLT 284, at 289L.
3 Above, at 291A–E. It was discounted, at 290F–H, by the possibility of the pursuer entering another pension scheme, or funding a pension himself. This last is surely an error, for the claim is one for the employer's contribution, not the employee's.
4 1991 SLT (Notes) 632.
5 The 'Ogden Tables' (*Actuarial Tables with explanatory notes for use in Personal Injury and Fatal Accident Cases* (3rd edn, 1998) contains in Tables 17–20 multipliers for loss of pension commencing at the ages of 60 and 65 and in Table 21 discounting factors for a term certain.
6 Damages for loss caused by breach of a Convention right under the Human Rights Act 1998 are subject to limits described in ch 3.

identified; and thirdly, that proportion should be apportioned between dependents if there are more than one. Clearly a calculational approach can be used for the first stage, but thereafter imponderables make estimates of a 'reasonable sum' unavoidable.

Deceased's lost income

In principle, this calculation is of the same nature as for loss of income in a personal injury action, with the same attendant difficulties. Where the deceased received a weekly wage, this calculation is likely to be relatively simple, as in *Dingwall v Walter Alexander & Sons Ltd*[1]. Where the deceased was a fee-earner or self-employed, it is likely to be more difficult, as in *Prentice v Chalmers*[2], where the deceased was a wealthy partner in a successful business, and there was dispute as to what 'quasi-salary', which varied somewhat over time, he should be taken to have drawn[3]. The effect of inflation was an issue, but was considered only in relation to the apportionment of income to the pursuer.

Apportionment to pursuer(s): the 'global sum'—the loss of support or dependency element

The pursuer or pursuers must show how much they were actually dependent upon the deceased, not what would be reasonable support, or whether support was required by law[4]. This proportion is commonly referred to as 'the global sum'[5], and in practice appears to be arrived at by a 'jury' or 'reasonable sum' approach. Remarriage or the prospect of remarriage of a widow has no effect, by virtue of the Law Reform (Miscellaneous Provisions) Act 1971, s 4, which adds an air of unreality to some cases, for instance *McKinnon v Reid*[6].

It is calculated as an annual sum. To cover loss between the date of the deceased's death and the date of proof, it therefore requires to be multiplied by 'the relevant number of years'. This is an application of the multiplicand/multiplier approach, and is paradoxical as a method of calculating past losses, occurring because the multiplier is deemed to operate from the date of death (confusing past and future losses)[7]. It may, however, be estimated (or agreed)

---

1 1980 SC 64, 1979 SLT (Notes) 100. Overturned on appeal on other grounds: see 1981 SLT 313 and 1982 SC (HL) 179.
2 1985 SLT 168.
3 Above, at 178, Lord Grieve noted the 'salaries drawn by the partners were small in comparison with their share of the profits, and it appears ... that both parties were inclined to let their share of the profits accumulate in their respective capital accounts'. At 176, Lord Dunpark in passing noted that the widow (the first pursuer) had received return of the deceased's capital in the business amounting to £190,000. This was excluded from calculation of loss of support.
4 In *Prentice v Chalmers* 1985 SLT 168, at 177, Lord Grieve suggested that in addition to 'the sums used by the deceased for family support, and ... the sums available to him for family support [c]onsideration has also to be given to the circumstances in which the family lived, and the general standard of living which they enjoyed'. This has to be understood in the light of the argument in that case about inflation, discussed below.
5 Because it is apportioned among pursuers.
6 1975 SC 233.
7 In *Dingwall* 1981 SLT 313, in the Inner House, at 314, Lord Justice-Clerk Wheatley described this as a formula adopted only in recent years.

as a percentage, for instance, 75 per cent in *Worf v Western SMT Co Ltd*[1]; 70 per cent in *Campbell v Gillespie*[2]; 60 per cent in *Dingwall*; and 55 per cent in *Davidson v Upper Clyde Shipbuilders*[3]. It is not clear what these varying percentages reflect, although responsibility for children appears to be one factor.

Five particular issues arise. Firstly, the support expenditure on the pursuer or pursuers must be disentangled from the deceased's personal expenditure. Secondly, there may be expenditure on common services (for example mortgage or rent payments). Thirdly, there may be income from both the deceased and the pursuer expended for individual or common (or reciprocal) purposes. Fourthly, the degree of dependency may vary from time to time depending upon the actual circumstances of the pursuer, as well as the hypothetical circumstances of the deceased. Fifthly, is any account to be taken of inflation?

Personal expenditure and support expenditure

In practice, the loss of support is usually calculated negatively, and heroically, in one of two ways. In the first, a proportion may be deemed to be spent on the pursuer, as in *Porter v Dickie*[4], where Lord Ross simply considered 'it would be reasonable to regard one half of [the relevant income] as required for the support of the pursuer'. (Indeed, he did so despite the pursuer, who had earned £46 per week, after the deceased's death receiving £30 per week unemployment benefit and then £22.10.) In the second, a proportion deemed to be spent by the deceased on him or herself may be deducted, as Lord Hunter and Lord Dunpark did in *Prentice v Chalmers* decided accepting the Lord Ordinary's proportion of one third[5].

Common expenditure

The distinction between personal expenditure and support expenditure conceals a complication. Some expenditure is on goods and services used by both deceased and pursuer, for instance rent or mortgage payment.

This is a problem if the first method of determining personal expenditure is used, as in *Porter v Dickie*[6]. Lord Ross concluded that half the income was spent on support of each of the couple and, despite noting the rent paid, he ignored it in his calculations, although it would continue to have to be paid. Had he taken common expenditure into account he would have had to compare the effect of paying rent on the joint income[7] with paying rent (albeit

---

1 1987 SLT 317, at 319.
2 1996 SLT 503, at 511.
3 1987 SLT 329, at 332–333.
4 1982 SLT 234 at 235.
5 1985 SLT 168 at 173 and 174. Albeit this was after a deduction for an annual contribution to the deceased's mother, the fifth-named pursuer, who was not a reclaimer. It is not clear why her lost support was deducted before the deduction for the deceased's own expenditure. There is also reference to the expense of the first-named pursuer's car and the loan to the church (at 173), but these do not figure in the calculation.
6 1982 SLT 234, particularly at 235.
7 Ie £32.67 per fortnight for a net weekly joint income of £104 (leaving £87.66 per week for the couple, ie £43.83 each).

now with a rent rebate) on a single income[1]. However, it is not a problem if the second method is used. In *Prentice v Chalmers*, the Inner House as a whole accepted simply that a third of expenditure was attributable to the deceased's personal expenditure, so two thirds was 'support'. *Brown v Ferguson*[2], discussed below, might suggest that 25 per cent was the appropriate deduction.

Income from both deceased and pursuer

The question might be more complicated where both pursuer and deceased have an income. In *Porter v Dickie*, effectively, this was again ignored. Having heard evidence that 'the pursuer and the deceased pooled their resources'[3], Lord Ross simply treated the total as a joint income, from which the proportion for loss of support was to be deducted, and despite its reduction when the pursuer received unemployment benefit. A significant effect of this is that a higher paid spouse may suffer a negative loss of support. Indeed, in *Porter v Dickie*, on this ground Lord Ross deduced that for a certain period 'the pursuer would suffer no loss'.

However, in *Brown v Ferguson*[4], Lord Sutherland said that '[t]he normal approach to the position where both spouses are earning is to add the incomes together and deduct say 25 per cent as being for the maintenance of the deceased. The net figure so arrived at less the earnings of the surviving spouse forms the loss of dependency'. The facts of that case were in fact complicated, and concern future dependency, so are discussed below.

Varying dependency in general

Clearly the degree of dependency may vary from time to time, because the pursuer's needs might vary (for example, a progressive illness), because the deceased's income might be anticipated to change (which might alter the proportion spent on dependents[5]) or because the pursuer's own income might change (which might also alter the proportion spent on dependents).

Such variation is not always dealt with the same way. In *Porter v Dickie* the fact that the pursuer had been made redundant between the time of the accident and proof, affecting his income, was in effect not assumed to affect his degree of dependency on the joint income (although given the changes in his income, this had a consequential effect on his dependency on the deceased's). The issue came up in different form in *Prentice v Chalmers*, discussed below in relation to the varying dependency of children.

---

1 Ie a rent of £14 per fortnight (as the pursuer now received a rent rebate) for a weekly income of £30 on unemployment benefit initially (leaving £21 per week for the widower), and then £22.10 (leaving £15.10 per week).
2 1990 SLT 274.
3 1982 SLT 234. At 234, the learned editor of the SLT recorded that '[t]he pursuer always handed over his whole pay to the deceased who had managed his finances'.
4 1990 SLT 274 at 275.
5 It was assumed in *Prentice v Chalmers* 1985 SLT 168 that the deceased's increasing income had not altered the proportion devoted to the pursuers' support, but that any decrease that might have occurred in the future would have resulted in an increase in the proportion in order to maintain the actual amount. Actual profits of the business were arguably irrelevant given that, *ex hypothesi*, the partnership was *res inter alios acta*.

However, in that case, and in *Brown v Ferguson*, it is chiefly a question of future variation.

The effect of inflation

Inflation was the major issue in *Prentice v Chalmers*[1]. The pursuer contended that the figures for the degree of dependency were historic ones, and the rate of inflation between the accident and proof should be taken into account. Uncontradicted evidence on the Retail Price Inflation Index (RPII) showed it had increased by 57.28 per cent.

Lord Hunter, Lord Dunpark and Lord Grieve agreed that the deceased would have maintained his family's standard of living despite the inflation, so would have spent an increasing proportion of it on support. Despite some doubts on how far inflation should be taken into account, and a clear attempt to distinguish the situation from that of inflation for future damages, they relied on the RPII figure. In reasoning fully described only in Lord Dunpark's opinion[2] they concluded that the 'global sum' for each past year should be the average of that for the first year, plus 157.28 per cent of the second, and so on. This average was to be multiplied by the number of years over which the past loss had occurred.

Apportionment between pursuers

Spouses and children etc

If there is more than one pursuer, the 'global sum' must be apportioned between them, typically, surviving spouse and children.

In *Prentice v Chalmers*, the Lord Ordinary, having apportioned two-thirds of the deceased's income as the 'global sum', further apportioned 60 per cent of that to the widow and 40 per cent among the three children. The Inner House substituted 75 per cent and 25 per cent. It is not clear how either conclusion was arrived at. Lord Hunter referred to the family's ages, and added simply that 'looking at the requirements of the respective members of the family and the total amount available, the proportion of the global sum allotted to the [widow ... is] ... substantially too low'[3]. Lord Dunpark[4], referred to the widow having to maintain the children. However, as he recognised, this seems to prove too much. If the widow was responsible, why pay anything to the children at all? In the event, the children's 25 per cent then required to be split between them, which was done in a surprising fashion, as described below in relation to future loss of support.

Without reference to *Prentice*, in *Campbell v Gillespie*[5] having accepted an allotment of 70 per cent to dependency, Temporary Judge Robertson accepted two-thirds of this to the widow and one-sixth each to the children, as this seemed 'reasonable'.

1 1985 SLT 168, particularly at 173, 175, 178–179.
2 Above, at 176.
3 Above, at 174.
4 Above, at 174 and 176.
5 1996 SLT 503, particularly at 511I–J.

Varying dependency of children

Prentice v Chalmers also raises the difficulty of varying dependency again. As explicated in Lord Dunpark's judgment the Inner House determined the relative continuing length of dependency of each and applied it retro-spectively. The basis of this calculation is discussed below in relation to future damages, but the outcome was that the three children received 5/24ths, 7/24ths and 12/24ths respectively from the 25 per cent of the global sum apportioned to them.

This is an aspect of the apparent confusion between past and future losses, discussed below; does not seem backed by any principle; and has strange effects. Older children receive less damages for past loss of support because they will be independent sooner in the future. Why should a child of 16, in order to be compensated for four and one third years past loss of support from her father, during all of which time she was considered dependent, receive £2,900; but a child of 14 receive £4,060 for the same period; and a child of 6 receive £6,960 for the same period? Moreover, this calculation fails to take account of actual past variation, for instance a child entering higher education.

Deductions

As noted, the deceased's income is calculated net of tax. Compensation from other compensation systems is discussed in ch 6.

Future lost support from deceased's employment income

Quantification takes place initially on the same principles as for loss of income. The modification attributable to applying the multiplier from the date of death, blurring past and future losses, produces significant differences in application.

Multiplicands

The multiplicand is, in principle, the annualised loss of support, subject to the usual difficulties. A good example is *Worf*. Apportionment to and between pursuers, varying dependency, and deductions are discussed below.

Multipliers

The same principles apply as in future loss of income, including the use of a tariff of multipliers[1] modified by individual circumstance[2], and again, *Worf* is a good example. However, this is subject to the multiplier operating from the date of death rather than the date of proof, which has the effect of reducing it.

This factor was subject to appeal in *Dingwall v Walter Alexander and Sons Ltd*[3]. In the Outer House Lord Jauncey applied a multiplier of 13, but

---

1 See Bennett *Personal Injury Damages in Scotland* (1999) App V(C)6.
2 Again, the Law Reform (Miscellaneous Provisions) Act 1971, s 4 prevents remarriage or the prospect of remarriage being taken into account, but interestingly, the possibility that there might have been a divorce can.
3 1979 SLT (Notes) 100.

deducted 3.1 to take account of the past loss, so in fact applied one of 9.9 for the future. The Inner House reversed his decision on liability, but pronounced obiter on multipliers in loss of support cases[1]. Lord Justice-Clerk Wheatley observed that such damages were no innovation, but suffered from additional imponderables compared with loss of income, that is, the length of time the deceased would otherwise have lived, and the length of time the claimant would live. Thus, while in non-fatal cases, the multiplier rightly operated from the date of proof, because past losses could be quantified then, the extra imponderables prevent that in fatal cases. Lord Robertson also considered past loss of support 'notional' and the date of proof immaterial[2].

In fact, this conclusion seems manifestly wrong. Firstly, Lord Wheatley's first extra imponderable in fact operates in both a loss of support claim and a loss of income one, and the second does not seem to create a new dimension of uncertainty. Secondly, past loss of support does not appear any more 'notional' than one for past lost income. Thirdly, although the date of proof may be more immaterial because in other cases it can be delayed until prognosis is clear, the more important difference is between relatively certain past loss and necessarily speculative future loss. Finally, dating multipliers from the date of death confuses past and future losses, and is likely to mean that the pursuer either receives nothing for past loss, or receives reduced damages for future loss. Nevertheless, this formula has been applied in other cases, such as *Porter v Dickie*, *Prentice v Chalmers* and *Campbell v Gillespie*.

Apportionment to and among pursuers

Apportionment operates in the same rough and ready way, but the proportions as between surviving spouse and children may not be the same as for past loss. For instance, in *Worf*, apportionment was 75 per cent/25 per cent for past loss, but 70 per cent/30 per cent for future loss. This is likely to represent reduced expenditure by a widow on dependent children.

Varying dependency

Variation of dependency is more clearly a problem of future loss. In *Brown v Ferguson* Lord Sutherland suggested the normal formula of adding spouses' income and subtracting 25 per cent for the deceased's personal expenditure, which answers questions about both common expenditure and double incomes. The formula required modification on the facts. The deceased was wife of the pursuer, was not working after the birth of her child, but would have returned to work. The couple and child lived in rented accommodation, but had bought a plot of land, and intended to build a house on it. The mortgage would come out of the deceased's salary, with a view to it being paid off in about seven years, during which time they would live off the pursuer's income. Lord Sutherland therefore decided, in effect to vary the multiplicand by adding half the deceased's earnings for the seven years and the whole of her earnings thereafter to the pursuer's earnings, and deducting the 25 per cent from that.

---

1 See 1981 SLT 313, IH. Lord Jauncey's actual multiplier was approved: see Lord Justice-Clerk Wheatley at 314, Lord Robertson at 317, and Lord Kissen at 319.
2 1981 SLT 313, IH, at 314, 316–317.

Varying future dependency of different children is a complicating factor because they are likely to cease dependency at different times. The problem was addressed in *Prentice v Chalmers*[1] where the pursuers' argument for a fixed sum multiplied by the number of years of dependency, in other words, a common multiplicand with different multipliers, was rejected by the Inner House[2]. Lord Dunpark declared the children to have five, seven and 12 years of dependency respectively, apparently to the age of 21. These years of dependency totalled 24. The global sum had been arrived at by assuming two-thirds of the deceased's annual income was for support of the family, and that 25 per cent of this was to be apportioned to the children. The children therefore received 5/24ths, 7/24ths and 12/24ths respectively of that sum.

Deductions

As noted with past loss of support from employment, the deceased's income is calculated net of tax, and compensation from other compensation systems is dealt with in ch 6.

Future loss of support from deceased's pension income

There may be a claim for loss of support on the ground of a reduced pension, occupational or private. It should not be confused with loss of pension rights, discussed above.

This can only be a claim for future loss, and three periods require to be distinguished, as *Davidson v Upper Clyde Shipbuilders*[3] explained. Firstly, a pension may be paid to a dependent for the period from the breadwinner's death until his or her expected retirement date. By definition, it is not reduced by the breadwinner's death before retirement, so cannot found a claim for damages. (It might, indeed, be a deduction from compensation for loss of support from employment income, although it is very unlikely to be deducted, as *Davidson* showed, and as discussed in ch 6).

Secondly, a pension may be paid from the expected date of the breadwinner's retirement to his or her expected date of death. It is likely to be reduced by the breadwinner's death before retirement, as that will reduce the number of contributions made. Thus it could found a claim for damages for loss of support from pension income, but this could only be for future loss. Such a claim was central to *Davidson*. Lord Milligan accepted the pursuer's contention that the multiplicand should be a 55 per cent apportionment of the full annual pension income her husband would have received, and the multiplier should be 6.5 since he would have been expected to live for 13 years after retirement[4]. (The very important question in *Davidson* of deductions is considered in ch 6.)

Thirdly, a pension may be paid from the expected date of the breadwinner's death to the dependent's expected date of death. This is the usual 'widow's pension'. It might be reduced by the breadwinner's death before retirement,

---

1 1985 SLT 168 at 176.
2 That the eldest was at university was mentioned, but ignored.
3 1991 SLT 329.
4 Above, at 333F–J. See also *Parry v Cleaver* [1970] AC 1 [1969] 2 WLR 821, [1969] 1 All ER 555 and *Auty v National Coal Board* [1985] 1 WLR 784, [1985] 1 All ER 930.

as that will again reduce the number of contributions made. Thus again, it could found a claim for future loss. (This did not arise in *Davidson* as it was agreed that the pursuer would not in fact receive a reduced pension for this period.)

Multiplicand and multiplier

The multiplicand is calculated on the same basis as loss of pension rights for an injured pursuer, as laid down in *Mitchell v Glenrothes Development Corporation*, with subject to deductions and apportionment of the share to the dependent. A multiplier is provided by the usual means.

Davidson v Upper Clyde Shipbuilders provides an example. The pursuer received the half pension her late husband's scheme gave a surviving widow, with a multiplier of 6.5 to cover a predicted 13 years from the husband's expected date of retirement to his expected date of death.

Deductions

Compensation from other compensation systems is dealt with in ch 6, and the law provides an extraordinary outcome in respect of lost support from pensions.

Apportionment to and among pursuers

Apportionment arises in respect of loss of support from pension as much as from earnings. In *Davidson v Upper Clyde Shipbuilders* Lord Milligan simply applied the same proportion as he had decided upon for loss of support from earnings, that is, 55 per cent. However, in *Campbell v Gillespie* Temporary Judge Robertson decided that, while the appropriate proportion for loss of support from earnings was 70 per cent, from pension it was only 50 per cent. No explicit reasoning was offered, but it may reflect that by retirement pension, children would be independent[1].

PERSONAL LOSSES: *SOLATIUM* AND 'LOSS OF SOCIETY'

Solatium and 'loss of society' are commonly dealt with separately but it is useful here to deal with them together.

QUANTIFICATION OF *SOLATIUM* IN GENERAL

Solatium is not amenable to a calculational approach. It is 'substitute or solace' compensation, not 'equivalence'. Quantification therefore operates through a mixture of form of tariff and jury approach[2].

---

1 1996 SLT 503, at 516.
2 Damages for loss caused by breach of a Convention right under the Human Rights Act 1998 are subject to limits described in ch 3. In particular, no award, or only a token, may be given for non-pecuniary loss: see eg *Abdulazíz, Cabales and Balkandali v UK* (1985) 7 EHRR 471, para 69.

Precedent, tariffs and consistency

The tariff approach, including the special form of law report listing in extra-ordinarily comprehensive and complicated form the classes of physical and mental injury, was described in ch 4.

In practice, therefore, a person claiming *solatium* must search through such collections to find the most similar preceding awards, which may be then subjected to a multiplier from the Retail Price Inflation Index[1] to produce current value, and modified up or down in the light of differences from the instant case. To this extent, a *solatium* award is right or wrong insofar as it conforms to tariff.

Juries and consistency

However, as discussed in ch 4 in relation to the 'jury' or reasonable sum approach, there is also strong authority for regarding *solatium* as 'a jury matter' (even where there is no jury). This explains a reluctance of the Inner House to lay down principles for awards, or even overturn *solatium* awards which do not conform to tariff.

Girvan v Scottish Farmers Dairy (No 2), the leading case, which encouraged the use of juries, was discussed at length in ch 4. It requires to be noticed here only that jury awards are as much precedents as judicial ones although they might vary considerably from judicial ones and as between themselves; that they should probably not be subjected to the Retail Price Inflation Index to produce a current value[2]; and that consistency is likely to decrease.

Allocation to past and future

Solatium damages are commonly broken into past and future components. Thus, in *Currie v Kilmarnock and London District Council*[3], the jury's award was split into £30,000 for the 30 months preceding trial and £61,000 for the future.

This has considerable significance. Division is made to allow interest on damages for past loss. However, while the loss is recognised as continuing into the future (unlike losses of asset) it is not dealt with on an annuity approach (unlike other damages for future loss). Thus, *solatium* is in practice treated as something between a one-off loss like property damage on the one hand, and a continuing loss like nursing care on the other.

EXAMPLES OF QUANTIFICATION OF *SOLATIUM*

Quantification of physical and psychological pain and suffering

There is no clear authority on the factors to be taken into account in quantify-ing *solatium* for physical pain, for instance. Clearly perceived intensity, duration, and perhaps the manner of infliction, are relevant, and can be inferred

---

1 Reprinted in McEwan and Paton *McEwan and Paton's Damages for Personal Injuries in Scotland* (2nd edn, 1989, looseleaf updated). However, this approach was doubted in respect of jury awards by Lord Hope in *Girvan v Inverness Dairy Farmers (No 2)* 1998 SC (HL) 1 at 12G–H, 1998 SLT 21, 1998 SCLR 72, referring to his opinion in *Currie v Kilmarnock District Council* 1996 SC 55.

2 See above.

3 1996 SC 55.

from the special forms of law report listing *solatium* cases. There may be a question of 'net pain and suffering' where some set-off occurs. Although a majority in the House of Lords approved this approach in *McFarlane v Tayside Health Board*. It seems to have influenced their conclusion as it did explicitly for a minority[1]. This conclusion may be confined to its unusual facts. As length can project into the future, awards for future pain are clearly competent.

However, for all examples of physical pain, disfigurement, physical disease or illness, psychological suffering and unhappiness, the best guide to likely levels of *solatium* are the published tariffs of quasi-precedents.

Quantification of wounded feelings and affront

Too few precedents exist to infer factors to be taken into account in quantifying *solatium* for wounded feelings and affront, or for a tariff to emerge, with two possible exceptions. Nevertheless, no doubt perceived intensity, length and, no doubt, manners of infliction, are relevant. The exceptions are defamation, and 'additional damages' under the Copyright, Designs and Patents Act 1988 for 'flagrant' infringement of copyright[2].

Defamation

Paucity of precedent, lack of tariff, and variety of awards

At common law there is very little indication as to what is an appropriate figure, or even what factors are to be taken into account. In *Winter v News Scotland Ltd*[3], the Inner House said there was no tariff for defamation awards. Lord Morison, giving the opinion of the court, considered that the test in a jury trial was what a reasonable jury would award[4] and that comparison should not be made with personal injury awards[5].

Not surprisingly, therefore, extraordinarily different awards were made in the two most similar cases of the few reported in recent decades, and in other cases there are differences hard to explain.

The two most similar cases were *Anderson v Palombo*[6] and *Fraser v Mirza*[7]. In *Anderson*, a police constable was charged with breach of the peace as a result of the false complaint by someone known to have made false complaints before, and was awarded £200 by Lord McDonald. In *Fraser*, another police constable might have been refused a transfer on account of a complaint from a person whose evidence Lord Marnoch found less than wholly credible[8], and was awarded £5,000.

---

1 (1999) Times, 26 November, HL. See the opinions of, on the one hand, Lord Slynn of Hadley and, on the other, Lord Millett.
2 Infringement of 'moral rights' under the same legislation apparently attract damages, which would appear to be a form of *solatium* for wounded feelings and affront, but no indication is given of how they might be quantified. A tariff might be developed, but a jury approach seems inevitable.
3 1991 SLT 828.
4 The court's attention was drawn to an award of 1881 of £2,500, an enormous sum in current spending power.
5 1991 SLT 828, at 831A, 831B and 831E.
6 1986 SLT 46.
7 1992 SC 150, 1992 SLT 740 and 1993 SC (HL) 27, 1993 SLT 527.
8 And who was apparently, at least till this case, a prominent citizen and JP.

Other cases hard to explain include *Muirhead v George Outram & Co Ltd*[1] and *McCluskie v Summers*[2]. In *Muirhead*, a solicitor whose professional competence was doubted in newspaper articles whose publisher refused to correct or to apologise, was awarded £3,000 by Lord Grieve. In *McCluskie*, a trade union and Labour Party official accused of perjury in a letter of limited circulation was awarded £7,500 by Lord Murray. In *Smith v Graham*[3], Lord Allanbridge said, obiter, that he would have awarded £2,000 to someone falsely accused of assault in a club[4].

Jury awards

Juries awards are exemplified by *Winter*. The *Sun*[5] published in both Scotland and England an allegation that the pursuer, a prison officer, had a sexual relationship with an inmate. The owners contended the allegations to be substantially true, but were found liable in a jury trial. The judge warned the jury that they should not seek to punish the defenders. They awarded £50,000.

Factors increasing awards

Certain factors have been suggested to increase awards, including the eminence of the pursuer (though not his or her goodness) and badness of the defamatory statement[6].

The first of these was evident in *McCluskie* where Lord Murray referred to the trust placed in the pursuer and his 'high public standing'[7]. It may also explain the apparent generousness of *Gilbert v Yorston*[8], where a semi-literate and less than credible allegation obtained £1,500 for the Chief Executive of the Orkney Islands Council. The awards in *Muirhead* and *Anderson* might suggest solicitors and police officers are not eminent, as such. Perhaps it is eminence in a profession, rather than of it.

The second factor figured in *Winter* where Lord Morison said that the more scurrilous the nature of allegations, the greater the injury[9]. This might explain *Fraser*, but accentuates the disparity with *Anderson*.

Other possible factors, possibly subsumable under 'badness', include the affront or injury to the pursuer[10], effect on employment and health[11], repetition[12],

---

1 1983 SLT 201.
2 1988 SLT 55.
3 1981 SLT (Notes) 19.
4 That is, a club properly-so-called, not a nightclub open to the public. However, it was not a 'gentleman's club', but a pigeon racing one.
5 A tabloid newspaper.
6 Eg Thomson *Delictual Liability* (2nd edn, 1999) p 259.
7 1988 SLT 55, at 55H.
8 1997 SLT 879, 1996 SCLR 1122.
9 1991 SLT 828 at 829I–K.
10 In *Winter* 1991 SLT 828, at 839K, Lord Morison said '[i]t is difficult to conceive of a more wounding attack'.
11 In *Anderson v Palombo* 1986 SLT 46, at 49F, Lord Macdonald said there was 'no question of damage to [the pursuer's] career or prospects', while in *Fraser*, the pursuer thought his transfer to the Serious Crimes Squad prejudiced, and Lord Marnoch said the case 'was much closer to . . . *McCluskie* than [to *Anderson*]'.
12 Mentioned by Lord Justice-Clerk Grant in *Stein v Beaverbrook Newspapers* 1968 SC 272, at 278, 1968 SLT 401.

the words used and manner of publication[1]. Finally, the very use of a jury may be a factor in the size of award[2].

Malice as a factor not increasing defamation awards

Malice on the part of the defender does not increase damages. This follows directly from the principle of *restitutio in integrum*, and was confirmed in *Stein v Beaverbrook Newspapers Ltd* by Lord Justice-Clerk Grant[3].

Factors decreasing awards

Certain other factors decrease damages. The opposites of the factors increasing damages will tend to decrease[4]. It has also been suggested that a person seeking only to clear his or her name will only receive a nominal sum, and that an already tainted character, immediate retraction and apology, provocation, and damages obtained by the pursuer from another defamer for the same defamation, may mitigate[5].

No authority is offered for the first factor, but an already tainted character was discussed in *C v M*[6]. The allegation was that the pursuer, a married woman, had an illegitimate child. The defender claimed not *veritas*, but that she herself had told him that and related things, so suffered little loss. Lord Clyde, giving the opinion of the Inner House, found that since she had put her character in issue, this was relevant. The question was also raised in *Winter*.

Immediate retraction and apology figured in *Morrison v Ritchie*[7]. The *Scotsman*[8] had carried a false report of a birth to a too-recently married couple. The newspaper staff were morally innocent and had carried out usual precautions. Lord Moncrieff, giving the opinion of the Inner House, said, albeit obiter, that in such circumstances 'the jury are quite entitled, if they think fit, to award a comparatively small amount, or it may even be a nominal amount ...'[9]. In *Stein* Lord Justice-clerk Grant made similar remarks[10].

Provocation might be thought to be a factor in *C v M*, and like assertions were made in *Winter*[11]. Finally, damages obtained from another defamer

---

1 In *Winter v News Scotland Ltd* 1991 SLT 828, at 829L–830B, Lord Morison referred to the language and style used, and the large circulation obtained.
2 It is possible that in *Winter*, the jury was influenced by the fact that the defender was a newspaper, that it had considerable means, and may have wished (although warned it should not) to punish it.
3 1968 SC 272, at 277–278, 1968 SLT 401.
4 But cf the argument in Nicholson *Sentencing: the Law and Practice in Scotland* (2nd edn, 1992) para 9.21, that lack of a criminal record and previous good character are not mitigating factors but the neutral starting point. Non-repetition of defamation, for instance, should not decrease damages.
5 Thomson *Delictual Liability* p 259.
6 1923 SC 1 particularly at 4–5, 1922 SLT 634.
7 (1902) 4 F 645, 9 SLT 476.
8 A broadsheet newspaper.
9 (1902) 4 F 645 at 652.
10 1968 SC 272, at 278.
11 Thomson *Delictual Liability*, at p 259, cites *Paul v Jackson* (1884) 11 R 460, although it is not clear that this supports the proposition.

mitigates by virtue of the Defamation Act 1952, s 12. This reflects the principle *restitutio in integrum,* assuming each repetition by a new person is not a new defamation.

Additional damages under the Copyright, Designs and Patents Act 1988 for 'flagrant' infringement

As discussed in relation to loss of profit on intellectual property, 'additional damages' may be awarded under s 97(2) of the Copyright, Designs and Patents Act 1988 (continuing earlier provisions). Two particular situations where this is appropriate are indicated. One is where there is benefit accrued to the defender. The other, which partakes of *solatium,* is where the infringement is 'flagrant'.

'Flagrant' is indicated by 'the existence of scandalous conduct, deceit and such like [including] deliberate and calculated ... infringements' it was held in the English case *Ravenscroft v Herbert*[1]. Thus in *Williams v Settle*[2], a photographer sold wedding photographs in the plaintiff's copyright containing the image of her father in law who was subsequently murdered. These pictures appeared in the national press causing her great distress. In reliance of the equivalent provision in previous legislation, a County Court judge awarded damages he himself described as 'very vindictive'. These were upheld on appeal, the Court of Appeal equating 'vindictive' with the 'exemplary' and 'punitive' damages known to English law. This approach was, however, doubted in *Beloff v Pressdram*[3], albeit obiter. There was a careful survey of the statute and its operation upon the facts of the case, limiting its ambit to 'exemplary' damages such as might be appropriate for insult and lack of regret. In *Nichols Advanced Vehicle Systems Inc v Rees, Oliver*[4] the breach of copyright was by former employees in positions of responsibility. It was described as involving 'stealing a march ... and inflict[ing] loss and humiliation which are difficult to compensate and difficult to assess' and as 'actuated by greed or cowardice, or gullibility' and involving 'deceit and treachery'. 'Additional damages' were held appropriate, even though paid to a company.

In *Redrow Homes Ltd v Bett Brothers plc*[5], the nature of such damages was considered by two Scottish judges in the House of Lords. Lord Jauncey of Tullichettle expressly reserved his position as to whether they were 'by nature punitive or purely compensatory' and Lord Clyde considered them 'exemplary, or, more probably, aggravated damages'. Lord Hope of Craighead offered no opinion. Thus the conclusions of *Ravenscroft* may remain applicable, though it is not clear whether *Williams, Beloff,* or *Nichols* remains the better guide, and the whole question is hostage to debates in English law as to the meaning of 'exemplary', 'punitive' and 'aggravated'.

---

1 [1980] RPC 193, at 208.
2 [1960] 1 WLR 1072, [1960] 2 All ER 806.
3 [1973] 1 All ER 241, particularly at 264j–272h.
4 [1979] RPC 127, particularly at 140, 141.
5 1998 SC (HL) 64, particularly at 69C–D and 71C–D.

As a matter of construction, the House of Lords decided that such 'additional damages' can only be awarded where other damages are already awarded.

Loss of faculties and loss of amenities

Subject to the special case of pursuers in a coma or persistent vegetative state, there is, as with pain and suffering, no clear authority of factors to be taken into account, though perceived intensity, duration and perhaps manner of infliction, are relevant.

Thus for all examples the best guide to levels of *solatium* are the published tariffs of quasi-precedents.

Loss of expectation of life

Traditionally, awards for *solatium* for loss of expectation of life were 'restricted to a conventional sum', that is, a token payment only, as Lord Justice-Clerk Wheatley noted in *Dalgleish*. Indeed, given the propensity to award an un-differentiated sum for all forms of *solatium*, it has been difficult to know what even a 'conventional' sum was thought to be.

Section 9A of the Damages (Scotland) Act 1976 has narrowed the range of situations in which *solatium* is payable to 'aware' pursuers only (over-turning *Dalgleish* in part), as described in ch 2, and thereby intending to replace conventional sums by requiring the suffering in consequence of knowledge of the loss be taken into account[1]. This requires an answer to whether awareness of shortly impending death attracts a larger award because of the proximity, or a smaller one, because of the brevity of the awareness, which the courts have not provided[2]. It does appear that the deceased was aware in *Beggs v Motherwell Bridge Fabricators Ltd*[3] for Lord Eassie was 'uncertain whether it was truly the intention of the legislature in enacting [the new provision[4]] that the courts should be required to carry out the difficult—and often distasteful—task of trying to assess the feelings of pain and apprehensions of mortality of someone so abruptly and severely injured as to be in imminent and real danger of death within a few minutes'. He awarded £250 because 'despite the intensity of that pain and distress, the brevity of its suffering dictates that the award be of mod-est proportions'[5].

However, s 9A(3) declares that a court making such an award 'shall not be required to ascribe specifically any part of the award to loss of expectation of life'. Thus, courts are able to continue to avoid explaining what they have done.

---

1 Scottish Law Commission *Report on the Effect of Death on Damages* (Scot Law Com no 134) (Cm 1848) (1992) paras 4.14 and 4.20.
2 Nor did the Scottish Law Commission.
3 1998 SLT 1215, particularly at 1223L–1224A, 1997 SCLR 1019.
4 In fact this was a claim by the executor under s 2 of the Damages (Scotland) Act 1976 (as substituted by s 3 of the Damages (Scotland) Act 1993), the victim having died before the action was raised.
5 Cf, however, *Wells v Hay's Exor* (Lord Osborne, 25 November 1998, unreported, but discussed in Forsyth *Transmissible Solatium After Death: a re-appraisal* 1999 SLT (News) 45–50 and Hajducki *Death Payments – a new approach* 1999 SLT (News) 77–79.

QUANTIFICATION OF 'LOSS OF SOCIETY' AWARDS

Common law provision

'Loss of society' awards are effectively the origin of modern *solatium*, although it was a mere 'acknowledgement payment'[1]. A widening occurred with cases such as *Kelly v Glasgow Corporation*[2] in which the sums awarded were not negligible[3].

Statutory provisions

Section 1(4) of the Law Reform (Miscellaneous Provisions) Act 1971 incorporated the requirement to disregard a widow's 'remarriage ... or ... prospects of remarriage' in assessing damages for the death of her husband which applies to loss of society as well as loss of support, presumably producing the same bizarre result as in *McKinnon v Reid*.

Common law *solatium* was replaced by a 'loss of society' award in s 1(4) of the Damages (Scotland) Act 1976, following a Scottish Law Commission report. Whatever the intentions of that report, as noted in ch 2, there was dispute as to whether or not this did expand the common law and offered compensation instead of 'acknowledgment' in cases such as *Dingwall*. Following the interpretation in such cases, s 1(4) was amended to its present broader form, including distress and anxiety in contemplation of the death; grief and sorrow caused by the death; and loss of society and guidance.

No cases on the amended version appear to be reported. However, some of those on the common law still have some authority, for instance, in *Inglis v London, Midland and Scottish Rly*[4] and *Kelly*[5]. In *Inglis* while the Lord President would 'lay down no scale of awards', he declared 'I think it is relevant to take account of the [deceased] child's age and any circumstance which would naturally tend to increase the parent's sympathy and affection for the child'. The Inner House view in *Kelly*, per Lord President Cooper[6], was that firstly, early death of a pursuer reduces his or her claim; but secondly, a death rendering children orphans increases a claim; and thirdly, the younger a child, the greater its damages. In other words, damages vary with the duration of the experience of the loss, and this is not balanced out by younger children suffering less intensity of grief.

Those cases on the more limited original form of the statutory claim still also have some authority. Lord Justice-Clerk Wheatley, in *Dingwall* listed as relevant factors: the relationship between the parties, their respective ages, the circumstances in which they lived with respect to each other, and any other

---

1 Per Lord Justice-Clerk Wheatley in *Dingwall v Walker Alexander & Sons Ltd* 1981 SLT 313. This harmonises with the limits imposed on non-pecuniary damages for a breach of a Convention right under the Human Rights Act 1998, as described in ch 3.
2 1949 SC 496, 1951 SLT 183. Affmd 1951 SC (HL) 15.
3 The husband received £250, which would have been larger but for his premature death, and the children, from £150 to £350. At that time, £250 might have been greater than the husband's annual income: cf *Riddell v Reid* 1941 SC 277, 1941 SLT 179 where the deceased was earning £3/10/– per week (ie about £175 pa), and his wife received £750 for *solatium* and loss of support.
4 1941 SC 551, particularly at 560.
5 Ie *Kelly v Glasgow Corporation* 1949 SC 496, particularly at 499–500.
6 Affirmed by the House of Lords at 1951 SC (HL) 15.

relevant factor[1]. This is unfortunately so all-inclusive as to be unhelpful (while ignoring *McKinnon v Reid*). It also flows from what is probably overall a minority opinion.

Examples of factors which have been taken into account include drunkenness and minor violence in *Wilson v Chief Constable, Lothian and Borders*[2]; the ages of the pursuers and the length of future lost society in *Davidson v Upper Clyde Shipbuilders*[3] (echoing *Kelly*); life expectancy in *Fowler v Greater Glasgow Health Board*[4] (again echoing *Kelly*); effect on the pursuer's mental health in *Phillips v Grampian Health Board (No 2)*[5]; the pursuer's indifference in *Wotherspoon v Strathclyde Regional Council*[6]; and major violence and separation with remaining affection in *Morrison v Forsyth*[7].

However, it is clear from *Davidson* that a sort of tariff has emerged. There, as noted in ch 4, Lord Milligan carefully compared seven characteristics on nine comparable cases with a view to determining the appropriate level of damages.

---

1 1981 SLT 313 at 316.
2 1989 SLT 97.
3 1987 SLT 329.
4 1990 SLT 303.
5 1992 SLT 659, 1991 SCLR 817 (even where death was anticipated).
6 1992 SLT 1090.
7 1995 SLT 539.

6. The interaction of damages with other compensation systems

In addition to delictual damages, there is a range of other systems which may provide compensation for a delict victim. These include commercial insurance; contractual 'sick pay' and occupational pension arrangements; redundancy payments; charitable[1] assistance; the social security system; the national heath service; and a number of particularistic schemes such as the Criminal Injuries Compensation Scheme. Atiyah has remarked on the United Kingdom's 'plethora of systems'[2]. Their existence raises a number of questions about the relationship between delict and these other systems.

DAMAGES AND COMMERCIAL INSURANCE

The relationship of delictual damages and commercial insurance must be looked at in three parts: the overall interaction of the two compensation systems; the relationship between damages and first party insurance; and the relationship between damages and third party insurance.

THE OVERALL INTERACTION OF DELICTUAL DAMAGES AND INSURANCE[3]

Differences between delictual damages and insurance are clear, and they may appear simple alternatives[4]. However, the relationship is in fact intimate and symbiotic, and depends on the conventional distinction between 'first' and 'third party' (or 'liability') insurance. Essentially, 'first party' insurance is just 'all non-liability' insurance.

'First party' insurance

One can insure 'first party' against almost any harm, including *damnum* to oneself caused by another's *injuria*, and claiming is normally enormously easier and cheaper than by delict. Such insurance is common for property, so victims of property loss choose it[5] when they have the choice. Such

---

1 In a non-technical sense.
2 Cane (ed) *Atiyah's Accidents Compensation and the Law* (6th edn 1999) p 315.
3 The argument here owes much to *Atiyah* ch 9.
4 See eg *Atiyah* pp 245–250.
5 *Atiyah* pp 7–8.

insurance is rare for personal injury[1], which is one reason why delict actions are so much more common in this area when victims have the choice. Delict and 'first party' insurance are thus in practice negatively correlated.

In cases where there is indemnity insurance, the victim's insurer may decide to sue, having been subrogated to the victim's rights[2]. Thus the incidence of insurance further influences the incidence of delict actions. Moreover, if the insurer waives its right to sue (as in 'knock for knock' agreements), the victim may sue but does so at his or her own expense, runs the risk of having the case taken over by the insurer (who may settle it), and would have to pay damages obtained over to the insurer[3]. The two systems are not simple alternatives.

'Third party'[4] (or 'liability') insurance

One can also insure against the *damnum* to others caused by one's own *injuria*. This form of insurance thus depends on the existence of delict, so the two are positively correlated.

Commonly a pursuer will not sue unless the defender is 'third party' insured (or is a large enough body to 'self-insure', ie carry the costs without insurance). Indeed, the positive correlation is reinforced by third party insurance being compulsory in some important areas. This is not in order to not protect the insured, but to ensure the delict victim gets compensated. They are plainly not alternatives.

A conclusion

Thus, at least in relation to personal injuries, delict begins to look like a complicated and inefficient way of transferring compensation from insurer to victim, or even insurer to insurer, simply a means by which insurance companies settle accounts. The sums may be paid by the wrongdoer's third party insurer to the victim, but may also be from the wrongdoer's third party insurer to the victim's first party insurer.

Atiyah further observes that a considerable amount of legislation on delict, including the Law Reform (Contributory Negligence) Act 1945, is only explicable in terms of the wide-spread use of 'third party' insurance[5]. Indeed, he suggests that the common law of delict as a whole has changed significantly (though not fundamentally) to reflect this. Such changes include the growth of negligence and the objectivisation of the duty of care[6], not to mention the very level of personal injury awards.

---

1 It is common for life, but there, special considerations apply.
2 Subrogation is the principle by which an insurer indemnifying an insured acquires the insured's rights to sue the wrongdoer. It is not available for personal accident or life insurance.
3 Indeed, in a 'knock for knock' case, the damages would be obtained from the defender's insurer, to whom they would be paid back by the pursuer's insurer: see *Hobbs v Marlowe* [1978] AC 16, [1977] 2 WLR 777, [1977] 2 All ER 241.
4 Presumably so called because the beneficiary is 'third party' to the insurance contract.
5 *Atiyah* pp 199–202.
6 *Atiyah* pp 202–208.

THE RELATIONSHIP BETWEEN DELICT AND 'FIRST PARTY' INSURANCE: NON-DEDUCTION AND OVERCOMPENSATION

Where both delict and first party insurance can be claimed, while they are negatively correlated in practice, the two are not alternatives, in that a pursuer can use both[1]. Moreover, if delict is used, in broad terms, compensation by first party insurance (including life assurance) is not taken into account in quantifying damages. Thus those who so insure and sue will commonly be doubly compensated, making nonsense of the principle of *restitutio in integrum*. This appears to be true whether the claim is for loss of assets; consequential expenditure; loss of profits, earnings or support; or *solatium* and loss of society.

Scots authority

This principle seems to have been assumed in *Forgie v Henderson*[2] (allowance from a friendly society) and *Morrison & Milne v Bartolomeo & Massa*[3] (assignation of insurance rights). Clearer, but still implicit, statements came in *Port Glasgow & Newark Sailcloth Co v Caledonian Rly*[4] (whether insurance companies should be sisted as pursuers) and *Stewart v Duncan*[5] (prejudicial statements to a jury). The most direct statement is in *Smith v Comrie's Exrs*[6], where Lord Mackintosh compared the situations of rights on succession and insurance money in their effect on damages, but this is an unappealed Outer House decision.

Relying in part upon English common law, this position was approved by the Scottish Law Commission[7]. Nevertheless there is little authority on the relationship of first party insurance and damages in the common law[8], although this principle still appears to apply outside personal injury and fatal accident cases.

English authority

English common law has been clearer, although it has depended upon the meaning of the Fatal Accidents Acts (which introduced loss of support actions into England and Wales) and the distinction between 'general' and 'special' damages. While providing reasoning, it has nevertheless avoided engaging

---

1 Subject to subrogation, which means that in respect of indemnity insurance, if the pursuer simply claims on the first party insurance, the insurer can sue after paying out.
2 (1818) 1 Murray 410.
3 (1867) 5 M 848.
4 (1892) 19 R 608, 29 SLR 577.
5 1921 SC 482, 58 SLR 325, 1921 SLT 292.
6 1944 SC 499, 1945 SLT 108.
7 *Damages for Personal Injuries: report on (1) admissibility of claims for services, (2) admissible deductions* (Scot Law Com no 51) (HC Paper 557 (1977–78)) paras 65–72.
8 *Bews v Scottish Hydro Electric plc* 1992 SLT 749, 1992 SCLR 448 has to be seen as concerning payments of a benevolent character, discussed below.

with the fundamental contradiction between *restitutio in integrum* and non-deduction of insurance payments.

The principal authority is *Parry v Cleaver*[1]. In it, and other cases, four overlapping arguments have been used: that the insurance is a contract, which should be kept; that if insurance payments were deducted, the wrongdoer would benefit; that the insurance payment is too remote from the *injuria*; and that the insurance contract is *res inter alios acta*[2]. None of these seems wholly sufficient, but they have produced the orthodoxy applied in practice.

Statute on the relationship between damages and first party insurance

In relation to personal injury, the common law is now partly replaced by the Damages (Scotland) Act 1976, s 1(5)(b) and the Administration of Justice Act 1982, s 10(a). The former[3] stipulates that, in assessing loss of support, no account shall be taken of 'any insurance money, benefit, pension or gratuity which has been, or will be, paid as a result of the deceased's death'. 'Insurance money' includes return of premiums, 'benefit' includes friendly society and trade union payments for the relief and maintenance of dependants, and 'pension' includes a return of contributions and payment of a lump sum[4]. The latter stipulates that, in personal injury actions, no account shall be taken in assessing damages of 'any contractual pension or benefit' which presumably includes insurance contracts.

Also, the Policyholders Protection Act 1975 was passed to provide protection to insurance policyholders generally upon the insolvency of their insurance company. The Policyholders' Protection Board has a duty to indemnify or otherwise assist or protect policyholders prejudiced by such companies, and the power to make levies upon insurance companies and others to finance it. There is no 'central fund', so any levy must be imposed ad hoc and after the event.

THE RELATIONSHIP BETWEEN DAMAGES AND THIRD PARTY INSURANCE: KEEPING DELICT GOING

The delict system, as discussed above, in practice relies heavily upon third party insurance. Commonly, damages would not be paid without it. Making motor vehicle and employment insurance compulsory produces an enormous quantity of detailed regulation of the relationship, some of which requires discussion.

---

1 [1970] AC 1, [1969] 2WLR 821, [1969] 1 All ER 555.
2 Ie 'something done between other persons [than the two parties in question]'.
3 Which is subject to the Damages (Scotland) Act 1976, s 1(5A) which specifically declares that an award of provisional damages does not prevent liability for loss of support, but that any part of that award for 'future patrimonial loss' shall be taken into account when damages for loss of support are assessed. This seems to mean that provisional future damages can be deducted from past loss of support.
4 It is not clear whether 'insurance' qualifies 'benefit ... [etc]', but such cases are dealt with below in relation to damages and employment pensions.

Compulsory third party motor vehicle insurance, 'third party rights', and the Motor Insurers' Bureau[1]

Compulsory third party insurance

Third party motor vehicle insurance was made compulsory by the Road Traffic Act 1930. The current provision is complicated both structurally and substantially.

The requirement for third party insurance

By s 143 of the Road Traffic Act 1988 (subject to certain exceptions) a person using, or causing or permitting another to use, a motor vehicle on a road must be covered by third party insurance complying with the Act[2]. By s 147, no policy of insurance has effect until a certificate in the prescribed form and with the necessary information[3] has been delivered (although the certificate itself is not a contract). There are exceptions, principally for organs of government, which 'self-insure'[4].

The insurance required

Section 145(2) of the Act, read with s 145(5) and (6), requires a policy issued by an authorised insurer[5], and s 145(3)[6] requires the policy to insure against 'any liability which may be incurred by [the insured] in respect of death or bodily injury to any person or damage to any property caused by or arising out of the use of the vehicle on a road in Great Britain', and also specifies liability for emergency treatment[7]. Very many drivers are 'permitted drivers' on the policy of a family member or employer, and s 148(7) requires insurers to indemnify them, although they are not parties to the contract[8].

There are exceptions where compulsory third party employment insurance operates and otherwise, under s 145(4) and (4A)[9], and an exception exists for drivers from overseas, who are dealt with through the 'green card' system[10].

---

1 Motor vehicle insurance is complicated by the prevalence of 'comprehensive' insurance providing first party insurance against personal injury, damage to or loss of the policyholder's car, damage to and loss of its contents, damage to its garage and contents, and legal expenses of pursuing claims, as well as third party insurance against personal injury to a third party and damage to a third party's property.
2 Or security fulfilling the requirements of the Road Traffic Act 1988, s 146. See also s 155.
3 See the Motor Vehicle (Third Party Risks) Regulations 1992, SI 1992/1217 (as amended), especially Sch 1, Forms A–F. They require details to determine validity and cover, and minimum legibility.
4 RTA 1988, s 183 (Crown vehicles); s 144(2) (local authority, police authority, NHS etc vehicles): see also the Nuclear Installations Act 1969, s 21(5) (as amended). See further RTA 1988, s 143(4) (invalid carriages) and s 144(1) (deposit of security).
5 Ie one carrying on business within the Insurance Companies Act 1982, Sch 2, Pt 2, Group 2, who is a member of the Motor Insurers' Bureau.
6 As amended by the Motor Vehicles (Compulsory Insurance) Regulations 1992, SI 1992/3036.
7 See RTA 1988, ss 155 and 158(5), also s 154.
8 As potential defenders rather than pursuers, they are not 'third parties' in the standard sense.
9 Added by the Motor Vehicles (Compulsory Insurance) Regulations 1992, SI 1992/3036.
10 See the Motor Vehicle (International Motor Insurance Card) Regulations 1992, SI 1992/992 (as amended): see also the Road Traffic Act 1988, s 145(3)(aa) and the Motor Vehicle (Compulsory Insurance) (No 2) Regulations 1972, SI 1973/2143.

The significance of compulsory third party insurance for the pursuer

Compulsory third party insurance means that a pursuer can usually expect that damages will be paid, irrespective of the means of the driver. However, of itself, it does not give the pursuer any rights under the insurance contract, nor assist where the insurer is insolvent, or the contract avoided by the insurer by reason of breach or misrepresentation. These problems are dealt with below in relation to 'third party rights'. Nor does compulsory third party insurance, of itself, assist where the driver has no contract of insurance at all, or is unknown. These problems are dealt with below in relation to the Motor Insurers' Bureau.

'Third party rights'

By definition, the pursuer is third party to the insurance contract, so has rights under it against neither insured nor insurer[1]. However, third party rights have been created statutorily[2].

Rights to discover the insurer

By s 154 of the Road Traffic Act 1988, a person against whom a claim on compulsory third party insurance is made is required to tell the claimant on demand whether or not he is insured, and if he is, to give particulars from the certificate of insurance or identify it.

Rights to make a claim under the contract

Section 148(7) of the Act stipulates that compulsory third party insurers are 'liable to indemnify the persons . . . specified in the policy in respect of any liability which the policy purports to cover in the case of [them] . . .'[3], giving third parties a right to sue.

Further, s 151(5) requires that (subject to conditions) if judgment is obtained against a person insured under a compulsory third party policy on liability which is covered by that policy, the insurer is obliged to disburse the whole sum payable under the judgment in respect of death or bodily injury, and some or all in respect of property damage[4], together with interest and expenses, 'to the persons entitled to the benefit of the judgement'.

So far as passengers are concerned, s 149 renders of no effect any antecedent 'agreement or understanding' to waive third party rights, and further removes the *volenti* defence in respect of them.

---

1 No *jus quaesitum tertio*, ie third party right under the contract, seems to have been argued for although the contract is nothing if not for the third party's benefit. Policies are also commonly governed by English law, which does not recognise such rights.
2 Although they have to a large extent been overtaken by the creation of the Motor Insurers' Bureau Agreements.
3 This stipulation negatives, as well as the common law, the apparent requirement of the Life Assurance Act 1774 (which also applies to at least some third party insurance) that in order to claim, a beneficiary must be named in the policy as having insurable interest.
4 Ie, where the sum is less than £250,000 the whole sum plus interest: where the sum is greater, either the same proportion of the sum is payable as £250,000 bears to the whole sum, or the difference between sums already paid and £250,000, in both cases plus interest.

Rights upon insolvency of insured or insurer

Contemporaneous with the Road Traffic Act 1930 was the complementary Third Party (Rights Against Insurers) Act 1930. This provided that if the insured became insolvent, his or her rights under a policy of insurance were transferred (subject to certain limits) to the third party in a sort of statutory assignment[1]. Section 153 of the Road Traffic Act 1988 now also provides that such insolvency shall not affect the insurer's liability to pay out.

The Policyholders Protection Act 1975, as noted above, goes further and ensures that, on liquidation of an insurer, compulsory insurance claims are fully met.

Rights in relation to breaches of specific terms of the contract

Section 148(1) of the Road Traffic Act 1988 stipulates that certain contractual conditions, effective as against the insured, are not effective as against a third party. They are a somewhat haphazard list of conditions relating to the condition of the driver and of the vehicle, but not relating to use of the vehicle, or permitted drivers (so such conditions remain valid as against the pursuer). Also, s 151, obliging the insurer to pay the third party where judgment is obtained against the insured, does so '[n]otwithstanding that the insurer may be entitled to avoid or cancel . . . the policy . . .'. Other conditions are similarly treated by s 148(5) and s 150.

Rights where the contract has been obtained by misrepresentation or non-disclosure

The principle of *uberrima fides*[2], fundamental to insurance, means that misrepresentation or non-disclosure of a material fact goes to the root of the contract. However, the third party's need for protection is no less in such a case. The compromise arrived at is that, by s 151(2)–(4) the insurer can avoid a policy obtained by misrepresentation or non-disclosure of a material fact and decline to pay out to a third party on such a policy, but only on stringent procedural conditions.

The Motor Insurers' Bureau[3]

The limitation on compulsory third party insurance in relation to those claiming against drivers whose insurance contracts were in fact avoided; against drivers who were not insured at all, and against unidentified drivers, were obvious from the first. They were addressed as early as 1937[4], although only

---

1 Transfer of rights occurs only after liability has been established, but declarator can be sought before that: *McDyer v Celtic Football & Athletic Club Ltd* 1999 SLT 2, at 10C and 10L–11B, per Lord MacFadyen.
2 Ie 'utmost good faith' on the part of the insured in apprising the insurer of relevant considerations.
3 Motor Insurers' Bureau, 152 Silbury Boulevard, Central Milton Keynes, MK9 1NB: Company Reg no 412787. It is unfortunate that the address given in the MIB Agreements (and in associated legislation) is out of date. In general, see Williams *Guide to Motor Insurers' Bureau Claims* (3rd edn, 1999).
4 Report of the Committee on Compulsory Insurance (Cmnd 5528 (1937)), particularly Pt III.

in 1946 was the Motor Insurers' Bureau ('MIB') set up and an agreement between it and the Minister of Transport instituted. The current versions of that agreement are the 'Uninsured Drivers Agreement' of 1988[1] and the 'Untraced Drivers Agreement' of 1996[2]. In practice these have partly replaced 'third party rights'.

The nature of the MIB

The MIB is 'in many respects, an extraordinarily anomalous institution, which operates partly within and partly outside the legal system'[3]. It is a private company limited by guarantee, wholly owned by the insurance companies and underwriting syndicates who undertake motor vehicle business, and relations between them are governed by the 'Domestic Regulations' which are a contract between itself and its member institutions, incorporated into its Articles of Association[4]. On the other hand, its function is to extend the protection of compulsory third party insurance, so motor vehicle insurers are obliged as a condition of their licence to become members of it; it operates through 'Agreements' which are contracts with the Government; the 'green card' system depends entirely upon its existence; and it is mentioned in various pieces of legislation. Also, there are in strict law no rights of third parties against it, although it is regularly sued.

The 'Uninsured Drivers Agreement'

The 'Uninsured Drivers Agreement' applies where there has been death or injury in a road accident for which a known driver was liable, and either that driver had a contract of insurance which was avoided by the insurance company by reason of breach of a specific condition, or misrepresentation or non-disclosure, or he or she had no contract of insurance at all. Thus liability has been determined, and the only question is who pays.

In such cases, subject to certain limitations and exceptions, and certain conditions, by virtue of cl 2 the MIB will pay what should be covered by the third party insurance required by s 145 of the Road Traffic Act 1988.

It does not pay out for losses not so covered, for example those covered by compulsory third party employment insurance, or caused by Crown vehicles. Clause 6 also stipulates that it does not pay out for some losses which are so covered, for example where the claimant knew or ought to have known that

---

1 Motor Insurers' Bureau (Compensation of Victims of Uninsured Drivers): Text of an Agreement dated 21st December 1988 between the Secretary of State for Transport and the Motor Insurers' Bureau together with some notes on its scope and purpose (HMSO, undated): reproduced in Williams *Guide to Motor Insurers' Bureau Claims* (3rd edn, 1999) Appendix.

2 Motor Insurers' Bureau (Compensation of Victims of Untraced Drivers): Text of an Agreement dated 14th June 1996 between the Secretary of State for Transport and the Motor Insurers' Bureau together with some notes on its scope and purpose (Department of Transport/HMSO, 1996: ISBN 0 11 551850 9): reproduced in *Williams*, Appendix.

3 *Atiyah* p 211.

4 A chief aim of the Domestic Regulations is to apportion sums paid out among members. In broad terms, where there is no insurance at all, the MIB 'Central Fund' pays out (cl 7). Where there is, but it is voidable or otherwise creates no liability for the insurer in law, the insurer nevertheless pays (cl 5). In effect, this means that the insurer cannot treat the contract as vitiated.

the vehicle was stolen or unlawfully taken. There are other limitations on its operation, such as an 'excess' of £175 and ceiling of £250,000 on property losses.

Clause 5 requires that a claim has already been pursued against the defender, and there are other procedural conditions. The MIB undertaking requires judgment of a court, but accepts settlements.

The 'Untraced Drivers Agreement'

The 'Untraced Drivers Agreement' applies where there has been death or personal injury in a road accident, but no driver has been traced. Thus, no liability has been, or can be, determined.

In such cases, subject to certain exceptions and limitations, and certain conditions, by clause 1 the MIB will pay what should be covered if, on the balance of probabilities, the untraced driver would be liable[1].

There are various exceptions, for example relating to stolen or unlawfully taken vehicles, and conditions precedent requiring the reporting of the accident etc.

There can be no requirement of a claim already pursued, nor of judgement since, by definition, there is no defender. The MIB therefore investigates and adjudicates itself according to one of two processes, with appeal to an 'arbitrator'[2].

Enforceability of MIB Agreements and decisions

The MIB Agreements are contracts under seal between the Secretary of State and the MIB, and have no statutory backing. The MIB is not party to relevant litigation. The Agreements therefore appear unenforceable by the third party.

However, although there is no reported Scottish decision on the matter, there are several English cases, for instance *Coward v MIB*[3], in which a claimant has sued the MIB on the Agreements. However, this has not passed without adverse comment[4].

Compulsory third party employment insurance, third party rights and lack of central funds

Though recommended long before compulsory third party motor insurance[5], compulsory third party employment insurance was only introduced by the Employers' Liability (Compulsory Insurance) Act 1969, and is considerably less effective.

---

1 The current Agreement applies only to deaths and injuries arising on or after 1 July 1996. (Nb a deed of variation dated 4 October 1996 amends the 1996 Agreement by correcting cl 28(b) to refer to 1 July: see *erratum* slip included with the 1996 Agreement). Those arising before then are dealt with according to the slightly different 1972 Agreement, as amended by the 1977 Supplemental Agreement.
2 See MIB claim form 'Compensation for Victims of Untraced Drivers' and 'Notes for the Assistance of Claimants on the "Untraced Drivers Agreement"'.
3 [1963] 1 QB 259.
4 In *Albert v MIB* [1972] AC 301, [1971] 3 WLR 291, [1971] 2 All ER 1345, at 1354, per Lord Dilhorne.
5 Holman Gregory Report on Workmen's Compensation Legislation (Cmnd 816) (1920).

Compulsory third party insurance

The requirement for third party insurance

Section 1 of the 1969 Act requires every employer conducting business in Great Britain to insure against specified third party liability to employees, and the Act is extended to certain offshore working[1]. 'Employee' is defined in the traditional form by s 2(1), which leaves some difficulties in relation to such things as 'loaned' employees.

As well as the exclusion of independent contractors and of employment outwith Great Britain (save under the offshore regulations), specified family members are excluded[2]. So is much of the public sector and a heterogeneous collection of other bodies and employments, by the Act itself, by delegated legislation under it[3], and by other legislation[4].

The employer is required to display the certificate of insurance in a certain form and allow inspection of it[5].

The insurance required

The insurance must be with an authorised insurer[6], and must be 'against liability for bodily injury or disease sustained by an employee arising out of and in the course of his employment in Great Britain in that business' (or in relevant areas in the case of offshore workers). 'Bodily injury', 'disease', business' and especially 'arising out of and in the course of employment', are all subject to interpretation.

The policy must not contain certain conditions, roughly equivalent to those excluded vis-a-vis third parties in the compulsory motor insurance legislation[7]. Regulations also require cover for at least £2m, a figure which has not changed in the 30 years since it was fixed.

'Third party rights' and lack of central funds

Unlike with compulsory motor vehicle insurance, there are no 'third party rights' in employers' liability insurance, subject to two small exceptions. Firstly, the requirement to display the certificate of insurance (however misleading) enables the pursuer to discover who the insurer is. Secondly, the Third Parties (Rights Against Insurers) Act 1930 (discussed above in relation

---

1 Offshore Installations and Pipeline Works (Management and Administration) Regulations 1995, SI 1995/738.
2 Employers' Liability (Compulsory Insurance) Act 1969, s 2(2).
3 EL(CI)A 1969, s 3, as amended, and the Employers' Liability (Compulsory Insurance) Exemption Regulations 1971, SI 1971/1933, as amended.
4 Eg the Sex Discrimination Act 1975, s 53(4), Sch 3, para 10.
5 EL(CI)A 1969, s 4 and the Employers' Liability (Compulsory Insurance) General Regulations 1971, SI 1971/1117, regs 5–7 (as substituted by SI 1975/194). As the contract may be void and not all limitations on it appear, the certificate can be misleading. In *Dunbar v A&B Painters* [1986] 2 LL Rep 38, at 43, Balcombe LJ approved Deputy Judge Pratt's observation that '[i]t is now apparent that the certificate is not worth the paper it is written on'.
6 Ie a person or body of persons lawfully carrying on in Great Britain insurance business of any class relevant for Part II of the Companies Act 1967 and issuing the policy or policies in the course therefor: EL(CI)A 1969, s 1(3)(b): a different definition from that in compulsory motor insurance legislation,
7 EL(CI)A 1969, s 1(2) and SI 1971/1117.

to compulsory motor insurance) operates in respect of the defender's insolvency. (The Policyholders Protection Act 1975 also applies).

However, the pursuer cannot claim directly from the insurance company at common law[1] nor compel the defender to claim from the insurer. Nor is there any protection against insurance contracts avoidable by reason of failure to disclose material facts, misrepresentation or otherwise[2]. Nor yet do the prohibited terms cover all possible objectionable terms, for instance ones limiting insurance in risky situations.

Further, there is no equivalent to the Motor Insurers' Bureau to ensure payment where the employer is for any reason uninsured.

Other examples of compulsory third party insurance

There are other examples of compulsory third party insurance, also designed to ensure that damages are paid, in the Riding Establishments Act 1964, s 1(4A)(d) and Nuclear Installations Act 1965, s 19.

DAMAGES AND EARNINGS AND 'SICK PAY'

Earnings actually received are not lost, so reduce any claim for lost earnings. 'Sick pay' does likewise, for the alternative is double compensation. This is entrenched in statute by the Administration of Justice Act 1982, s 10, proviso (i), which refers to 'any remuneration or earnings', so far as personal injury actions are concerned (and it is difficult to see the issue arise in respect of any other claim)[3].

On the basis of a House of Lords case on the English common law, *Hussain v New Taplow Paper Mills*[4], this is so even if sick pay (and later 'topping up' pay in a lower paid job) is funded by the employer's first party insurance scheme, and so might fall to be regarded as an insurance benefit which, by virtue of s 10(a) of the Act, is not to be deducted. The reasoning of *Parry v Cleaver*[5] (discussed below in relation to employment pensions) was distinguished on the ground that that case concerned a pension paid after employment ceased. Thus the basic principle that the plaintiff could not claim for what he had not lost re-asserted itself. Lord Bridge of Harwich admitted that such borderline cases produced a variety of results and Lord Reid concluded that the common law treated this as a matter of 'justice, reasonableness and public policy', and that the decision depended upon the 'intrinsic nature' of the benefit, not its source[6].

---

1 And may be barred by the Life Assurance Act 1774, as noted in relation to compulsory motor insurance.

2 As occurred in *Dunbar v A&B Painters* [1986] 2 LL Rep 38 where the misrepresentation was made by the insured's broker, as agent without the assent of the insured.

3 *Davidson v Upper Clyde Shipbuilders Ltd* 1990 SLT 329 concerned the effect of a pension on a loss of support claim. However, it appears to have been implicitly amended by the Social Security (Recovery of Benefits) Act 1997, s 17, as noted below.

4 [1988] AC 514, [1988] 2 WLR 266, [1988] 1 All ER 541.

5 [1970] AC 1.

6 [1988] 2 WLR 271 at 271–272 respectively.

However, there are two complications. One is that such payments by an employer may be paid on the express condition that they are repayable if damages are obtained[1]. The Scottish Law Commission[2] favoured non-deduction of non-contractual examples, as effectively benevolent payments, and considered it would be unsatisfactory to distinguish contractual ones. Purely benevolent examples are discussed below, and contractual examples are now declared by s 10(e) of the Administration of Justice Act 1982 to be non-deductible (subject to contrary agreement). Thus double compensation is only avoided in respect of such 'returnable payments' if they are actually returned.

The other is that sick pay may be 'statutory sick pay', that is, in brief, sick pay required to be paid by employers if there is no contractual sick pay[3]. Nothing in the 1982 Act requires that to be treated differently from contractual sick pay, but it appears as one of the benefits recoverable from damages for lost earnings in the Social Security (Recovery of Benefits) Act 1997, discussed below, and therefore 'recovered' rather than simply deducted. This does not denote a change of principle[4].

DAMAGES AND EMPLOYMENT PENSIONS

Employment-based contractual or quasi-contractual benefits, such as employment pensions, may be paid to those who cease work as a result of delictual injury, or to dependents of those who die.

PENSIONS TO INJURED PERSONS

Whether such pensions paid to the injured person are to be treated as sick pay (and deducted from damages for loss of earnings) or commercial insurance (and not so deducted) fell to be decided in the unsatisfactory English House of Lords decision of *Parry v Cleaver*[5]. The facts were somewhat complicated but, essentially, a police constable had contributed to a police pension fund which entitled him to a pension if discharged as disabled. He was so discharged and the question was whether the pension should be deducted from damages. The House of Lords decided by a bare majority that such pensions were to be treated as commercial insurance, seemingly whether voluntary or compulsory, contributory or non-contributory, transferrable or non-transferrable.

The Scottish Law Commission agreed with this conclusion[6], and it became entrenched in s 10(a) of the Administration of Justice Act 1982 in personal

---

1 Such an arrangement is understood to be common with local authorities.
2 Scot Law Com no 51, paras 62–63.
3 See the Social Security Contributions and Benefits Act 1992, ss 151–155 and Statutory Sick Pay (General) Regulations 1992 SI 1992/894.
4 But, as noted above, SSCBA 1992, s 10 proviso (i) seems to have been implicitly amended by s 17 of the Social Security (Recovery of Benefits) Act 1997 so as to exclude statutory sick pay: see the discussion of social security benefits below.
5 1970 [AC] 1.
6 Scot Law Com no 51, paras 65–72.

injury actions (an equivalent having already appeared in s 1(5) of the Damages (Scotland) Act 1976 for loss of support actions[1]). The position was underlined at common law in England and Wales by *Smoker v London Fire and Civil Defence Authority*[2].

The effect is double compensation, made more remarkable where the defender or defendant who must pay the damages is the employer who pays the non-deducted pension (as was the case in *Smoker*, where this fact was held irrelevant).

PENSIONS TO DEPENDENTS

Whether such pensions paid to the dependents should be treated the same way is dealt with by s 1(5)(b) of the Damages (Scotland) Act 1976, which specifically provides that 'any insurance money, benefit, pension or gratuity ... paid as a result of the deceased's death' is not to be taken account of in assessing loss of support. This provision was noted above in relation to insurance as such[3]. It seemingly extends the commercial insurance principle to other payments received.

As noted in ch 5, three periods have to be distinguished. They are: from the deceased's actual death until his or her expected date of retirement; from that date until the deceased's otherwise expected date of death; and from that date until the dependent's expected date of death. The provision was considered in *Davidson v Upper Clyde Shipbuilders Ltd*[4]. There, a widow received a pension from her deceased husband's employer's contractual pension scheme for the first period, and would for the second and third. She also sued the employer in respect of his death, claiming loss of support.

In respect of her claim for loss of support from her deceased's husband's earnings for the first period, it was agreed that s 1(5)(b) meant the pension was not to be deducted from the damages.

In respect of her claim for the second period, she argued that s 1(5)(b) operated in the same fashion. The defender (relying on *Parry v Cleaver* and another English case, *Auty v National Coal Board*[5]) argued that as she was already receiving the pension for this period, she would in fact suffer no loss (or at least only a small difference between the pension she was receiving and her apportionment of the pension she would have received) and that s 1(5)(b) did not apply. Lord Milligan found that it did apply, so the pension received was not deducted from the damages.

In respect of the third period, there was no dispute, because it was common ground that there would be no loss then[6].

Double compensation is therefore again clearly effected, again more remarkable because the pension was paid by the deceased's employer who was also the defender, so the same source provided both compensations.

---

1 Following *Report on the Law Relating to Damages for Injuries Causing Death* (Scot Law Com no 31) (1973).
2 [1991] 2 AC 502, [1991] 2 WLR 1052, [1991] 2 All ER 499.
3 Including its relationship with the Damages (Scotland) Act 1976, s 1(5A).
4 1990 SLT 329.
5 [1985] 1 WLR 784, [1985] 1 All ER 930.
6 Although it is not clear that D(S)A 1976, s 1(5)(b) would not operate then, too.

DAMAGES AND REDUNDANCY PAYMENTS

Redundancy payments have nothing to do with delict as such. However, it may happen that a person ceasing work as a result of delictual injury might receive such a payment incidentally, and the question arises as to whether any payment for this falls to be deducted from damages for loss of earnings.

The Scottish Law Commission, having toyed with the idea that such a payment is a form of wages, plumped for the view that as redundancy has no connection with the relevant delict, redundancy payments should not be deducted from damages[1], and the Administration of Justice Act 1982, s 10(d) requires that no such payment be taken into account[2].

This is not, however, double compensation, because the payment and the damages compensate for different losses.

DAMAGES AND PAYMENTS OF A BENEVOLENT CHARACTER

Injured people, and the dependants of those killed, are a traditional object of charity. Many obtain benefits in kind or services from relatives and friends[3] which would be impossible to take into account in assessing damages. Some receive benefits from ad hoc 'disaster funds'. In any event, charitable[4] payments have been, along with insurance, regarded as classic examples of receipts which should not be deducted from any form of damages at all.

The leading case is often regarded as *Redpath v Belfast and County Down Rly Co*[5], concerning a serious railway accident for the victims of which the Mayor of Bangor started a relief fund. The Lord Chief Justice of Northern Ireland comprehensively stated his reasons for not deducting from damages payments from the fund, including effecting the donor's intentions, reduction of the defendant's liability, remoteness and collaterality, and the lack of benefit to the beneficiaries. English cases have followed this principle, including *Parry v Cleaver*.

There is very limited Scottish authority on the point. The facts of *Dougan v Rangers Football Club Ltd*[6] are similar to those of *Redpath*, in that it was litigation following the Ibrox disaster in which the widow and children of a person killed sued Rangers Football Club, and the Lord Provost of Glasgow had set up an 'Ibrox Disaster Fund'. A potentially significant difference from *Redpath* was that the defenders in the action were donors of about 14 per cent of the fund and therefore averred that they had wholly or partly satisfied the pursuers' claims, so that, in effect, their donation was interim payment of damages.

---

1 Scot Law Com no 51, paras 84–87.
2 The Social Security (Recovery of Benefits) Act 1997, s 1, Sch 1, Part I, para 6 now says the same thing. The relationship of the Administration of Justice Act 1982, s 10, and SS(RB)A 1997, is not wholly clear, as noted below in relation to social security payments.
3 See (English) Law Commission *Personal Injury Compensation: how much is enough?* (Law Com no 225) (HC Paper 666 (1993–4)) and ch 3.
4 In a non-technical sense.
5 [1947] NI 167, particularly at 175.
6 1974 SLT (Sh Ct) 34.

Sheriff J Irvine Smith concluded that Scots law was no different from English law[1], and that deduction would be 'contrary to well established principle, inequitable and contrary to public policy ...'. He noted that while *Redpath* relied heavily on analogy with insurance contract and remoteness, more recent authorities tended to stress 'public policy' and 'inequity'.

The Scottish Law Commission broadly agreed with the sheriff's conclusion[2], emphasising that deduction might discourage such philanthropy[3] and fail to fulfil the donors' intentions. It took the point that differences of principle might arise if the defender were a donor, as in *Dougan*.

The statutory position is now found in the Administration of Justice Act 1982 in respect of the injured, and the Damages (Scotland) Act 1976 in respect of dependents. Section 10(f) of the former declares that, subject to agreement, payments 'of a benevolent character' are not to be taken into account, save (by virtue of s 10, proviso (iv)) where they are made by the defender directly (whether to the injured person or a relative), and not through a trust or other fund. Section 1(5) of the latter does not specifically refer to benevolent payments, but 'patrimonial gain or advantage' in s 1(5)(a) seems apt to cover them even if 'benefit, pension or gratuity' in s 1(5)(b) is not.

Perhaps surprisingly, the rich possibilities arising out of these provisions have not produced much reported litigation. However, the operation of s 1(5) arose in *Bews v Scottish Hydro Electric plc*[4]. Mr Bews' life was insured by his employer, which paid the premiums and was the beneficiary. However, a document of uncertain status stated that payments under it could be made to dependants 'at the discretion' of the employer in order 'to avoid hardship'. This was declared to be 'without prejudice to any claim upon [the employer]'. Mr Bews was killed at work and his dependants received about £55,000 by an exercise of the employer's discretion under that document. The dependants also sued the employer who raised a plea to the relevancy and claimed that if it were liable, the £55,000 should be deducted from the damages. Lord Abernethy concluded that the payment was not made 'as a result of the deceased's death' but of the employer's discretion. Thus s 1(5) did not apply. However, common law indicated, on the basis of *Dougan v Rangers Football Club*, and English and Northern Irish authority (some of which was discussed above), that it should not be deducted.

DAMAGES AND RIGHTS ON SUCCESSION

Inheritance is not a compensation system, but a person may benefit from another's death, by way of succession, thus benefitting from the death.

While there might have been some warrant in *Smith v Comrie's Exrx*[5] for deduction from damages of a person inheriting from a relative in respect of

---

1 1974 SLT (Sh Ct) 34 at 37. He also cited Windeyer J in *National Insurance Co of New Zealand v Espagne* 105 CLR 569.
2 Scot Law Com no 51, paras 57–58, 60–61.
3 An odd argument; is it the role of delict to encourage philanthropy?
4 1992 SLT 49, 1992 SCLR 448.
5 1944 SC 499, 1945 SLT 108.

whose death they might claim loss of support or loss of society, the position is now clear under s 1(5)(a) of the Damages (Scotland) Act 1976, which declares that no account is to be taken of 'any patrimonial gain or advantage which has accrued or will or may accrue ... from the deceased or from any other person by way of succession or settlement' in assessing damages for loss of support.

DAMAGES AND SOCIAL SECURITY BENEFITS

Social security is essentially a system of compensation for a wide variety of conditions, including some which constitute *damnum* caused by *injuria*, such as injury and inability to work[1]. Thus it overlaps with damages, and most pursuers receive some social security payments. Indeed, this may be an important source of interim income[2]. However, social security operates largely independently of damages, and does not have the intimate and symbiotic relationship with it that commercial insurance does. Yet the outcome of the relationship it does have is paradoxically different, since the overriding consideration in the relationship is avoidance of double compensation.

The social security system has been described as 'a ragbag of provision based on differing, sometimes conflicting and anachronistic principles'[3]. There is a wide variety of possible benefits, contributory or not, means-tested or not, discretionary or not, and only available after an accident or not, to which different principles apply[4]. Thus the interlocking of damages and social security, while limited, is complicated.

BENEFITS AS THE BASIS OF CLAIMS

While social security benefits are usually compensation for *damnum*, if a delict disentitles from one, that loss itself is *damnum* caused by *injuria*, and can be sued for, as in *Webb v MacAuley*[5], where inability to work as a result of the accident meant disentitlement from family income supplement, and *Arnott v Bristol-Myers Co Ltd*[6], where the pursuer would have been able to claim income support regardless of her inability to work because of the accident[7].

---

1 Many benefits are concerned with Atiyah's 'redistributive' compensation, which is not the subject of delict: see *Atiyah* p 350. On 'redistribution justice', see now the opinion of Lord Clyde in *McFarlane v Tayside Health Board* (1999) Times, 26 November, HL.
2 See eg (English) Law Commission *Personal Injury Compensation: how much is enough?* (Law Com no 225) (HC Paper 666 (1993–4)) and ch 3.
3 Quoted in Ogus, Barendt and Wikeley *The Law of Social Security* (4th edn, 1995) p 144).
4 *Atiyah* pp 285–294, usefully divides benefits into short term, long term, and widows' and dependants'. His types of compensation can be superimposed upon this, though he does not do this himself.
5 1988 SC 10.
6 1998 SLT 110.
7 This case was complicated by the relationship with the recovery of benefits legislation: see also *McKenna v Sharp* 1998 SC 297 (sub nom *McKenna v Chief Constable, Strathclyde Police* 1998 SLT 1161).

BENEFITS AND DOUBLE COMPENSATION

Where benefits are received as compensation for a loss which is *damnum* caused by *injuria*, the question of double compensation arises. There is a tortuous history of discussion[1] and legislation on this, most of which can safely be ignored[2].

Four approaches are or have been employed, that is: ignoring, deducting half, deducting all, and recovering, the benefits.

Ignoring

The Damages (Scotland) Act 1976, s 1(5) provided that no 'benefit' be deducted from damages for loss of support, and this is defined to include social security benefits generally. Thus all are ignored, and any double compensation is similarly ignored.

For personal injury actions, s 10(b) of the Administration of Justice Act 1982 provides that 'any pension or retirement benefit payable from public funds' be not taken into account. What benefits this covers is not authoritatively determined, but presumably retirement pensions are. Since they are not compensation for *damnum*, no double compensation results.

Section 10(c) provides that 'any benefit payable from public funds in respect of any period *after*[3] the date of the award of damages, designed to secure to the injured person or any relatives of his a minimum level of subsistence' is to be ignored. Again, there is no authoritative determination of what this covers, but it is intended to cover income support at least. As this relates to the period after damages are awarded, such a benefit is in respect of future damages, and thus might constitute double compensation. However, the provision must now be read in conjunction with the Social Security (Recovery of Benefits) Act 1997, discussed below.

In relation to any claim which is not for loss of support, nor personal injury, it is not clear what the law is.

Half deduction

A compromise reached in the Law Reform (Personal Injuries) Act 1948, s 2(1) was to deduct half of certain benefits[4] from loss of earnings for a certain period. This system was unsatisfactory but remained till 1989, and in respect of small claims until 1997[5].

Deduction

Section 10 provisos (i)–(iii), of the Administration of Justice Act 1982 provide that remuneration or earnings from employment (thus including statutory

---

1 But see Scot Law Com no 51.
2 Though payments made in pursuance of court orders and agreements made before 6 October 1997 fall under the previous system, for which see the Law Reform (Personal Injury) Act 1948, s 2(1) for payments under £2,500, and the Social Security Administration Act 1992 and Social Security (Recoupment) Regulations 1990, SI 1990/322 (as amended).
3 Emphasis added.
4 Originally industrial injury benefit, industrial disablement benefit and sickness benefit.
5 Social Security (Recovery of Benefits) Act 1997, ss 2, 33, Sch 3, para 1 and Sch 4.

sick pay, discussed above in relation to damages, earnings and sick pay; contribution-based jobseeker's allowance[1]; and any s 10(c) benefit (discussed above) 'payable in respect of any period *prior to*[2] the date of the award of damages') are to be 'taken into account', ie deducted. Thus, double compensation is avoided.

However, an inconsistent provision specifically relating to jobseeker's allowance and income support prior to an award of damages now appears in the Social Security (Recovery of Benefits) Act 1997[3] (discussed below), so the provision must be assumed implicitly repealed, at least in part.

Recovery

The Social Security (Recovery of Benefits) Act 1997 provides that, with effect from 6 October 1997, certain benefits paid to the pursuer can be recovered by the Government from the defender, who deducts them from the damages, in a form of statutory subrogation[4].

Section 6, read with s 1, states that if a defender is liable to a pursuer 'in respect of any accident, injury or disease' suffered by the pursuer, and the pursuer has received a listed benefit[5] then, subject to exceptions, he or she 'is liable to pay to the Secretary of State an amount equal to the total amount of [certain] recoverable benefits'.

'Listed benefits', defined in s 1(4)(c) and Sch 2, are of three sorts, matched respectively to loss of earnings[6], cost of care[7], and loss of mobility[8]. The amount of such benefits is 'recoverable'[9] if paid or likely to be paid during the 'relevant period'. Section 3 defines that as five years from the injury or onset

---

1 Previously 'unemployment benefit': see the Jobseeker's Allowance Act 1995, s 41(4), Sch 2, para 6.
2 Emphasis added.
3 Cf the position of statutory sick pay.
4 This scheme replaced a similar one found in the Social Security Administration Act 1992 Part IV and Social Security (Recoupment) Regulations 1990, SI 1990/332, having been introduced by the Social Security Act 1989. The current form was described by Lord President Rodger in *Wisely v John Fulton (Plumbers) Ltd* 1998 SLT 1026, at 1030B, as 'a rough and ready set of compromises' (though no worse than its predecessor).
5 Or is the MIB: Social Security (Recovery of Benefits) Act 1997, s 1(2)(b).
6 Disability working allowance, disablement pension payable under s 103 of the Social Security Contributions and Benefits Act 1992, incapacity benefit, income support, invalidity pension and allowance, jobseeker's allowance, reduced earnings allowance, severe disablement allowance, sickness benefit, statutory sick pay, unemployability supplement, and unemployment benefit. It also includes any income support paid with any of the above benefits.
7 Attendance allowance, the care component of disability living allowance, and disablement pension increase payable under ss 104 or 105 of the Social Security Contributions and Benefits Act 1992.
8 Mobility allowance and the mobility component of disability allowance. 'Loss of mobility' is not a common title for a head of damages, and in *Mitchell v Laing* 1998 SLT 203 it was interpreted to mean 'damages for patrimonial loss suffered by a person as a result of loss of mobility due to the accident' examples including taxi fares. This is clearly actual consequential expenditure.
9 Thus the provision is wholly or partly inconsistent with the Administration of Justice Act 1982 in respect of statutory sick pay (s 10, proviso (i)), jobseeker's allowance (s 10, proviso (ii)), and income support (s 10, proviso (iii)). Those provisions must be concluded to be amended or repealed to that extent: see also reference to s17 of the Social Security (Recovery of Benefits) Act 1997 below.

of disease, or until there is final discharge of any claim, or it is settled, whichever is sooner[1].

However, by virtue of s 8, recovery of any benefit can only be made in respect of the type of loss or cost with which it is matched which was received during the 'relevant period'[2], and if the amount of damages awarded for that loss or cost is less than the benefit received, recovery is only up to the amount of the damages. Thus, there is no *'virement'*, and no benefit can be recovered at all from damages for loss of assets, for future consequential expenditure, future loss of earnings, or *solatium*[3]. Also, certain payments are exempted from the scheme by virtue of Sch 2[4], including prescribed small payments[5].

The mechanism of recovery is that, by virtue of s 17, damages are assessed without reference to listed benefits[6]. Then, by virtue of ss 4–6, the defender must obtain from the Compensation Recovery Unit[7] a 'certificate of recoverable benefits', containing details of such benefits paid or likely to be paid, before paying damages and must pay the sum indicated by the certificate within 14 days. Section 5(6) requires the pursuer be given the details of the certificate on request; s 9 requires the defender to indicate to the pursuer that the damages are paid net of the recoverable benefits; and s 15 requires a court making an order to specify which head of damages any recoverable benefit is attributed to[8]. There is a system of review of, and appeal against, the certificates in ss 10-14[9]. Special regulations govern certain complex cases, and structured settlements[10].

A number of problems remain, including the position of benefits which are not 'listed benefits', how the 'relevant period' is to be calculated, what the effect of the legislation is on tenders, contributory negligence, and others[11]. However, in *Wisely v John Fulton (Plumbers) Ltd*[12], the First Division decided that calculating interest on damages was part of the process of assessing them. Therefore, s 17 requires that interest be calculated on the whole sum of damages, disregarding any benefits which would have to be paid to the

---

1 Ie, in relation to AJA 1982, Sch 2, column 2: in relation to column 1, it is five years: see *Mitchell v Laing* 1998 SLT 203.

2 Interpreted by the Inner House in *Mitchell v Laing* 1998 SLT 203 as the five year period without the alternative of the date of final discharge. This was necessary to make the Act work. The Secretary of State was not represented in the proceedings.

3 The possibility under the previous legislation of deducting benefits designed to replace income from any head of damages including *solatium*, which might thereby all be used up, was one reason for the current legislation.

4 See Social Security (Recovery of Benefits) Regulations 1997, SI 1997/2205, reg 2, including payments under s 1 of the Damages (Scotland) Act 1976, the Vaccine Damage Payments Act 1979, the Criminal Injuries Compensation Act 1995 and contractual sick pay.

5 At the time of writing, no small payment exemption had been made.

6 This is also inconsistent with s 10 provisos (i)–(iii) of the Administration of Justice Act 1982, which must be considered implicitly repealed or amended to that extent.

7 DSS, Reyrolle Building, Hebburn, Tyne & Wear, NE31 1XB.

8 Court of Session Practice Note of September 15 1997 provides a Schedule of Damages for use in relevant cases: 1997 SLT (News) 253, and it is understood that sheriffs principal have issued similar guidance: see Bennett *Personal Injury Damages in Scotland* p 38 (also App IV).

9 *Boal v Secretary of State for Social Security* 1998 SLT 639 may apply, *mutatis mutandis*, to the new legislation.

10 Social Security (Recovery of Benefits) Regulations 1997, SI 1997/2205, regs 9 and 10.

11 See eg McGuire *Compensation Recovery* (1997) 42 JLSS 352–354, and Paton *Damages and the recovery of benefits* 1998 SCOLAG 41–43, and 1998 SCOLAG 107.

12 1998 SLT 1026.

Compensation Recovery Unit. Moreover, interest must be included in the sum of 'Compensation for earnings lost during the relevant period' in Sch 2.

DAMAGES AND NATIONAL HEALTH SERVICE BENEFITS

The national health service is a compensation system, and three questions arise in its relationship with damages. Firstly, since comprehensive national health service benefits are universally available, should damages pay for medical benefits at commercial rates? Secondly, should national health service benefits resulting in reduced non-medical expenditure reduce damages? Thirdly, can the national health service recover its expenses from a defender?

USE OF MEDICAL SERVICES AT COMMERCIAL RATES

The principle of minimisation of damages ought to require that medical services at commercial rates not be used. However, the view has been taken that this would improperly restrict the liberty of the individual.

Thus s 2(4) of the Law Reform (Personal Injuries) Act 1948, which remains in force subject to minor amendment, provides that in an action for personal injuries, the reduction of costs created by use of the national health service shall be disregarded. The Scottish Law Commission considered that this drafting precludes the defence that the services were unnecessary or the expense unreasonable, and recommended the provision be repealed, leaving a simple 'reasonableness' test[1].

EFFECT OF REDUCED NON-MEDICAL EXPENDITURE

In-patients receive bed and board free at the point of consumption. Thus normal expenditure is reduced. This could be taken into account in calculation of loss of earnings, a principle accepted in relation to reduced living expenses in a different context in the English Court of Appeal case *Shearman v Folland*[2]. The issue was raised again in *Daish v Wauton*[3] where, after reviewing authority, the Court of Appeal concluded that the principle would treat wastrels better than conscientious people, so that national health service benefits should be regarded in the same light as public benevolence or commercial insurance, and disregarded.

However, in the event, s 11[4] of the Administration of Justice Act 1982 provides that in a personal injury action 'any saving to the person which is attributable to his maintenance wholly or partly at public expense in a hospital, nursing home or other institution shall be set off against any income lost by him as a result of the injuries'. The 'set off' can only be against future

1 Scot Law Com no 51, paras 81–83.
2 [1950] 2 KB 43.
3 [1972] 2 QB 262.
4 The effectively identically drafted s 5 operates in England and Wales.

loss of income and no other head of damages. The provision does not seem to have been the subject of reported decisions.

RECOVERY OF EXPENDITURE

The Road Traffic Act 1988, s 157 allows a hospital to recover expenses incurred in treating a pursuer from a compulsory third party motor insurer who is paying out in respect of an insured, up to a certain level, in a form of secondary statutory subrogation. Section 158 does something similar for a doctor treating a road traffic emergency.

DAMAGES AND CRIMINAL INJURIES COMPENSATION AND CRIMINAL COURT COMPENSATION ORDERS

CRIMINAL COURT COMPENSATION ORDERS

Compensation orders made by criminal courts are provided for in the Criminal Procedure (Scotland) Act 1995, ss 249–253. They allow a court in some circumstances, when convicting a person, to make a compensation order for 'any personal injury, loss or damage caused, whether directly or indirectly, by the acts which constituted the offence'. The power reflects the fact that such acts are likely to constitute delicts, actionable as such in principle, but not worth it in practice.

There is no guidance in the legislation as to quantification, and orders are in fact rare.

Section 253 requires that compensation orders are not to be taken into account in assessing damages, but where a compensation order has been made, damages in fact payable are reduced by the amount of the order already paid, and/or the court's leave is required for any order for payment of the damages beyond the difference between the award and the compensation order.

CRIMINAL INJURIES COMPENSATION

The Criminal Injuries Compensation Scheme was also created at least in part because of the practical impossibility of victims of crimes of violence successfully suing their aggressors.

The current scheme is found in the Criminal Injuries Compensation Act 1995 and delegated legislation thereunder. The Act is skeletal, s 1 empowering the Secretary of State to 'make arrangements for the payment of compensation to, or in respect of, persons who have sustained one or more criminal injuries'. These arrangements are to be called the 'Criminal Injuries Compensation Scheme'. Most of the detail is found in eponymous delegated legislation (approved by Parliament, but not a statutory instrument) dated 12 December 1995.

The details of the Scheme are beyond the scope of this work[1]. However, the scheme covers 'personal injuries' which are 'directly attributable to' certain types of criminal act. These are essentially violent crimes, but include fire-raising, poisoning and trespass on a railway line. The Criminal Injuries Compensation Authority[2] operates the Scheme, which gives 'standard amounts', in effect *solatium* payments, from an explicit 25-point tariff. The tariff levels, ranging from £1,000 to £250,000, are an attempt to reflect contemporary forensic *solatium* levels. In addition, there may be awards for certain past and future losses of earnings to be calculated on similar principles to damages, and if such an award is made, so may one for certain actual and notional past and future consequential expenditure.

Various grounds for reducing awards exist. These are wider than apply in relation to damages (including 'conduct and character' for instance), but one (under paras 48 and 49 of the Scheme) is a pound-for-pound reduction for any damages awarded or settled already, or in the future. There is no provision to deduct *solatium* only from the 'standard amount', etc (as applies for recovery of social security benefits). There appears to be no authority in relation to deducting Criminal Injuries Compensation from damages, and given paras 48 and 49, it is not clear how a court (which might regard such payments as more like social security than commercial insurance or charitable payments) would approach the matter.

OTHER STATUTORY SCHEMES

There are other ad hoc compensation schemes, such as those under the Vaccine Damage Payments Act 1979 and Pneumoconiosis etc (Workers Compensation) Act 1979. Both provide lump sums to limited groups who in practice would be unable to sue in delict. Had a beneficiary so done, no doubt a court would also have regarded the payment as more like social security than insurance or charity.

---

1 See eg Brown, Hiram *et al Claiming criminal injuries compensation* … (1997), Foster *Claiming compensation for criminal injuries* (2nd edn, 1996), Miers *State compensation for criminal injuries* (1996).
2 Tay House, 300 Bath Street, Glasgow, G2 4JR.

7. Negotiations

Since a very high proportion of cases claiming damages settle out of court either before an action is raised at all or at some stage during the action's progress through the courts, the negotiation process is an increasingly important one. Thus it is important to have a clear idea of the most effective way to conduct discussions with a view to settlement of the dispute.

It cannot be said that there is only one possible approach to the gentle art of negotiating, because each person will have his or her own ideas of what is the correct one but whatever is the ultimate approach there are important characteristics which must be included in the method if the end of reaching a fair settlement is to be achieved.

The purpose of this chapter is to give some pointers to the essential ingredients of a successful negotiation and to discuss some of the pitfalls.

COMMENCING THE NEGOTIATIONS

PREPARATION

Like in all things in life it is essential to be properly prepared before facing the opposite number in the negotiations. This book is dealing with damages but of course it is necessary to cover all aspects of the case when preparing for the discussions because the negotiations will cover liability, prescription, causation and many other aspects of the general law of reparation or contract as well as damages. Unless one is to be placed on the back foot it is worth trying to identify those which are relevant and likely to feature in the case in hand and research them, at least to the extent of a working knowledge, before serious discussions begin. Time spent at an early stage covering the basic circumstances will pay off as the case proceeds. The following paragraphs give some examples of basic matters which would be worth considering in most cases before the case proceeds very far.

Clear instructions

It is self-evident that before any meaningful argument about any matter can be put forward there must be a clear understanding in the mind of the negotiator of the basic details of the accident in the case of reparation, or the nature of the breach of contract or other cause of the loss. This is not always easy and there is a temptation to gloss over the details and hope that they will become clearer as time goes on. That should always be avoided because it allows an advantage to the other side which cannot always be retrieved and which inevitably affects the decision as to when to settle the case and at what figure.

It is always a good idea to ascertain any relevant background information which might help with the negotiation. For example, basic details of the injured person's lifestyle so that the effect of the injuries on that person might be assessed could be helpful in personal injuries cases.

Circumstances

Establishing the details of the incident is equally important. Very exact details of the way in which an accident took place often require to be discussed and regulations and statutory provisions apply to quite specific situations. Both sides will find it useful to know as much about the cause of the loss as possible. To be in any other state of knowledge gives away an advantage to the other side and makes for inefficient negotiation.

Evidence

The Civil Evidence (Scotland) Act 1988 removed the need for corroboration in civil cases and so it is legitimate to proceed on the basis of the complainer's evidence alone if necessary but it never does any harm in presenting an argument on behalf of one party to be in a position to present evidence vouching a proposition which is being put forward. Thus where there are witnesses to an accident, particularly where they are 'independent', it is worth while finding out who they are and, most importantly, what they are able to say about the incident involved.

This applies both to the establishment of liability and to the establishment of any loss. Of course the persons negotiating will not see or hear any evidence from witnesses so that they will not necessarily accept what the witness might be saying. There is however scope for examination of statements or vouchers or for the investigation of witnesses' positions by the other side. Often a stage of agreement can be reached much more quickly if both sides know the likely state of the evidence. The establishing of what witnesses were present or what documentary evidence exists in relation to important matters at an appropriately early stage pays dividends in time and effort later.

In breach of contract cases evidence of the terms of the contract and how it should be interpreted as well as the circumstances of the alleged breach or evidence that the contract has been correctly honoured is often difficult to obtain later but its existence at an early stage often sets the tone of the negotiations and allows a proper conclusion to be reached more speedily.

The law

Once there is a clear idea as to the facts in the case it is important to apply the law to the facts as they are known so as to work out in the first place whether the circumstances admit of any potential liability on the part of any person and, if so, to what extent. Consideration in reparation cases would have to be given to the question of whether there is common law liability and if so what the duties are which are breached. Similarly it is important to discover the statutory provisions, if any, which apply and which individual regulations might be breached in the circumstances of the case. As will be apparent later, it is also important to see that the breach of any particular regulation is what caused the loss in any particular situation.

In breach of contract cases the law of contract would have to be looked at to establish whether or not the contract could legally be said to have been breached. This is the time in defamation cases to look at the words used to ascertain whether they are defamatory and to formulate the argument for and against saying that they are. It is pointless starting negotiations on any of these matters without having a clear idea of the legal position as well as the factual position in which each side is placed.

Damage

Most important in the context of this book, it is essential to establish the damage which has flowed from the injury and to come to clear conclusions for the basis upon which the individual claims are made. At an early stage, of course, the full details of the loss and, it may be, even the categories of loss will not always be known, but nevertheless it may be possible to list a number of headings or even likely headings under which claims may subsequently be made if the circumstances justify it.

Now comes consideration of such matters as causation, remoteness and whether the claim is for economic loss or physical loss. In many cases such questions are easy to resolve but it seems that negotiators can forget to give the question consideration at all and thus find themselves well into a negotiation before turning to consider the question for instance, as to whether the person alleged to have committed a delict owed a duty to the person said to have suffered the loss or whether the loss claimed to have occurred can be said to have flowed from the alleged delict.

It is not the function of this book to cover in detail any of the aspects of the law relating to these matters of principle but in the field of economic loss, for instance, the question of how wide is the duty to compensate has been discussed in a series of cases which arose from the Braer disaster[1]. Similarly the question of whether a loss could properly be said to have flowed from the breach of duty was discussed in *Lomond Assured Properties Ltd v McGrigor Donald*[2], where loss of rental in respect of buildings not yet completed was sought in a claim for professional negligence. The question is often easy to resolve and does not require close scrutiny but in some cases the question requires consideration at an early stage.

Quantification

Quantification is probably the most important matter in the context of this book but of course it is important in relation to every negotiation that each side prepares in advance the calculation of the loss as it sees it so that it can be ascertained quickly where the areas of dispute are and, since it is a negotiation, the areas, if any, where the parties may be prepared to make concessions which might help to settle the matter. Each side will have to consider the damage which the claimant suffered and come to a conclusion as to what that amounts to. To do so it will be necessary in, for instance, cases of personal

---

1 Eg *Landcatch v International Oil Pollution Compensation Fund* 1999 SCLR 709.
2 1999 SCLR 568, at 576D.

injuries, to make a list of possible headings of damage that might be suffered in such a case. A typical list might be:

1. Solatium;
2. loss of earnings to date;
3. future loss of earnings;
4. loss of pension rights;
5. loss of employability;
6. claim for necessary services;
7. loss of personal services;
8. loss of property (including uninsured losses in road accidents, emergency treatment, clothing and other articles damaged in the accident);
9. expenses of travelling to medical treatment, physiotherapy etc;
10. expenses of medical equipment or appliances and adaptation of house or car to take into account any disabilities;
11. cost of future nursing and nursing home if required.

These are some of the common headings under which claims may be made but the individual circumstances of each case may result in further claims being appropriate. For instance the claimant may have expertise in a particular sport or hobby in which the injuries prevent future participation and he may wish to claim for loss of opportunity to excel or continue to excel in that activity.

Similar lists can be adopted for cases of breach of contract or defamation but the circumstances of each case will be so different that it is unprofitable to try to develop a standard list for such cases. In each instance it would be necessary to identify the likely headings which would apply and carry out a calculation based on the principles set out above of the amount to be claimed under each. This will bring out a total claim as a starting-off point for negotiations. Of course the individual headings will no doubt change as the information improves, and it will have to be borne in mind clearly that the figures are for negotiation purposes and are not written in stone

GATHERING THE EVIDENCE

General

It may be necessary to gather evidence in relation to the merits of the action and to see witnesses and obtain statements which may in some cases be used in the negotiation, but that is not the subject of this work. The important evidence for the purposes of this chapter is that which vouches the loss which has been sustained.

In general it will consist of vouchers of some sort certifying damage but may also consist of statements of opinion from experts in the relevant field in the form of reports. These might come from doctors, psychologists, surveyors, accountants, engineers or other experts in some field. These vouchers or reports are of no real value if they cannot be accepted by the other side so before experts are instructed it is important to check their credentials to see that the qualifications they have provide a proper basis for their opinion, that they are not being asked to go outside their sphere of expertise and that they have sufficient experience in the field to stand up to scrutiny.

If the report is submitted by the other side there is always an economic advantage in being able to accept its terms if possible but before doing so it is important to check the credentials, qualifications, expertise and experience of the expert if he or she is not known. Similarly, the vouchers such as estimates should come formally written, preferably on letter-headed paper and officially signed by the person completing them, so that their reliability can be assessed, at least superficially, by the other side.

Medical reports

Where injuries are relatively minor or where treatment has chiefly been provided by the claimant's General Practitioner then the report can be obtained from that doctor. If so the letter requesting the report should clearly state the questions that have to be addressed and the information which is required to be covered so that the doctor is able to address it properly. Care should be taken to ensure that the doctor has the appropriate permission to give the information.

If the injuries are more serious then a report from a consultant in the field of medicine concerned might have to be obtained. The particular field concerned is not always immediately apparent and it is often necessary to have a report from more than one such expert. The choice of individual surgeons or physicians will be a personal matter but questions of accessibility, cost and experience in the particular aspect of the case will be considerations, as will the likelihood, if known, of the particular expert's opinion being accepted for the purposes of the other side.

In some cases it will be profitable to see whether a particular list of experts might be agreed as acceptable in particular cases so that the likelihood of a second opinion being insisted in would be reduced with the resultant saving of time and expense. The letter instructing the report is important. It must clearly state to the expert what aspects of the patient's treatment the opinion is to cover, whether a prognosis is required, whether an opinion is required as to whether the patient will be fit for work, and if so what kind and when, and whether any pre-existing condition or previous accident has a bearing on the condition so as to affect the quantification of damages.

Failure to give all the information might result in the report's failing to cover an important point and since the written report is to be used without the opportunity to supplement it with additional verbal information this can have a deleterious effect on the negotiations. Of course, some extremely eminent doctors are not very good witnesses and sometimes the choice of which expert to choose may come down to a comparison of who performs best in the court because, if the negotiation fails and evidence has to be led, then the witness whose report is used may have to give evidence if the report cannot be agreed.

Other expert reports

Medical reports were dealt with separately for no other reason than that they are more commonly required and as a result there is a formidable body of doctors of all specialities experienced at giving suitable reports. When it comes to experts in other fields, however, the picture is more complicated. The subjects which require an expert witness are legion but many of them occur only occasionally and as a result there is often some doubt as to how to get hold of a suitable expert and then whether the person chosen is sufficiently expert in the subject to be accepted in evidence.

Some experts, for example handwriting experts and accident investigators, advertise in the legal journals. Others can be found on lists of persons willing to carry out forensic work, such as analysts and chemists and yet others can be found by contacting professional bodies such as the Royal Institution of Chartered Surveyors or the Royal Incorporation of Architects in Scotland. University departments often contain experts in all sorts of unusual subjects or can suggest people from other university departments who do the type of work required.

Great care has to be taken with the selection of the appropriate expert and even greater care with his instruction which will often require a meeting or meetings to acquaint him with the exact subject matter upon which his opinion is required, and to ascertain that the question is within his expertise and that he has specific academic or professional qualifications in the subject. Beware the client who tells you that he has spoken to an expert who will be able to deal with the subject matter and agrees totally with the client's point of view. Sometimes they may be right but more often than not the 'expert' does not have qualifications in the subject or has been persuaded to venture beyond his expertise by the client or, when carefully questioned, is not so definite about the point as was first thought.

Many fringe experts, such as dry rot operatives or builders, are persuaded to a client's point of view without fully realising what has happened and if taken at face value their evidence can lead to an embarrassing situation in negotiations or, worse still, at a proof. The same care has to be taken when instructing such experts that enthusiasm for the client's point of view does not lead to an attempt to persuade the expert to adopt a sympathetic view of the clients case which is not justified. Such an approach would lead to problems later. It has to be remembered that experts are also anxious to obtain the work.

Where the reports have to come from persons who would not be expected to have professional or academic qualifications, it is nevertheless prudent to check that the person has some skill or knowledge in the subject under discussion. An estimate for repairs of a car or the valuation of a car is much more useful if the mechanic has served an apprenticeship and attended courses on the vehicle concerned and the valuer has long experience selling such models.

Vouchers and receipts

The same principles apply in connection with the production of vouchers. The best possible type of voucher available should be obtained. The grubby, hastily scribbled pencil receipt may in some cases be all that exists and will have to do but where possible proper certified vouchers should be produced. Where there is control over the obtaining of a voucher, such as an estimate for repairs, it is better to obtain one if possible from a garage that can issue an official estimate with some authority. This means a garage with at least some commercial experience behind them rather than a one-man business which started work from home two weeks ago.

Similarly, the persons who actually issue the estimate should be the persons who have the expertise or the experience so that there is no question about their authenticity. Difficulties often arise in relation to estimates for the putting right of damage to buildings or the reinstatement of below-standard work because it is often difficult to find one person who is an expert in all the skills required to be covered and persons who describe themselves as 'builders' often have no formal qualifications and rely purely on experience. While they may get the job done on site, in some ways they are little more than experienced 'do-it-yourself' exponents when it comes to giving evidence. If their report is put up against experienced journeymen or professional witnesses it will compare unfavourably.

In contract cases or cases where damages are sought for destruction of items such as furniture, pictures or antiques there is often no shortage of volunteers for the job of valuer but, once again, care has to be taken to select a genuine expert whose opinion can be expected to prevail.

CONDUCTING THE NEGOTIATIONS

COMMENCEMENT

Most negotiations commence with the intimation of a claim by the claimant. This is usually done in writing and there generally follows a correspondence while the grounds for liability are set out and attempts are made to rough out the basis of a claim as best as is possible given the state of information available as to loss at that early stage.

Once both sides have had a chance to investigate the liability aspect it is probably worth having a meeting to see if there is likely to be any measure of agreement on that question. It is probable that unless there are very clear indications of liability the defender is unlikely to want to indicate anything more than a hypothetical admission of liability at that stage unless it is clear that the claim is reasonably small and might be able to be settled early to avoid unnecessary and unjustified expense.

In most situations the defender will want to preserve his position in relation to both the question of quantum and liability so as to strengthen his bargaining position. He will wish to retain the element of uncertainty and risk in relation to liability which will contribute to his ability to settle the case when and if he is ready to offer.

Meantime, the claimant should be gathering the vouched evidence of the claim so as to be ready to present it when the time comes. This will take a period of time which will vary considerably depending upon when the evidence becomes available. For example, in some cases the true medical position in relation to recovery might not be available for some years, while in others the evidence might be readily available.

At some stage it might become clear that the information is available about the various elements of the claim which would enable a worthwhile discussion to take place and a meeting or meetings should be arranged then to discuss the matter. It is impossible to be any more definite about procedure because the negotiations could take an endless number of forms; it might be settled during the correspondence by an offer in settlement being made which is acceptable; it might end with a steadfast rejection of the claim; or it might drag on with tantalisingly close discussions until the Prescription and Limitation of Actions (Scotland) Act 1973 forces an action to be raised. All that really matters is that it is remembered that the purpose of the negotiations is to reach a satisfactory settlement of the claim at as early a time as is possible.

'WITHOUT PREJUDICE'

Negotiation is all very well when it succeeds but if it does not then what can be made of the information provided during the discussions?

All parties to a negotiation will rightly be concerned that by entering into negotiations they might inadvertently provide the other side with useful ammunition in a later court action. That fear might inhibit open and properly wide-ranging negotiations and, indeed, might prevent the parties putting forward their full position and supporting facts unless they thought that settlement was imminent. It cannot be said that this worry prevents all negotiation but there is clear evidence in decided cases of information in letters written with a view to settlement being used against the writer in subsequent court procedure.

In these circumstances a practice developed over the years of attempting to avoid that risk by using a formula to indicate that the letter was written for the purpose of trying to reach a settlement and without admission of liability. Over the years the formula was often reduced to the addition, usually at the end of the letter of the words 'Without prejudice'[1]. For a time it was thought that the addition of these words had the effect of rendering the letter inadmissible in proceedings following on an unsuccessful negotiation.

The justification for that view must be doubted because as far back as 1852 in England there was concern about the practice of attempting to use such correspondence for evidence of some fact contained therein. In *Jones v Foxall*[2], Romilly MR lamented 'I find the offers were in fact made without prejudice to the rights of the parties, and I shall, so far as I am able, in all cases, endeavour to repress a practice which, when I was first acquainted with the profession, was never ventured upon, but which, according to my experience in this place, has become common of late – namely, that of attempting to convert offers of compromise into admissions of acts prejudicial to the person making them. If this were permitted, the effect would be that no attempt to compromise a dispute could ever be made.'

It seems that the Master of the Rolls' efforts were fruitful as, indeed, well they might have been, because there were few cases on the subject for some considerable time. Indeed in 1984 Oliver LJ justified the approach as resting upon public policy[3]. The underlying aim was that parties should be encouraged as far as possible to settle their dispute without the resort to litigation. Meantime, however, in Canada in 1971 the warning was given that

---

1 One version of the full text would be something like: 'This letter is written purely in an effort to settle the matter and is entirely without prejudice to [client's] rights and pleas and is not to be construed as an admission of liability'.
2 (1852) 9 Beav 388.
3 See *Cutts v Head* [1984] 1 Ch 290, [1984] 2 WLR 349, [1984] 1 All ER 597.

'[c]ontrary to popular belief in some quarters the shibboleth that 'without prejudice' written on a letter protects it from subsequent use as an admission is not accurate'[1] and in Scotland in *Watson-Towers Ltd v McPhail*[2], Lord Wylie said 'These terms do not, in my view, infer a hypothetical admission or concession for the purpose of securing a settlement but are a statement of fact. The use of the expression 'without prejudice' does not in my view protect the letter from subsequent use as an admission of fact'.

The same sentiments were expressed by Lord Sutherland in the case of *Daks Simpson Group plc v Hermannus Kuiper* where he says:

'"Without prejudice" in my view means without prejudice to the whole rights and pleas of the person making the statement. If, however, someone makes a clear and unequivocal admission or statement of fact, it is difficult to see what rights or pleas could be attached to such a statement other perhaps than to deny the truth of the admission which was made. I see no objection in principle to a clear admission being used in subsequent proceedings, even though the communication in which it appears is stated to be without prejudice'[3].

The question was discussed in the Inner House in the case of *Richardson v Quercus Ltd*[4] where the opinion of the court was given by Lord Prosser. There was a dispute in that case as to whether a letter in fact contained an unequivocal admission but it was held that if the terms of the letter were an unequivocal admission then the addition of the words `without prejudice' would not prevent its being used in subsequent proceedings.

It is clear from these authorities that the words 'without prejudice' are not the complete protection that some may have thought. When the writer began practice most solicitors qualified their letters sent for the purpose of negotiations and, it is believed, many thought that by doing so the letter was immune from becoming a production.

It may be that few such letters contained unequivocal admissions, or that there was an acceptance of the view that they should not be used but it is fair to say that there was not an avalanche of cases where letters protected by these words were founded on. When *Watson-Towers Ltd* was reported it caused some concern in some solicitors' offices and some began to add a sentence to the end of the previous disclaimer along the following lines: 'Any statement of fact contained in this letter is purely hypothetical and is written purely for the purposes of attempting to reach a settlement and is not to be construed as an admission of the fact'. Whether it would have the desired effect is not known because no-one has tested it, so far as is known. It did make the letter rather cumbersome, especially when the content of the rest of the letter was short.

It might make a lot of sense if the addition of the words 'without prejudice' did have the effect of preventing the letter being used against its writer. In that way negotiators could write letters quite fully without the prospect of their remarks made in the course of the negotiation being used against them. When negotiations in industrial tribunals are being carried out under the auspices of

---

1 See *Kirschbaum v 'Our Voices' Publishing Co* (1971) 1 OR 737.
2 1986 SLT 617 at 618L–619A.
3 1994 SLT 689 at 692C–D, 1994 SCLR 373 (Notes).
4 1999 SCLR 133.

the conciliation officer there is a complete embargo on the use of any information obtained as a result and so parties are free to negotiate without worry as to the possible consequences. Certainly the negotiations protected there are carried out in a special stage of the procedure and under the auspices of an official but it is not claimed that any disadvantage is suffered by any party as a result of being unable to use information, whether admission or not, gained at negotiation. It might be said that the pursuer would suffer by being unable to use an admission of fact made in negotiation and would have to struggle to prove it although it was already admitted in negotiation. On the other hand negotiations between persons in damages claims are not done through the medium of a third party and so there is less need for protection because any admission would be made spontaneously and without the likelihood of its being provoked by the intervention of a third party. It is probably rare that a situation would arise where a defender would make an admission in negotiation and then steadfastly refuse to admit it when an action is raised. However the admission would in any event have been obtained purely as a result of the fact that the negotiation had taken place so it is suggested that no prejudice would be suffered even if he did.

In these circumstances it seems clear that it would be of significant assistance to negotiators if they knew that their discussions would remain private and that even their admissions of fact could not be founded on if they were made purely for the purpose of attempting to negotiate a settlement.

DISCLOSURE

Another thorny problem for negotiators is how much information to give away when discussing the case. Some negotiators want to try to keep back as much information as possible to try to retain a perceived advantage. The information could consist of facts relating to liability, extent of the loss, fitness for work or contributory negligence. Every negotiator will have his or her own method of approach, and it is not really possible to lay down any formula. However full disclosure of the pertinent parts of the argument will have to be made at some stage in the negotiation and except in very rare situations all the information which is known by the parties should be laid before the other side during any meeting arranged to discuss the claim.

It is self-evident that the claimant will have to demonstrate liability, causation and quantum of damage and deal with any argument about remoteness and contributory negligence. Therefore sufficient information will have to be laid before the defender's side to convince the negotiators that the claim is valid and little can be gained by trying to keep back damaging information in the hope that the other side does not find out. If it does at a later stage it casts doubt on the whole negotiation and might affect future negotiations in relation to other claims.

That is not to say that it is appropriate to confess all the perceived weaknesses in the claim but positively misleading information should not be proffered and information which negates a possible claim which might in other circumstances have been open to the claimant should not be withheld. The putting forward of untrue information knowing it to be untrue would be not only unprofessional but criminal as well.

MEETING THE OPPOSITION

As previously stated, most negotiations commence with a correspondence setting out the parties' initial points of view. In smaller claims it is possible that an offer in settlement can be made and accepted in the course of the correspondence. In larger claims once sufficient information has been obtained by each side to make a meeting worthwhile, one should be arranged to discuss the claim.

At such a meeting it is worth establishing at the outset what matters are not in dispute. Is liability accepted? If so is contributory negligence to be argued? Are any of the heads of damage able to be agreed, even on a provisional basis? For instance, can estimates for repairs be agreed? Or past loss of wages? Then it is possible to move on to discussion of the matters in dispute. Often that will involve discussing liability and reaching a conclusion on that, and then moving on to discuss damages.

On many occasions it is not possible to reach a conclusion on both matters, perhaps because the information about damages is not complete as there is doubt about future treatment, or a medical decision on the claimant's future ability to work cannot yet be made. In these circumstances the question of liability can be discussed and any contribution by the claimant thrashed out. Most negotiators acting for defenders concede the question of liability only for the purpose of the negotiation and reserve their position for the future in the event of settlement not being reached. The value of that depends on how strong the case on liability is because the spectre of liability hanging over the claimant will be significant only if there is genuine doubt about liability. On other occasions the defender will not want to concede finally the question of liability, even for the purpose of the negotiations, because there is serious doubt about the success of the claim and he does not want to lose the element of litigation risk as a bargaining tool. Thus discussions on damages will proceed purely on a provisional basis.

At this stage the discussion will cover the vouchers and reports collected during the preparation period. It may be that it will be obvious that further expert evidence is required either because the defender does not accept the terms of a report, or because a point is not clear, or because the evidence has to be updated. Where possible it is best to leave the meeting to discuss the claim until reasonably positive medical evidence is obtained. However, for reasons of limitation of actions that may not always be possible in cases of serious injury.

In the same way the defender may not be prepared to accept some of the vouchers and may set out views as to what would be necessary to convince him that the element of the claim was sufficiently vouched. The claimant would have to decide if he was able or prepared to produce what was required.

Sometimes there is difficulty as to who is to make the running in the negotiation. Of course each negotiation is different and it will depend on the strength of each side's case as to who takes the lead. The matter is often most sharply raised when the time comes to discuss figures and often each side wants the other side to make the first move and set out its idea of how the claim should be calculated. Indeed, it often seems that there are cases where negotiators rely on the other side to do the work in the first instance and then check out the figures once the claim is quantified by the other side. It is much more sensible for each side to work out the quantification as they see it, using such previous authorities or examples as can be found. Nor is it sensible to come to a conclusion as to the appropriate figure and then substantially increase it if the calculation is for the claimant or reduce it if for the defender. It is submitted that more pressure is put on the other side by a sensible figure than by one which is completely inaccurate.

It goes without saying that each side will adopt the previous examples which suit its purposes and the discussion and negotiation can much more sensibly centre on coming to an agreement as to which of them give a fair and reasonable settlement for the claim in hand.

INTERIM PAYMENTS

In appropriate situations it may be possible to negotiate interim payments. These are appropriate where large outlays have to be incurred shortly after the accident but there is a likelihood that damages will not be able to be assessed for some time. No such payment can be made unless liability is established and care has to be taken that the amount to be paid does not exceed the amount ultimately agreed.

In these circumstances the sums to be paid will be a small proportion of the likely end payment and of course, any argument about contributory negligence has to be taken into account. There can be no hard and fast rule about when an interim payment can be claimed but it is easier to justify in a big claim, especially where substantial early expenditure is necessary and there is to be a delay beyond the control of the pursuer in settlement.

SETTLEMENT

The purpose of the negotiation is, of course, to reach a settlement of the claim. That will obviously involve an element of compromise on the part of the negotiators, sometimes in relation to matters which seem adequately vouched and fairly incurred. Both parties will have to bear in mind the litigation risk in pursuing the case through the courts, both in relation to the question of liability and in relation to quantum of damages.

The less convincing the argument for liability and the greater the hostage to fortune in the evidence that can be produced, the more willing the claimant will have to be to concede reductions in the claim. The skill is identifying where the bottom line is and where the risk of going to court becomes worthwhile, or puts sufficient pressure on the other side to make a payment.

Indeed, despite all the careful preparation and despite the work involved in putting the claim into proper categories, settlement often is reached purely on an economic basis by calculating not the true value of the claim, but the cost of not settling and becoming involved in a court action with its implications in relation to expenses, time and effort devoted to servicing the action. This is particularly so if the negotiations are taking place after the court action has commenced and the parties are trying to settle to avoid the expense and risk of a proof.

The most important factor to the claimant is the final figure which is reached. He usually has little regard for the method of calculating it and so there is often room for manoeuvre in relation to the method of calculation. Often one whole branch of the claim can be abandoned while a concession in relation to another might be made by the defender.

The benefit recovery provisions must always be borne in mind by the claimant. If settlement is reached purely by means of a financial payment, then a discharge has to be prepared. This usually acknowledges that the payment is in full settlement of the claim and is made without admission of liability. After signature by the claimant, payment can be made.

If the settlement is reached after the court action is raised, then the action has to be dismissed. That is achieved by lodging a joint minute requesting the court to grant absolvitor with no expenses once the settlement has been made. In some cases, such as in actions involving breach of contract or cases where the claim is for damage for encroachment on land or the like, the settlement might not involve the payment of money but an agreement to carry out work or physically put right the damage, perhaps by taking back defective goods and replacing them. In these cases it might be necessary to draw up a minute of agreement setting out the method of settlement.

It is important to recognise the difference between a joint minute disposing of the action and the minute of agreement settling it. The former is a request to the court made jointly by the parties to dispose of the action after settlement, and must contain a request which it is competent for the court to grant, such as dismissal or decree for an agreed sum. The latter is a contract between the parties for settlement. On some occasions a minute of agreement has been lodged with the obvious intention of having the action disposed of but the terms of the settlement reached contain provisions which the court could not order in the action before it. The agreement would have to be regarded as an enforceable contract between the parties rather than the method of finishing the action and the distinction is important.

EXPENSES

In all settlements the question of expenses is an element which requires careful consideration. Recovery of the expenses of an unsuccessful negotiation incurred before the action is raised will not be possible in a subsequent action[1] but settlement of a successful negotiation can, and usually does, include an element for expenses. Since it is a matter of negotiation, no hard and fast rules can be laid down and each case depends on the terms upon which the parties are prepared to settle. In the normal reparation claim negotiated by solicitors, a separate element is agreed for expenses including solicitors' fees and outlays for medical and other reports.

In reaching a settlement, however, the question of expenses must be kept in mind and if a settlement seems likely then the question must be addressed so that both parties are aware of what is agreed in relation to the principle of expenses and the method by which they are to be calculated. Many insurance companies have standing arrangements for the scale of fees and outlays that will be paid in the claim but if one does not exist then the question has to be settled by agreement.

---

1 *Clyde Nail Co Ltd v AG Moore & Co* 1949 SLT (Notes) 43.

Appendix

The main purpose of chapter 7 was to give an overview of the mechanics of carrying out the negotiating of a claim for damages but without providing a negotiator's manual. While a structured approach is necessary, it is undesirable to fence it in with fixed rules or practices which might prove stultifying.

The approach to damages is of course more formal and rule-bound when an action has to be raised in court. The record in the action must set out the elements of the claim so that the defender can see how it is to be calculated and what elements of damages the pursuer avers must be taken into account. Clear averments of causation and duty must be specified and any unusual claims must be specified with averments that set out the circumstances justifying the recovery of the particular sum claimed.

It is not the purpose of this book to deal with the procedure in court actions in relation to damages actions but some styles for the articles of condescendence in relation to the elements or heads of damage might help to clarify matters. It cannot be emphasised too strongly that the purpose of the pleadings is to give fair notice to the defender of the claim which is being made against him and for that purpose it is vital to set out the heads of damages in a way which will enable the defender to be informed of the way the claim is constructed and to be clear about the different heads of damage claimed. For instance, there must be averments explaining that future loss of earnings is claimed and upon what basis, or whether a claim for services is being made. If provisional damages are claimed then circumstances justifying such a claim must be set out[1]. It is not necessary or appropriate to detail all the evidence that is to be led to demonstrate that any particular claim is valid. The skill is to give fair notice of the heads of damage without clogging up the pleadings with all the details of the evidence to be led.

Where solatium is claimed it is not necessary to include in the pleadings the specific sum which is claimed but it is necessary to set out the circumstances of the pursuer and the nature of the injuries and the difficulties encountered by the pursuer as a result. Where loss of wages is claimed, again it is unnecessary to aver the total sum but the basis for calculation must be set out by averring the pre-accident wage and the period of loss of earnings as well as the post-accident wage if that is different[2]. If disadvantage on the labour market is claimed then the basis on which that claim is made has to be set out, but the details of the evidence to be led to prove it do not.

In cases where there is a big claim, it is worth considering setting out the different elements in separate articles of condescendence devoted to one separate head of damages because then it is easier to concentrate on the averment required for each branch of the claim and for the defender to

---

1 See *Paterson v Costain Mining Co* 1988 SLT 413, 1988 SCLR 71.
2 See *Jamieson v Alan McNeil & Son* 1974 SLT (Notes) 9.

consider each branch and form a view on it. In any event, the averments of loss should always be in an article of condescendence devoted to damages and separate from those setting out the facts and liability.

An example of articles of condescendence for an action of personal injuries follows. It covers a number of the possible heads of damages:

6. As a result of the accident the pursuer suffered loss, injury and damage. He sustained a comminuted fracture of the left femur and dislocation of the left hip. He suffered a fracture of the left elbow. There was damage to the tendons of the left leg. He suffered severe pain and inconvenience. He required to have the fracture of the left femur and the dislocation of the left hip reduced under a general anaesthetic, and on 23 September 1998 he required to undergo a further operation to re-set the fracture and to insert metal pins in the bones because the fracture of the femur had failed to unite. He had to remain in hospital for three weeks and then required to return for examination and treatment at weekly intervals for a further six weeks. His arm and leg were in plaster for six weeks and 12 weeks respectively. He required to undergo painful physiotherapy for ten weeks. He continues to suffer severe pain and inconvenience. His left leg is now 2.5 cm shorter than the right. He walks with a limp and requires to use a stick. He cannot walk on rough ground or negotiate steps. Rotation of his left leg and movement of the left elbow are restricted. His disability is permanent. The pursuer was a keen golfer and had won a number of club competitions. He is now unable to play golf. He was also a keen hill walker and is now unable to pursue that hobby.

7. As a result of the accident the pursuer lost wages. At the time of the accident the pursuer was employed as a crane driver. He was earning £350 per week. A detailed statement of earnings will be produced. He was unable to continue working as a crane driver and as a result lost wages and continues to lose wages. He is unlikely ever to return to work as a crane driver because he is unable to climb ladders or sit in the confined space of a cab for any length of time. He is unfit for heavy work or that which involves standing or operating machinery. He is unlikely ever to be able to do so. He became fit for light work on 20 September 1999. He has no formal training for any type of work other than in the building trade.

8. Prior to the accident the pursuer carried out extensive maintenance and DIY work throughout the family home. He decorated the home and carried out electrical repairs and plumbing work. In 1997 he completed the construction of a conservatory and in 1998 he built an extra bathroom. He removed fireplaces in two bedrooms and re-plastered the walls. The pursuer also maintained and planted the garden of the house which extended to one-third of an acre. He is unable to carry out any similar work and any such work will require to be carried out by tradesmen. The annual cost of having tradesmen carry out the work done by the pursuer is £2,000. Further, the pursuer carried out decoration and general main-tenance work for his sister who resides alone at 13 Black Street. In the years 1996 and 1997 he decorated three rooms and installed extra sockets in two others. The cost of the works carried out by him if done by trades-men would have been £500 in 1996 and £450 in 1997. All of the foregoing work was done gratuitously by the pursuer. He claims damages in terms of the Administration of Justice Act 1982, s 9.

9. The pursuer was discharged from hospital on 10 October 1998. He was unable to carry out numerous every day activities as a result of his injuries. He was unable to dress himself. He was unable to make his way to and use the toilet alone. He was unable to use a knife and fork or bathe himself until mid-December 1998. Thereafter he still required assistance to get up stairs and with some items of clothes. He was unable to drive and to get in and out of a car. His wife assisted with all these tasks except for driving which was carried out by his sister. She took the pursuer on shopping trips one day per week and on at least two other occasions each week drove the pursuer to other appointments and leisure trips. The total time spent by the pursuer's wife in providing these services to the pursuer was 14 hours per week. The total time spent by the pursuer's sister was five hours per week. A reasonable rate of remuneration would be £5 per hour for both the pursuer's wife and his sister. All of the foregoing services are necessary services which the pursuer claims in terms of the Administration of Justice Act 1982, s 8[1].

---

1 See *Ingham v John G Russell (Transport) Ltd* 1991 SLT 739, 1991 SCLR 596.

Index